THE BAD CITIZEN IN CLASSIC

This book provides a fresh perspective on Athenian democracy by exploring bad citizenship, as both a reality and an idea, in classical Athens, from the late sixth century down to 322 B.C. If called upon, Athenian citizens were expected to support their city through military service and financial outlay. These obligations were fundamental to Athenian understandings of citizenship and it was essential to the city's well-being that citizens fulfill them. The ancient sources, however, are full of allegations that individuals avoided these duties or performed them deficiently. Claims of draft evasion, cowardice on the battlefield, and avoidance of liturgies and the war tax are common. By examining the nature and scope of bad citizenship in Athens and the city's responses – institutional and ideological – to the phenomenon, this study aims to illuminate the relationship between citizen and city under the Athenian democracy and, more broadly, the tension between private interests and public authority in human societies.

Matthew R. Christ is associate professor of classical studies at Indiana University. He is the author of *The Litigious Athenian* (1998).

THE BAD CITIZEN IN CLASSICAL ATHENS

MATTHEW R. CHRIST

CAMBRIDGE UNIVERSITY PRESS
Cambridge, New York, Melbourne, Madrid, Cape Town, Singapore, São Paulo, Delhi

Cambridge University Press
32 Avenue of the Americas, New York, NY 10013-2473, USA

www.cambridge.org
Information on this title: www.cambridge.org/9780521730341

First published 2006
Reprinted 2008
First paperback edition 2008

Printed in the United States of America

A catalog record for this publication is available from the British Library.

Library of Congress Cataloging in Publication Data

Christ, Matthew Robert.
The bad citizen in classical Athens / Matthew R. Christ.
p. cm.
Includes bibliographical references and index.
ISBN-13: 978-0-521-86432-9 (hardback)
ISBN-10: 0-521-86432-1 (hardback)
1. Citizenship – Greece – Athens – History. I. Title.
JC75.C5C45 2006
323.60938'5 – dc22 2006007787

ISBN 978-0-521-86432-9 hardback
ISBN 978-0-521-73034-1 paperback

To Elizabeth Burch Lambros

CONTENTS

Acknowledgments *page* ix
Abbreviations xi

Introduction: The Other Athenians 1

1 **The Self-Interested Citizen** 15
Self-Interest and Athenian Citizenship 16
Human Nature and Self-Interest 16
Democratic Citizenship and Self-Interest 24
Citizenship Strategies: Self-Interested Citizenship 35
Civic Responses: Compulsion and Persuasion 40

2 **The Reluctant Conscript** 45
Draft Evasion and Compulsory Military Service 46
Motives 48
Opportunities 52
Conscription and Draft Evasion through a Tragic Lens 65

3 **The Cowardly Hoplite** 88
Cowardice on Campaign 91
Muster 93
Desertion 94
Endurance of Hardships 95
On the Brink of Battle 96
Battle 99
Rout 103
Victory 109

Cowardice on the Home Front 111
The Hoplite's Homecoming 112
Legal Accountability for Cowardice? 118
Courage and Cowardice in Democratic Discourse 124
Epitaphioi 125
Courage, Cowardice, and Political Leadership 128
Case Study of Demosthenes 132

4 **The Artful Tax Dodger** 143
Financial Obligations: Rules and Institutions 146
Selection 148
Exemptions 151
The Liturgical Class 154
A System under Pressure 155
508/7–432 B.C. 156
431–404 B.C. 161
403–321 B.C. 165
The Limits of *Philotimia* 171
Costs 172
Rewards 176
Fairness 184
Compulsion 188
Choices and Strategies 190
Concealment of Property 191
Assignment of Financial Obligations 194
Performing a Liturgy 199
Representation of Public Service 200

Conclusion 205
Bibliography 211
Index of Ancient Citations 227
General Index 243

ACKNOWLEDGMENTS

My work on this book began in 1998, with the presentation of a paper entitled "Cowards, Traitors, and Cheats in Classical Athens," at a symposium at Oberlin College in honor of my dear friend and former colleague Nathan Greenberg. Since that time, I have presented parts of my work-in-progress to audiences at Northwestern University, Ohio State University, University of Chicago, and University of Minnesota, as well as at the meetings of the American Philological Association; I have benefited greatly from their suggestions and comments. Indiana University generously provided me with leave time for work on this project through an Arts and Humanities Initiative Grant in 2002/3 and with support for materials and other research costs through Grants-in-Aid in 1998 and 2002.

I am grateful to my colleagues at Indiana University and other institutions who provided encouragement and insights as I worked on this project; to my family and friends for their support and many kindnesses; to Beatrice Rehl at Cambridge University Press and the anonymous readers of my manuscript, whose suggestions and criticisms were extremely helpful; and to Peter Katsirubas and Mary Paden at TechBooks.

In this book, ancient passages that are cited on specific points are given *exempli gratia* rather than as comprehensive listings of all testimonia, unless otherwise indicated. Translations in the text are adapted from Collard, Cropp, and Lee (1997); Freeman (1948); Grene (1987); Krentz (1989); MacDowell (1990); Sommerstein (1980–2001); Todd (2000); and the Loeb Classical Library. Chapter 2 is an expanded version of my article "Draft Evasion Onstage and Offstage in Classical Athens," *Classical Quarterly* n.s. 54 (2004) 33–57 (Oxford University Press).

ABBREVIATIONS

Abbreviated references to ancient authors and works are based primarily on those used in *A Greek-English Lexicon*^{9} (H. G. Liddell and R. Scott, with revisions by H. S. Jones and R. McKenzie), Oxford, 1996. Comic fragments are cited from the edition of Kassel and Austin (1983–), unless otherwise noted. Tragic fragments are cited from the editions of Snell (1971) and Radt (1985), except for fragments of Euripides, which are cited from Nauck^{2} (1964) unless otherwise specified. Fragments of the Presocratics are cited from H. Diels and W. Kranz, *Die Fragmente der Vorsokratiker*^{6} (3 vols., Zurich, 1951–1952); those of historical writers from F. Jacoby, *Die Fragmente der griechischen Historiker* (3 vols. in 15, Leiden, 1923–1958). Fragments of Tyrtaeus and Solon are cited from M. L. West, *Iambi et Elegi Graeci*^{2} (2 vols., Oxford, 1989–1992).

Abbreviated references to modern scholarship are to the Bibliography at the end of this book. Abbreviations of periodicals in the Bibliography follow the system of *L'Année philologique*, with a few exceptions: I use *AJP* instead of *AJPh*, *CP* instead of *CPh*, and *TAPA* instead of *TAPhA*.

Introduction

THE OTHER ATHENIANS

The remarkable spread of democracy in the late-twentieth century has led to renewed interest in the roots of western democracy in ancient Athens. This study examines a facet of the Athenian experience that has received less scholarly attention than it deserves: the nature and scope of bad citizenship in classical Athens (508/7–322/1 B.C.) and the city's responses, institutional and ideological, to this. Good citizenship is not ubiquitous in modern democracies, and it was not in democratic Athens. This presented the city with practical challenges, as it sought to limit the scope for bad citizenship through its administrative structures and legal institutions. At the same time, however, bad citizenship challenged Athenian ideals concerning the relationship between individual and state, and elicited a range of ideological responses from the city. How Athens responded to these diverse challenges within a democratic framework is fundamental to our understanding of it.

Although Athenian citizenship bore numerous responsibilities, implicit and explicit, for the exclusive group of adult men who possessed it, this study focuses on two formal obligations that were central to it. Citizens were expected, if called upon, to perform military service as hoplites and to support the city financially in a variety of ways; as Athenian sources pithily put it, citizens were to serve their city with "person and property."[1] While these obligations could potentially

[1] On the centrality of these two obligations to Athenian citizenship, see e.g., [Arist.] *Ath. Pol.* 55.3; Sinclair 1988: 49, 54–65; Manville 1990: 9; Hansen 1991: 99–101; cf. Whitehead 1991: 149. A model citizen can be said to be one who carries out both obligations willingly (Lys. 20.23; Dem. 54.44; Is. 4.27–8; 7.41–2), a bad citizen one who evades both (Isoc. 18.47; Lys. 6.46; Is. 4.29; 5.46). For the ideal of service with

be imposed on any citizen, in practice they did not fall equally on all individuals. Only those able to afford hoplite equipment – perhaps half of the citizen body in the fifth century B.C. – were subject to conscription as hoplites. A much smaller segment of the citizen population, perhaps five percent of the total, was obliged to pay the irregular war tax (*eisphora*) and to perform and finance expensive public services (liturgies). Despite the fact that only a part of the citizen body was liable to these diverse obligations at any one time, civic ideology places their performance at the core of good citizenship; indeed, the city relied heavily upon its citizens to carry out these duties.[2]

In focusing on these two fundamental civic duties, I do not mean to suggest that Athenians viewed citizenship narrowly and exclusively in terms of the performance of these formal obligations.[3] In fact, citizen norms and ideals in Athens encompassed a wide range of behaviors: for example, a model citizen was one who respected his parents, obeyed the city's laws, and operated within the parameters of sexual norms. As scholars have observed, to be a father-beater, a law-breaker or abuser of litigation (sykophant), or another man's passive sexual partner (*kinaidos*), was not simply socially reprehensible in the eyes of Athenians but an inversion of citizen ideals.[4] I focus on the formal duties of Athenian citizenship and breaches of them because they form a critical nexus for inquiry that curiously has not, to the best of my knowledge, been considered in a book-length study. If we can better understand these core elements of Athenian citizenship, we stand in a better position to appreciate the broader experience of Athenians as citizens as well.

"person and property," see Dem. 10.28; 42.25; cf. [Arist.] *Ath. Pol.* 29.5, with Rhodes 1981: 382–3.

2 On Athenian civic ideology's slighting of those who served (normally not by conscription) in Athens' fleet, see Loraux 1986: 212–13; Strauss 1996, 2000; Pritchard 1998; Roisman 2005: 106–9; on its privileging of hoplites over members of the cavalry, see Spence 1993: 165–72.

3 I agree with McGlew (2002: 6) "that democratic citizenship does not lay itself fully bare in legal definitions and formal actions . . . " For similar caveats on interpreting Athenian citizenship too narrowly, see Connor 1994: 40, and Euben, Wallach, and Ober 1994b: 3; cf. Adeleye 1983; Winkler 1990: 54–63; Hunter 1994: 106–11.

4 On fathers and sons in Athenian civic ideology, see Strauss 1993; on law and litigiousness, see Christ 1998a; on citizen sexual norms, see e.g., Winkler 1990: 45–70, but cf. Davidson 1998: 167–82.

Athens could not have flourished to the extent that it did during the classical period if citizens in large numbers had not carried out these basic obligations. It would be a mistake to infer from Athens' overall success as a city-state, however, that it was not troubled by bad citizenship.[5] It is not the intent of this study to debunk positive evaluations of the Athenian democracy, but rather to provide a realistic and plausible picture of the complex, and often tense, relationship between individual and state in democratic Athens.[6] Much source material points to persistent social concern in Athens over citizens' avoidance or deficient performance of their duties. The topics of draft evasion, cowardice on the battlefield, and avoidance of financial obligations crop up regularly in Attic oratory, comedy, and elsewhere. Consistent with these indications of social concern is the existence of numerous legal actions and procedures for pursuing those not fulfilling their obligations, and periodic reforms of the civic institutions governing military service and financial obligations.

While social concern in Athens over bad citizenship need not correlate directly with its prevalence, it is reasonable to suspect, along with Athenians, that bad citizenship was common. Setting aside any romantic preconceptions concerning the "Golden Age" of Athens or Athenian patriotism, we should not be surprised if Athenians, like other historic peoples, were not uniformly ready to subordinate their individual interests to those of the state, especially when their lives or fortunes were at stake.[7] If the phenomenon of bad citizenship is hardly

[5] When I use the term "bad citizenship" in this study, I mean bad citizenship specifically in connection with the formal obligations of citizenship.

[6] My goals are thus very different from those of Samons (2004), who seeks to challenge the generally positive evaluation of Athenian democracy in modern scholarship by exposing the defects of popular rule in Athens (4–13, and *passim*).

[7] Cf. Meier 1990: 142: "We have no reason to believe that the Athenians were peculiarly virtuous, unselfish, or worthy of emulation." Meier, however, is rather too ready in my view to believe that the political identity of Athenians induced them to a high degree to subordinate private interests to public ones (see e.g., 143: "a surprisingly large number of Athenians neglected their domestic interests to a quite surprising extent in order to play their part as citizens," and 146: "Political identity was realized in its purest form in fifth-century Athens. Many citizens spent a good deal of their lives performing their duties as citizens (and soldiers)."). Farrar (1996: 125) also goes too far in generalizing, "The benefits of citizenship at Athens were evident, and the democracy was able to sustain civic commitment (with few lapses) over two centuries."

unique to Athens, however, its sources, manifestations, and implications are intimately bound up with its cultural context. A host of questions arise as we seek to locate it and understand it within this milieu.

How did Athenians view their relation to the city and their obligations as citizens, and how might this have affected their behavior? What cultural and democratic values came into play as Athenians considered whether to conform with civic ideals of citizen behavior? How did concerns about self and property affect citizens' willingness to serve the city? What forms did bad citizenship take, and how prevalent were these? How did administrative structures and legal regulations discourage bad citizenship? How aggressively did the city or its agents seek to compel individuals to carry out their duties? To what extent did social pressures rather than legal or administrative mechanisms elicit compliance? How did civic ideology respond to the problem of bad citizenship? How did it deal with the paradox that free individuals under a democracy could be compelled to carry out civic duties?

Although the fragmented and limited ancient record does not always lend itself readily to answering these questions, this study seeks to explore bad citizenship, both as reality and idea, in classical Athens insofar as this is possible. Viewing Athens from this vantage point can help us appreciate the tensions surrounding democratic citizenship and the effect that these had not only on Athenian institutions but also on civic ideology. Concern over bad citizenship, as we shall see, profoundly shaped Athenian discourse about citizenship: it is no accident that repudiation of bad civic behavior went hand in hand with praise of good citizenship in Athens.[8] Indeed, the possibility and reality of bad citizenship were integral to citizen experience and had a profound impact on both civic life and public discourse.

While few scholars would deny the existence of bad citizenship in connection with civic duties in Athens, the subject has received little

[8] Cf. Hunter 1994: 110: "The competing stereotypes of the good and the bad citizen . . . are part of an ideology of citizenship." On the interplay of the ideal hoplite and his polar opposite in Athenian discourse, see Velho 2002; cf. Winkler 1990: 45–70.

in-depth attention. Although recent studies of Athenian democracy acknowledge the problem of bad citizenship, they have focused more on the institutions and ideologies that made democracy work than on the possibilities for circumventing the former and acting contrary to the latter.[9] While handbooks of Athenian law routinely mention the legal measures that Athenians adopted concerning evasion of civic obligations, detailed inquiry into bad citizenship and its wider significance lies beyond their scope. Likewise, recent commentators on the orators and comic writers are alert to bad citizenship, but extensive treatment of the subject would be tangential to their purposes.[10]

This book seeks to fill this gap in scholarship by considering closely three manifestations of bad citizenship in Athens, namely, draft evasion, cowardice on the battlefield, and evasion of liturgies and the war tax. Draft evasion has received very little study at all, despite its frequent mention in our sources.[11] Although cowardice on the battlefield has received some attention in treatments of the Greek hoplite experience (e.g., Hanson 1989: 96–104), the topic has not been examined closely within an Athenian context and in connection with basic citizen obligations under the democracy.[12] Evasion of liturgies and the war tax in Athens, by contrast, has drawn somewhat more attention (e.g., Christ 1990; E. E. Cohen 1992: 190–207; Gabrielsen 1986; 1994), but many questions remain open, including how pervasive this was and how successfully the city responded to the problem.

While this study seeks to address each of these forms of bad citizenship in its own terms, it will also examine how much these behaviors are kindred phenomena that are mutually illuminating. To the extent

[9] While two recent and engaging works on Athens treat matters relevant to bad citizenship, greed (Balot 2001a) and deception (Hesk 2000), their focus lies elsewhere.

[10] Handbooks of Athenian law: In my analysis, I draw on Lipsius 1905–15, Harrison 1968–71, MacDowell 1978, and Todd 1993. Commentators: I have found especially useful the work of MacDowell (1962, 1971, 1990), Olson (1998, 2002), and Sommerstein (1980–2002).

[11] I am not aware of any detailed study of the topic before Christ 2004, which appears with additions as Chapter 2 of this book.

[12] Roisman (2005: 105–29) provides a nice overview of the representation of military behavior in the Attic orators. My interest is in the interplay between the *realia* of Athenian military experience and the social processing of this at home through civic institutions and public discourse.

that these types of bad citizenship have attracted scholarly attention, they have been viewed largely in isolation from one another as more or less independent phenomena. The three forms of bad citizenship under consideration, however, were all rooted in the pursuit or protection of personal self-interests; emerged more prominently when citizen morale was low; and presented often similar institutional and ideological challenges to the city. By analyzing these deviations from good citizenship side by side, it is possible to identify their similarities and differences as citizen behaviors and civic problems.

In examining the topic of bad citizenship in Athens, it is important to acknowledge from the start that the ancient sources are often vague, tendentious, or alarmist in their treatment of it. Evidence for bad citizenship frequently derives from oratorical invective, comic jibes, or the snipes of critics of the Athenian democracy. If we take these sources too much at face value, we may come up with a distorted picture of democratic Athens as a city rendered helpless by bad citizenship and poised for decline and fall. V. Ehrenberg (1951), for example, relying upon an uncritical reading of comic sources, found "an almost complete lack of social conscience" (252) and "economic egoism" (373) among Athenians, intensifying over time (319, 336) and leading to the decline of Athens (368). To overlook this body of material, however, may lead to an equally mistaken picture of Athens that is akin to that advanced in Athenian patriotic discourse. W. K. Pritchett (1971: 1.27) goes so far as to generalize that in a Hellenic context, "The citizen identified his own interest with that of the state. His patriotism was shown no less in devotion on the battlefield than in financial sacrifice."[13] Our challenge is to make the most of the evidence that survives, without being taken in by hyperbole and distortion.

[13] Cf. Pearson 1962: 181: "[I]n Greek and Roman times alike, the ordinary citizen readily recognized his obligation not only to obey the laws of his state, but to be a 'good man,' so far as lay in his power, by serving his country in a military or civil capacity or by putting his wealth at the disposal of the state when it was needed." While Samons (2004) vehemently rejects the idealization of Athenian democracy, he oddly idealizes Athenian attitudes toward the state: "Athenian values associated with civic responsibilities and duties so thoroughly suffused the populace that the lives of individuals with ideological differences as vast as those that separated Socrates and Pericles still demonstrate the Athenians' dedication to the gods, their families, and their polis" (201; cf. 171, 185).

In light of the slippery nature of the source material, it is important in my view that we cast our net widely and seek to consider literary evidence from a wide range of genres – oratory, comedy, tragedy, history, and philosophy – as we look for recurring themes relevant to the assessment of bad citizenship. This cross-genre approach can help bring to the fore common features of the discussion of bad citizenship as well as throw into relief the distinctive preoccupations and perspectives of each type of source. This broad inclusion of source material makes it possible to see how much of what we encounter in different genres concerning bad citizenship reflects the shared experience of Athenian observers, even if their observations are filtered through different lenses. In attempting to evaluate critically material from so many different genres, I am indebted to my scholarly predecessors, who have thoughtfully engaged with the challenges of drawing inferences about Athens from particular genres.[14] While I am trying to elicit certain kinds of information from these sources, I do my best to respect the context in which information appears and how it is colored by genre and authorial vantage point. Although it is logical to give preference to contemporary sources in evaluating the Athenian experience of bad citizenship, occasionally I draw on later authors, for example, Diodorus Siculus (1st c. B.C.) and Plutarch (late-1st/early-2nd c. A.D.); these writers, who often draw on earlier authors, can usefully complement if not supplant contemporary sources; no significant part of my argument depends upon their testimony, however.

If the ancient sources themselves present obstacles to our inquiry into bad citizenship in Athens, so too can our preconceptions about Athenian values and behavior – in particular, assumptions about Athenian solidarity and patriotism. To come to a realistic assessment of bad citizenship in Athens, we must appreciate, first, that in any society, individuals seek ways to manipulate or circumvent rules that they regard as unfair, inconvenient, or a threat to their personal interests;

[14] My approach to the sources has been influenced especially by Dover 1974; Loraux 1986; Ober 1989, 1998; Goldhill 1990; Henderson 1990; Saïd 1998; Balot 2001a; Roisman 2005.

if a loophole in regulation or an administrative gap exists, it generally is found and exploited. In classical Athens, this common human tendency is abundantly clear in the sphere of litigation, where competing litigants shrewdly navigate around civic rules, regulations, and administrative structures in pursuit of their selfish interests (Christ 1998a: 36–9). Athenians were also prepared to act shrewdly, as we shall see, when it came to protecting or advancing their interests in the sphere of civic duties, where, as in litigation, life and property were at stake; patriotism could overcome narrowly selfish action, but it did not eliminate it.

Although it is difficult to determine the scope of shrewd behavior in connection with civic obligations, it is useful to ask in each area of civic duty what motives and opportunities Athenians had for falling short of civic ideals. While motive and opportunity do not in themselves prove that Athenians engaged in sharp practices, attention to these can help ground our assessment of contemporary claims about bad citizenship in the real circumstances of citizen experience. Where we find compelling evidence of both motive and opportunity for a particular type of bad citizenship, we should be alert to the possibility that it was common, and evaluate contemporary claims concerning its frequency in light of this.

An advantage of looking closely at the motives behind, and opportunities for, bad citizenship in Athens is that this allows us to move beyond the limited purview of many of the ancient sources, which characterize bad citizenship as the province of utterly perverse and marginal citizens, named or unnamed. These portrayals of the "otherness" of bad citizenship are interesting in their own right, as evidence of the Athenian tendency to scapegoat individuals for communal problems (cf. Sagan 1991: 168–85; Christ 1998a: 50–3). A survey of the range of motives behind different forms of bad citizenship and the diverse opportunities for these indicates, however, that the temptation to evade obligations or to fall short in performing them was not limited to utterly shameless or exceptional members of society. On the contrary, Athenians of all ilks and social classes could fall short of civic ideals of good citizenship for a variety of reasons and in many different ways. Behind the often sensational depictions of egregiously bad citizenship in our sources lies a more mundane reality of gradations of good and bad citizenship.

This study seeks first to locate bad citizenship within its cultural context in democratic Athens (Chapter 1). Although bad citizenship in Athens sometimes derived from ideological opposition to the democracy, more commonly it arose from basic personal concerns over self and property. Athenians were acutely conscious of the tug of self-interest on individuals, and frequently acknowledged and addressed this basic feature of human nature in public discourse. Consistent with this consciousness is how self-interest figures prominently in Athenian understandings of citizenship and its obligations.

Athenian democracy pragmatically acknowledged the legitimacy of personal self-interest, which was intimately connected with individual freedom, and incorporated this into its ideology of citizenship. While Athenians sometimes envisioned a citizen's performance of his duties as a spontaneous act of patriotism or as fulfillment of his filial obligation to his fatherland, they also conceptualized this as a conscious and calculated act that was consistent with individual self-interest. Citizens, according to this latter model, carry out duties for their democratic city because this benefits them as equal shareholders in it; they "give" to the city and "get" something in return for this.

Although this model of citizenship, which sought to harness individual self-interest for the common good, could be a powerful inducement to fulfill citizen obligations, the expectation of reciprocity between city and citizen that it fostered could prove problematic. When individuals felt that their personal self-interests were in danger and saw no reciprocal return for subordinating these to the public interest, they might feel justified in evading or falling short in their duties. Especially in hard times when the city's demands on its citizens were most acutely felt – and such times were not infrequent from the late-fifth century B.C. on, the temptation to hold back in performing civic obligations was strong. In good times as well as bad ones, however, Athenians often acted strategically to protect their interests and exercised shrewdness – which is intimately connected with personal self-interest in a Hellenic context – in determining how or whether to comply with civic expectations. Utterly unscrupulous individuals were not alone in acting strategically in their citizenship; even Athenians who complied with the city's demands on them often did so with an eye to protecting and advancing their personal interests.

Because citizen compliance with civic obligations could not be taken for granted, the democracy developed a range of mechanisms, administrative and legal, to compel citizens to carry out their duties. The democratic city, however, was not entirely comfortable with compelling free citizens to do their civic duties; Athenians, unlike Spartans, preferred to elicit good citizenship and discourage its opposite more through persuasion and exhortation than through coercion and "fear of the laws." Although public discourse, which was fostered by a variety of democratic institutions, facilitated this in a variety of ways, its persistent exhortation to embrace good citizenship and reject its dark alternative attests to the ongoing challenge of selfish citizen behavior.

After situating bad citizenship in its democratic context in Athens, this study turns to consider specific forms of it, beginning with draft evasion (Chapter 2). While Athenian civic ideology often insisted that citizens were eager to serve the city in time of war, most hoplites were in fact conscripts. Whenever modern democracies have employed conscription, draft evasion has cropped up; this was also the case in democratic Athens. Frequent allusions to draft evasion in forensic oratory and comedy make it clear that it was familiar. Although it is impossible for us to know how widespread evasion was, it appears to have been a real temptation and possibility that evoked considerable social concern.

There were many reasons why Athenians might seek to evade hoplite service, not least of which was the desire to avoid the very real risks of injury and death that accompanied service. While some embraced these risks out of a sense of duty and honor, others preferred a long life without glory to a short life with it (cf. Hom. *Il.* 9.410–16). As ancient observers fully appreciated, men diverge widely in how much they are attracted to honor. Once we understand that Athenians, despite the martial bent of Hellenic culture, were not uniformly drawn to military service, we can see that draft evasion was a natural option for those who did not wish to serve.

Although it was not a simple matter to evade the draft in Athens, it was probably easier than in most modern democracies, which possess elaborate bureaucracies for administering conscription and charge public agents with enforcing the obligation to serve. In Athens, conscription appears to have been fairly loosely administered, especially in the fifth century B.C., and no public agent was required to prosecute dodgers. In this setting, individuals seeking to avoid the draft could, with some effort, manipulate exemptions or exercise influence with the officials involved in administering conscription to win release from service. Some individuals went so far as to defy the system outright by not presenting themselves for service at muster. While prosecution for evasion by volunteer prosecutors was possible, this does not appear to have been very common.

Athenian concerns over compulsory military service and its evasion surface in an unexpected theater, literally, on the tragic stage. Athenian tragedians regularly bring before their audiences myths that focus on recruitment for military service and attempts to evade this. In presenting these mythological scenarios, tragedians reflect, and engage with, their contemporary milieu: attuned to the tensions surrounding contemporary conscription and its evasion, tragedians brought these on stage before large Athenian audiences.

While a conscript who appeared for muster fulfilled a basic obligation of his citizenship, the city expected him not only to serve but to do so honorably and, above all, without cowardice. Although Athenian hoplites were as courageous as any of their rivals, cowardice and less extreme shortfalls in courage were a real possibility for individuals and groups, and our Athenian sources convey a great deal of anxiety over this (Chapter 3). This high level of concern is not surprising, given the reliance of the city on the fighting mettle of its forces. At the same time, however, this may reflect the fact that deficiencies in courage were difficult to prevent because they often occurred spontaneously as a result of fear and panic rather than rational reflection. Furthermore, it could be difficult to detect individual lapses in courage, and awkward to address group shortfalls when, for example, an entire force was routed and fled the field.

To understand the place of hoplite courage and cowardice in Athenian citizenship, it is important first to consider these within the immediate context of a military campaign. While cowardice in the heat of hoplite battle was of fundamental concern to the city, concerns over courage and cowardice pervaded a campaign from start to finish. At all stages of a campaign, individuals and groups were conscious of how their actions were perceived by those present – friend and foe alike – and how, at a later time, upon their return to Athens, these might be interpreted. To protect or advance manly reputation required not only bold deeds but a presentation of self consistent with this; to some extent at least, men could shape how others assessed their courage. Paradoxically, while the manly competition to gain honor and avoid shame reached its climax on the battlefield, the conditions of battle could make it difficult to gauge the courage or cowardice of participants. This was especially true when, as often happened, an army was routed and abandoned the field indecorously amid chaos and confusion; in the immediate aftermath of defeat, the performance of individual and group was open to contestation and partisan interpretation.

If the performance of hoplites was open to dispute during a campaign, this was all the more true when Athenian hoplites returned home and made claims and counterclaims at a remove from the battlefield. On the home front the social dynamics of defending or enhancing reputation were transformed in the presence of civic institutions. Of particular interest is the city's disparate treatment of group and individual failures. On the one hand, the city chose to overlook the ignominy of defeated forces, allowing them to disband upon their return without public comment on their collective embarrassment. On the other hand, it allowed for prosecutions of generals of unsuccessful forces and of individual hoplites accused of cowardice; the former, however, were much more common than the latter, in keeping with a democratic political culture that was more comfortable holding the prominent and powerful accountable than it was average citizens.

Once the question of hoplite performance entered public discourse, it took on a life of its own that reveals little about battlefield behavior and a great deal about courage and cowardice as matters of civic concern and ideology. The Attic funeral orations, in praising the state's war dead, naturally focus on Athenian courage; at the same time, however, they can be read as polemic against cowardly behavior in battle and as exhortation to the living to behave honorably when called upon to serve the city. Other forms of public discourse more directly address cowardice. While group cowardice or shortfalls in courage are taboo subjects, individuals' deficiencies sometimes come under scrutiny and are held up for ridicule and shame. Of particular interest is the frequency of charges of cowardice against politically prominent individuals, like the orator Demosthenes. This is significant for understanding not only Athenian expectations of political leaders but also more generally citizen norms and ideals.

After considering bad citizenship in the sphere of military service, this study examines the response of wealthy Athenians to their obligation to pay the *eisphora* and carry out costly liturgies, including the trierarchy in connection with the city's navy and the *chorēgia*, which entailed providing a chorus for a civic festival (Chapter 4). The city's relationship with its wealthy benefactors was distinctly troubled in the classical period. This is reflected in the institutional history of the arrangements governing liturgies and the *eisphora*, and in the diverse complaints in our sources concerning these obligations. Although it was difficult for wealthy men to evade their financial duties altogether, they developed a range of strategies for protecting their fortunes from these.

Athens' complex arrangements governing liturgies and the *eisphora* took form gradually and, as best we can tell, amid controversy and conflict between wealthy citizens and the city. While this is best documented in connection with the fourth-century overhaul of many of these arrangements, tensions likely date back at least to the mid-fifth century when the newly empowered popular courts became the ultimate arbiters of cases involving attempts by wealthy men to win release from liturgical service through the legal procedures of *skēpsis* and *antidosis*. During the Peloponnesian War (431–404 B.C.), the introduction of the *eisphora* in 428 added further pressure to the relationship between the wealthy and the city, and tensions concerning financial obligations figured prominently in the oligarchic revolution of 411.

While wealthy Athenians were especially sensitive to the costs of their obligations, resentment could arise from other considerations as well. The rich expected public gratitude (*charis*) in the form of honor and civic privilege for their expenditure, and the city encouraged this expectation; in practice, however, it could be difficult for a wealthy man to reap public rewards for his sacrifice, and this could lead to alienation. Questions of fairness also arose among the wealthy over the fact that they exclusively bore the burden of financial obligations and over the manner in which these were allocated among the rich. The compulsory nature of financial obligations likewise could evoke resentment, because not all Athenians were subject to this compulsion, which could encumber an individual personally as well as financially.

Wealthy men had recourse to a range of strategies to reduce their liability to financial obligations. Probably the most common course was to conceal wealth from public view insofar as this was feasible, to avoid initial assignment to a financial obligation. Even after a wealthy man was assigned to a liturgy, however, he had a number of options to escape service or to minimize the expense of carrying it out. Wealthy Athenians became adept, moreover, at putting the best face on their liturgical records, regardless of the circumstances under which they came to carry out liturgies and the quality of their performance of these.

By exploring Athens' confrontation with bad citizenship in its diverse forms, we can better understand how this early democracy grappled with the challenge that individual interests posed to civic cohesion and cooperative enterprises. If Athens was largely successful in mustering citizen cooperation for its various endeavors, this could not be taken for granted: the city's ongoing efforts, institutional and ideological, to overcome citizen reluctance and resistance are testimony to the continuing challenge it faced. This study, I hope, will not only lead to a deeper understanding of the Athenian experience but also provide a mirror in which we may reflect on the equally complex relationship of individual and state in modern democracies.

I

THE SELF-INTERESTED CITIZEN

> All men, or most men, wish what is noble but choose what is profitable. (Arist. *EN* 1163a1)

Although bad citizenship in Athens could arise from a wide range of motivations, it was rooted in the individual's pursuit of self-interest. While few scholars would deny the presence of self-interest among Athenians, the role of self-interest in democratic citizenship in Athens has not been sufficiently explicated. Athenians were highly attuned to the tug of self-interest on the individual and the problems this could pose for their city. Democratic ideology did not seek so much to suppress the pursuit of self-interest as to exploit this: good citizenship, it proclaimed, benefits both the individual and the city. Because individuals varied widely in the extent to which they embraced this view and because shrewd, self-serving behavior was always a temptation, the city faced an ongoing challenge: to persuade and, if necessary, to compel citizens to perform their civic obligations.

This chapter seeks, first, to contextualize self-interest in Athens by surveying how Athenian sources treat this as a fundamental problem for human society. The frank and persistent treatment of the subject in a range of sources attests to the primacy of self-interest in Athenian understandings of human motivation and behavior. The chapter then turns to consider how Athenian civic ideology engaged with the problem of individual self-interest by portraying the relationship between citizen and city as a mutually beneficial one. While this ideology, which shrewdly appealed to citizens' self-interests, could be a powerful inducement to good citizenship, individual self-interest proved difficult to tame in practice. As compulsory duties were often in conflict with private interests, strategic behavior was naturally elicited from individuals. This was true not only as individuals determined whether or how to comply with civic demands upon them, but also as they chose how to represent their citizenship to the public. Finally, this chapter sketches some civic strategies, institutional and ideological, for encouraging good citizenship and controlling its opposite. Although the threat of civic compulsion helped induce citizens to carry out their duties, Athenians were ambivalent about forcing free men under a democracy to serve their city. They tended to prefer, therefore, to foster good citizenship and discourage its opposite through public discourse rather than to force it through bureaucratic and legal mechanisms.

SELF-INTEREST AND ATHENIAN CITIZENSHIP

Although the pursuit of self-interest is ubiquitous in human societies, each society differs in how it views and responds to self-interest as a threat to communal enterprises. The following analysis seeks not to provide a complete account of self-interest in Athens but rather to highlight features of it that bear on our understanding of citizen mentality and behavior in the sphere of civic obligations. Athenians regarded the pursuit of self-interest as a central feature of human nature and a primary determinant of behavior; their democracy, therefore, did not seek so much to overcome this as to redirect it in pursuit of the common good.[1]

Human Nature and Self-Interest

Greeks took for granted that individuals are ultimately selfish and regularly base their actions on what they perceive to be most advantageous

[1] I focus on Athenian views of self-interest, as this is key to understanding not only Athenian perspectives on human motivation but citizen behavior itself, which was likely influenced by the way Athenians regarded self-interest. For the debate in the social sciences over self-interest as an explanation for human behavior, see the essays in Mansbridge 1990a, and Amemiya 2005: 158–9.

personally. As K. J. Dover (1974: 81) observes in his seminal study of Greek values, "No Greek doubted . . . that an individual is very apt to give precedence to his own interest over the interests of others." While Greeks did not view this innate selfishness as an absolute obstacle to cooperation within human societies, they were acutely conscious of how individuals (even as they collaborated with others) remained attuned to their own interests and could thereby jeopardize group efforts.[2] This Hellenic perspective was expressed in and perpetuated by a shared poetic tradition, including Homeric epic where the problem of individual self-interest looms large (Balot 2001a: 59–70).

Classical Athenian perspectives on human nature and self-interest were influenced not only by the cultural heritage that they shared with other Greeks but by their common experiences as a people in the fifth century B.C.[3] The growth of democracy in Athens in the early part of the fifth century reflected and reinforced the egalitarian principle that the city should respect and consider the interests of all male citizens, not simply an elite few.[4] The Athenian naval empire, which took shape in the decades after the conclusion of the Persian Wars in 479 B.C., was among other things an exercise in the pursuit of collective interests (Th. 1.75; Plu. *Arist.* 25.2–3; *Per.* 12; cf. [X.] *Ath. Pol.* 1.16–17).[5] Athenians probably acted in part to preserve their individual stakes in the spoils of the empire when they restricted citizenship to individuals born of two Athenian parents (451/0 B.C.) ([Arist.] *Ath. Pol.* 26.4; Plu. *Per.* 37.2–5; Patterson 1981: 102–7; Whitehead 1991: 147). The experience of the Peloponnesian War (431–404 B.C.), however, brought conflicts

[2] While altruism was possible in this setting (see Herman 1998 and Konstan 2000), those engaging in it did not readily lose sight of their self-interests; this is especially true of civic benefactors (cf. E. E. Cohen 1992: 191), as we shall see in Chapter 4.

[3] A further influence on Athenians was the poetry of Solon, which grapples with the social and political problems posed by greed and self-interest in early-sixth-century Athens: see Balot 2001a: 73–98.

[4] On the balancing of competing interests as a central problem for Athens and the Greek *polis* in general, see Ober 1993: 136, 141–9. The topic of democracy and self-interest is taken up at length in the next section. On the prominent role of the idea of universal self-interest in the emergence of modern egalitarianism, see Holmes 1990: 284–5.

[5] Athenian imperialism, as an exercise in the pursuit of group interests, may well have made individual Athenians more ready to pursue their own self-interests within the city. As Balot (2004c: 91) observes: "Foreign policy helps to educate the desires and self-understanding of the citizenry . . . "

between individual and collective interests to the fore, as war, plague, and dislocation took a heavy toll on individuals. Those who joined in the oligarchic juntas of 411 and 404/3 B.C. acted in part to preserve or advance what they viewed as their personal interests (cf. Balot 2001a: 211–24).[6] While an intellectual like Thucydides, as we shall see, could view the history of fifth-century Athens explicitly in terms of the pursuit of self-interest, personal and collective, all Athenians must have been conscious of self-interest as a powerful force in their lives and the life of the city.[7]

The way that Athenians conceptualized and spoke about self-interest was deeply influenced by the sophists, itinerant intellectuals who began to arrive in Athens in the mid-fifth century.[8] The sophists were drawn to Athens in pursuit of profits in a market ripe for their intellectual wares (cf. Pl. *Prt.* 313c–e; X. *Mem.* 1.6.13), especially the teaching of rhetoric, which was essential for success in the democratic lawcourts and Assembly. Wealthy students, who could afford the sophists' steep fees, flocked to them (cf. Pl. *Ap.* 19e–20a) because they or their fathers calculated that this investment would pay off. The sophistic enterprise, founded on this self-interested relationship between teacher and pupil, not only armed students with rhetoric to pursue personal advantage but also schooled them in the rhetoric of self-interest, that is, how to build arguments exploiting the assumption that it is human nature for individuals – and by extension, states too – to pursue what is advantageous to them (e.g., Th. 1.75–6; cf. [X.] *Ath. Pol.* 2.19).[9]

Although sophistic doctrines concerning self-interest could, if taken to an extreme, constitute a challenge to conventional morality (Ant.

6 M. C. Taylor (2002: 95–6) points out that, according to Thucydides (8.48.3), self-interest also motivated many members of the *dēmos* to accept the oligarchic regime of 411.

7 On the intense discussion of self-interest in late-fifth-century Athens, see Balot 2001a: 136–233. Balot (181) goes too far, in my view, however, in contrasting the situation before the Peloponnesian War with that during it: "As long as the empire was successful, there was no conflict between the good of the polis and the good of the individual. Imperialistic success made it easy for individuals to identify themselves first and foremost as Athenian citizens." As we shall see in Chapter 4, the wealthy and the city were likely in conflict over liturgies well before the start of the Peloponnesian War.

8 On the sophists, see Guthrie 1971; Kerferd 1981; Romilly 1992; Wallace 1998b.

9 On the evaluation of individual and group behavior in similar terms, see Dover 1974: 310–11. Cf. Ober 1998: 68: "For Thucydides, the selves that naturally act to further their perceived interests are collectivities."

Soph. 87 fr. 44 D–K; Pl. *Grg*. 482e, 483b–d; *R*. 365c) and go beyond what a broad public was ready to embrace, the assumption that men naturally seek their own advantage was broadly appealing. Thus, when Plato criticizes cynical views of self-interest, he attributes these not only to the sophists but also to the mass of men (e.g., *Lg*. 731d–e).[10] While Plato's assertions about "most men" (e.g., *R*. 586a–b; cf. *Lg*. 831c) are tainted by his disdain for democracy and the average men whom it empowers (*R*. 555b–562a),[11] to all appearances the sophists found Athenians highly receptive to their pragmatic view of human nature.[12]

Abundant evidence of how much the Athenian public was intrigued by self-interest as a force in human society is provided by public discourse in Athens, that is, oratory and drama addressed to large Athenian audiences in public contexts. Because public discourse was tailored (to varying degrees, to be sure) to take into account the assumptions of popular audiences, it can provide clues to widely held Athenian views and concerns.[13]

The topic of self-interest crops up prominently in a wide variety of public settings in Athens, including the lawcourts, Assembly, and Theater of Dionysus. Those addressing Athenian audiences offer a range of perspectives on self-interest, sometimes appealing to it as justification for individual and collective behavior, sometimes criticizing those who pursue it to excess. In either case, the frequency with which they address self-interest points to its centrality in Athenian thinking concerning human motivation.[14]

Athenian litigation regularly brought before large panels of jurors the spectacle of individuals struggling to protect or advance their

[10] Additional passages are collected in note 23.

[11] Although Aristotle is sometimes equally cynical about "most men" (see note 23 in this chapter), he is less harsh at *EN* 1163a1, quoted at the opening of this chapter; cf. 1104b30; E. *Hipp*. 373–90.

[12] Cf. Balot 2001a: 238: "The views expressed by Plato's leading immoralists represented only an amplification of competitive values that were themselves deeply maintained even within Athenian democratic culture."

[13] On public discourse as a source for popular views and ideology, see Dover 1974: 1–45; Ober 1989: 43–9; Roisman 2005: 1–6.

[14] Elster (2002: 6–7) greatly overestimates in my view the "unavowability" of self-interest as a motivation in an Athenian context.

personal interests within a legal framework (Christ 1998a: 32–43). Self-interest often surfaces as an explicit topic within the self-interested claims advanced by litigants. For example, litigants sometimes generalize about the inherent selfishness of human nature. Thus one of Isaeus' clients asserts, "No man hates what profits him nor does he place others' interests before his own" (3.66; cf. Dem. 36.54). One of Lysias' clients invokes a similar view of human nature to defend his passive collaboration with the oligarchic Thirty in 404/3: "No man is naturally either an oligarch or a democrat, but rather each is eager to see established whatever constitution he finds advantageous to himself" (25.8; cf. 25.10; Isoc. 8.133; Wolpert 2002: 111–18). Antiphon, in his defense concerning his role in the oligarchy of the Four Hundred in 411, may (the text is partly mutilated) go so far as to suggest that Athenians are universally attuned to self-interest: in arguing that overthrow of the democracy would have been contrary to his own interests because he was much in demand as a speech writer under the democracy, he asks incredulously, "Am I, alone of the Athenians ([μόνος] Ἀθη[ναίων]), unable to recognize this or to understand what is profitable to me?" (fr. 1 Thalheim).[15]

Litigants' cynical assumptions about human nature extend to their understanding of how jurors will decide their cases. Litigants regularly assume that jurors will render a decision based not only on the justness of their claims but also on what is expedient for the Athenian people (*dēmos*) (Ant. 2.1.10; Lys. 19.64).[16] While litigants stop short of asking jurors to disregard justice and decide a suit solely on the basis of what will benefit them as members of the *dēmos*, the explicit appeal to expedience in a legal context is disconcerting to a modern audience. For an

[15] Although the key phrase "alone of the Athenians" is heavily restored, this would be consistent with the tone of its context. I doubt that Antiphon's assertions concerning self-interest would have seemed as brazen to an Athenian court as Balot (2001a: 217) suggests. It is certainly true, however, that litigants, when it served them, denied that they were motivated by crass self-interest and greed and attributed these motivations to their rivals (cf. Roisman 2005: 82; 173–6).

[16] On such arguments, see Dover 1974: 309–10; Ober 1989: 146–7; Christ 1998a: 40–3; Millett 1998: 232–3. The Old Oligarch, a critic of Athenian democracy, exaggerates in asserting: "In the courts they are not so much concerned with justice as with their own advantage" ([X.] *Ath. Pol.* 1.13).

Athenian audience, however, group decision-making, like individual decision-making, naturally entailed considerations of self-interest, and it was no crime to acknowledge this openly.[17]

Frank acknowledgement of this is even more pronounced in the Athenian Assembly. Whereas litigants in the courts appeal to their audiences primarily on the basis of what is just, with calculations of advantage thrown in as further grounds for a favorable verdict, speakers in the Assembly tend to focus on what is advantageous to the city (Arist. *Rh.* 1358b; Dover 1974: 311–12). To be sure, because Athenians wished to believe they were acting not only prudently but also fairly, speakers in the Assembly do not normally set advantage and justice against one another.[18] Nonetheless, they assume that the city's survival in a perilous world demands that expedience be the ultimate criterion for collective decision-making.

Attic tragedy and comedy likewise reflect, each in its own idiom, the Athenian preoccupation with self-interest as a human motivation. Through mythical plots set in the distant past and often outside of Athens, tragedy provided Athenians with a safe venue for reflecting on contemporary concerns about the city and life within it (Zeitlin 1990; Goldhill 1990; Saïd 1998). This was a natural place, therefore, for Athenians to consider the problematic ramifications of egocentrism for human relationships and society at large.

Athenian tragedians are very much attuned to the contemporary discussion of self-interest as a fundamental human motivation. At times, their characters explicitly address this. For example, the Tutor in Euripides' *Medea*, reflecting on Jason's pursuit of personal advantage, asks the Nurse: "Are you only now learning that every man loves himself more than others?" (85–6). Similarly, Sophocles' Oedipus poses the rhetorical question, "For what good man is not a friend to himself?" (*OC* 309). These comments concerning individual self-interest

[17] I am not persuaded by D. Cohen (1995: 115) that Athenians went so far as to assimilate justice and advantage in these contexts: the fact that speakers distinguish clearly between considerations of justice and those based on advantage suggests there was no fundamental confusion between the two.

[18] Thucydides' Diodotus (3.44) is exceptional in distinguishing so pointedly between advantage and justice.

are offered not as matters for debate – no interlocutor challenges them – but rather as pithy articulations of conventional wisdom (cf. S. *Aj.* 1366; *Ant.* 435–40; E. *Hel.* 999).[19]

If tragedians invoke the common view that the pursuit of self-interest is ubiquitous, however, they cast extreme egocentrism in a dark light. Thus, for example, Euripides' stalwart Iolaus posits at the opening of the *Heraclidae*: "the man whose heart runs unbridled toward profit (*kerdos*) is useless to his city and hard to deal with, being good only to himself" (1–4).[20] Elsewhere, Euripides calls attention to the dangers of the rhetoric of self-interest, by showing how individuals can exploit this to justify ugly and anti-social behavior. Thus Euripides' ruthless tyrant Polyphontes justifies his behavior on the grounds that "I am experiencing that which all mortals do; loving myself especially, I am not ashamed" (fr. 452, with Cropp, in Collard, Cropp and Lee, eds., 1997: 144). Similarly, Euripides' Eteocles and Polyneices dubiously invoke their personal interests as justification for jeopardizing their native Thebes (*Ph.* 499–525; 439–40; cf. Balot 2001a: 207–10).

While tragedians expose extreme selfishness as ugly and dangerous to human communities, they also sometimes show that it is not to the advantage of an individual to pursue self-interest without restraint. Thus, unabashedly self-interested parties – like Jason, Polyphontes, Eteocles, and Polyneices – often fare very poorly in tragedy.[21] Although tragedians frequently explore the problem of self-interested behavior through the excesses of Odysseus (e.g., S. *Ph.* 111; cf. Stanford 1963: 102–17), in Sophocles' *Ajax*, Odysseus advances a more moderate standard of behavior: he argues on the basis of what moderns might term enlightened self-interest that his enemy Ajax should be given a proper burial because he himself may someday benefit from

[19] Cf. also Men. *Mon.* 407 ("there is no one who is not a friend to himself"); Arist. *EN* 1168b10 ("a man is his own best friend"); Pl. *Lg.* 731d–e. The proverbial flavor of many of these utterances suggests an origin in popular wisdom.

[20] On *kerdos* and self-interest, see also S. fr. 354.1–5; *Ph.* 111; E. fr. 794.

[21] On the killing of Polyphontes in Euripides' *Cresphontes*, see Cropp, in Collard, Cropp, and Lee, eds., 1997: 121–5; fr. 459, which Cropp (147) places after the tyrant's death, may condemn his shameless pursuit of self-interest: "The kind of profits (*kerdē*) a mortal should acquire are those he is never going to lament later." Likewise, in Euripides' *Heracles*, the shamelessly self-interested Lykos (165–9) perishes.

this convention ("For whom am I likely to work if not for myself?") (1364–8). All may benefit, Sophocles suggests, from looking beyond their narrow and immediate interests.[22]

Old Comedy, like tragedy, invited Athenians to reflect on problematic features of their common experience (cf. Henderson 1990). Within a framework of outrageous humor and fantastic plots, comic writers reflected on the complexities of civic life through caricatures of both average and prominent citizens. Aristophanes, whose extant comedies constitute the bulk of our evidence for Old Comedy, regularly addresses the conflict between individual and collective interests within the city.

Aristophanes gleefully lays bare the selfish side of human nature. His comedies are full of characters who are intent on satisfying their appetites for sex and food and on acquiring money and power in order to do so; they are often ready to employ any means to achieve their ends, with little heed to the cost to others.[23] This selfishness pervades public as well as private life: powerful individuals struggle to win the affection of the masses to advance their own selfish ends (*Knights*); average men seek personal profit through payment for jury service (*Wasps*) or for attendance at the Assembly (*Ecclesiazusae*). While Aristophanes may present men as "worse than they are" (cf. Arist. *Poet.* 1448a) to amuse his audience, the fact that they were receptive to this dark view of human nature provides testimony to Athenian cynicism.[24]

If Aristophanic comedy frequently shows human selfishness in action, it often argues for the containment of this within civic life.

[22] Cf. Morris (1994: 357–8) on the interplay of short-term interests and long-term ones.

[23] Plato and Aristotle offer a similar picture of human motivation. Most men live to feed their own boundless appetites and desires (Pl. *R.* 505b; *Lg.* 918c–d; Arist. *Pol.* 1267b4; cf. Solon fr. 13.71–3) and pursue wealth (Pl. *Lg.* 870a-b; Arist. *Pol.* 1318b15) because it enables them to do so (Pl. *R.* 580e). Most men envy the tyrant because he can selfishly and without constraint satisfy his appetites (Pl. *Grg.* 471d–472a; cf. *Lg.* 874e–875b; Arist. *EN* 1134b; X. *Hier.* 1.9).

[24] For a more optimistic view of human nature, see Men. *Dys.* 718–22, where Knemon states after his rescue from the well: "By Hephaestus, I thought no man could be kindly to another – that's how very deluded I had become through studying all the different ways of life, how men in their calculations (τοὺς λογισμούς) angle for gain (πρὸς τὸ κερδαίνειν). That was my obstacle, but one man has succeeded now in proving me quite wrong . . ."

The *dēmos*, it asserts, must not tolerate those who selfishly fail to fulfill their civic duties (*V.* 1114–21; *Ra.* 1014, 1065–6; *Lys.* 654–5; cf. *Ec.* 746–876), or profiteers – especially politicians – who reap benefits at the expense of their fellow citizens (*Knights passim*). While Aristophanes seeks to incite Athenians to moral outrage against these selfish citizens, he also appeals directly to their collective self-interests. For example, Bdelycleon – whose name indicates that he, like the poet (*V.* 1029–37), hates the popular politician Cleon – insists that, if average Athenians could curtail the rapacity of politicians, they could themselves live off the fruits of empire (655–724; cf. *Eq.* 797, 1330; Balot 2001a: 196–200). Aristophanes, like orators addressing the Athenian Assembly, takes for granted that Athenians act collectively on the basis of their self-interests.

Plato, a native Athenian, and Aristotle, a resident of Athens for much of his career, reflect their Athenian context in treating human self-interest as a central problem within their ethical and political analyses. Although both philosophers regard the pursuit of self-interest as ubiquitous or nearly so, they condemn excess in this matter.[25] They do so, however, largely on prudential grounds: virtuous and just behavior is ultimately beneficial to an individual.[26] To justify their ethical and political perspectives on grounds other than individual self-interest – properly viewed, to be sure – would run against the grain of Hellenic and Athenian culture and fail to persuade an audience that was attuned to its self-interests.

Democratic Citizenship and Self-Interest

Athenian democracy, rather than seeking to suppress the individual pursuit of self-interest, pragmatically acknowledged its legitimacy. Two

[25] Pursuit of self-interest ubiquitous: Pl. *Lg.* 731d–e; Arist. *EN* 1142a, 1159a14, 1163a1, 1168b10; *Rh.* 1371b19. Condemnation of excess: Pl. *Lg.* 731d–e ("the cause of all moral faults [πάντων ἁμαρτημάτων] in every case lies in the person's excessive love of self"); Arist. *Pol.* 1263b1 ("the universal feeling of love for oneself is surely not purposeless, but a natural instinct. On the other hand selfishness [τὸ δὲ φίλαυτον] is justly blamed; but this is not to love oneself but to love oneself more than one ought.").

[26] See Pl. *Grg.* 522d–e; 527b; *Ap.* 30b; *R.* 369b–c; *Prt.* 327b; cf. Arist. *EN* 1160a10; Plu. *Sol.* 5; Heinaman 2004. For prudential ethics in Xenophon, see e.g., *Mem.* 3.9.4; *HG* 6.3.11.

key democratic principles, freedom and equality, reflected the high status of the adult, male citizen and his personal interests in Athens. Individuals were free to pursue their interests (cf. Th. 2.37.2) insofar as these did not threaten others or the community at large. Each individual enjoyed (theoretically at least) the same basic civic privileges as every other citizen, including equal votes in the Assembly and equal access to the many public offices that were distributed by lot; as equal shareholders in their city, individual citizens could lay claim to equal shares of public distributions whether in the form of wages for performing civic functions or more direct handouts (e.g., Dem. 10.45; cf. 3.33–4).[27] Democratic institutions helped ensure that these principles would be observed; the popular lawcourts, manned largely by average Athenians, allowed individuals to appeal on equal terms to the city's laws to protest assaults upon themselves or their interests by magistrates or private persons. The democracy's high regard for the individual and his interests set Athens apart from most other city-states and in particular from Sparta (Plu. *Ages.* 37.6).[28] Athenians were conscious of this fact and incorporated this into their ideology of citizenship.

[27] On individual freedom under Athenian democracy, see Hansen 1991: 74–81, 1996; Wallace 1994, 1996, 2004; D. Cohen 1997; cf. Raaflaub 2004; Sluiter and Rosen 2004; on equality and its limits, see Hansen 1991: 81–5; Raaflaub 1996; Cartledge 1996; cf. Hedrick 1994: 307–17. For democratic citizens as equal shareholders in the city, see Sinclair 1988: 23; Manville 1990: 7–11; Ostwald 1996; Schofield 1996; Ober 1998: 312–13. The fact that citizens shared in benefits could be said to obligate them to share also in the city's woes and burdens: see Lys. 31.5; Lyc. 1.133; cf. Th. 2.63.1; Pl. *Lg.* 754d–e.

Citizens possessed their shares automatically by virtue of their status as free men, not because the city was thought to bestow shares upon them as Plato's Socrates (*Cri.* 51c) envisions it. Athenians regarded themselves more as "possessors" of their city than as "possessions" of it, *pace* Ostwald 1996: 57, who maintains that in a Greek context, "Citizenship was neither a right nor a matter of participation, but a matter of belonging, of knowing one's identity not in terms of one's own personal values but in terms of the community that was both one's possession and possessor" (cf. Arist. *Pol.* 1337a25).

[28] I disagree with Seager 2001: 389: "The democracy demanded from the individual not merely solidarity but subordination: absolute obedience to the people, its institutions, and its appointed representatives, and unquestioning acknowledgement of the priority of the city's interests over his own and those of his family and friends." For a more balanced view of the relationship between citizen/*oikos* and *polis* in Athens, see Roisman 2005: 55–9; cf. Farrar 1992: 17 ("Athenian political life raised the possibility of maintaining a bracing tension between personal and civic identity"), and 1996: 112–13. On the related debate over how far separate private and public spheres can be distinguished in Athens, see Ober 1993: 142–3, and 1998: 148, with n. 57; Patterson 1998: 226–9.

Athenian civic ideology offered citizens diverse models for envisioning their relationship with the city. According to one frequently invoked model, the city stood in the role of father to its citizen sons: the fatherland (*patris*) benevolently nurtures and raises its sons and they, in return, obey and serve it as good citizens (Lys. 2.17; Dem. 18.205; 60.4; Lyc. 1.53; cf. Ar. *Lys.* 638–48).[29] This hierarchical model, based on the unequal relationship of father and son, justifies a basic and undeniable facet of the city's relationship with its citizens, namely, its authority over them; the subservience of citizen to city, it suggests, is as natural and necessary as the subordination of son to father.[30]

A different model of citizenship, however, envisions a more equal relationship between citizen and city based upon mutual self-interest. It presents good citizenship as a conscious and rational decision involving enlightened self-interest. A democratic polity, this model asserts, best protects and serves the interests of individual citizens; its citizens, conscious of this, willingly serve their city, because they benefit themselves in so doing. This framing of the give-and-take relation of Athenian shareholders to their city translates the powerful Greek idea of reciprocity to an egalitarian and democratic context.[31]

While Athenians were free to privilege one of these models over the other in their assertions about citizenship, they often invoked these together as complementary – if not entirely reconcilable – visions of the relation between citizen and city.[32] These models coexist in

[29] On this model, see Strauss 1993: 44–5, 49, 57–60. Plato, in advancing a more authoritarian model for the city, makes it not only father but master (*despotēs*) to its citizens (*Cri.* 50e; cf. 51b; *Lg.* 804d). For military service to the city as something owed to the nurturing motherland, see A. *Th.* 10–20, 415–16; E. *Heracl.* 826–7.

[30] On Athenian assumptions concerning father-son relations, see Dover 1974: 273–5 and Strauss 1993: 61–99.

[31] While reciprocity is also present in the relationship on which the father-son model of citizenship is based (a son is said to owe his father a debt of gratitude for raising him: see Millett 1991: 132–5, 289 n. 11), this relationship is inherently unequal and the reciprocity associated with it asymmetrical. On reciprocity in a Greek context, see the essays in Gill, Postlethwaite, and Seaford 1998.

[32] This is common, for example, in the Attic funeral orations, which are discussed below in the text. Cf. Lycurgus' appeal to each model in his prosecution of Leocrates: he portrays the Athenian citizen at one point as a dutiful son (1.53), and at another point as a friend (*philos*) who reciprocates the city's gifts to him (1.133).

Athenian civic ideology presumably because they reflect two important aspects of democratic citizenship. On the one hand, citizens were ultimately subject to the authority of their fatherland and obliged to carry out civic duties for it. On the other hand, it was important for democratic citizens to view good citizenship as consensual – an act of volition on the part of free men – and for this to be so it had to be compatible with the interests of individuals. This latter strand of Athenian civic ideology deserves closer attention, as it has broad implications for our understanding of citizen mentality. Let us consider first how this ideology of citizenship is articulated in our sources, and then probe some of the tensions embedded in it.

The historian Herodotus attributes Athens' rise to power after the expulsion of the Peisistratid tyranny (510 B.C.) to the fact that free individuals have a vested interest in supporting their city:

> So Athens had increased in greatness. It is not only in one respect but in everything that democracy (ἡ ἰσηγορίη)[33] is clearly a good thing. Take the case of the Athenians: under the rule of tyrants they proved no better in war than any of their neighbors, but, once rid of those tyrants, they were by far the first of all. What this makes clear is that, while held in subjection, they chose to play the coward (ἐθελοκάκεον) since they were working for a despot, but, once freed, each was zealous to succeed for his own self (αὐτὸς ἕκαστος ἑωυτῷ προεθυμέετο κατεργάζεσθαι). (5.78)

In embracing this view of Athens' success under democracy, Herodotus echoes the claims of Athenian civic ideology concerning the role of self-interest in motivating democratic citizens.[34]

[33] For this translation of the problematic ἰσηγορίη, see Forsdyke 2001: 333 n. 13 and Raaflaub 2004: 97, 222–3.

[34] On Herodotus' invocation of Athenian civic ideology in this passage, see Forsdyke 2001: 332–41; 348–9; Millender 2002: 47, 50. Thucydides (1.17), perhaps under the influence of Hdt. 5.78 (thus Hornblower 1991: 50), likewise views tyranny as an obstacle to a state's success, because tyrants have regard only for their own interests; cf. Th. 2.46.1; 7.69.2. For the view that free men have more fighting spirit than those under despots, see also Hp. *Aer.* 16 ("they run risks on their own behalf, and they carry off for themselves the prizes of bravery and likewise the penalty of cowardice"), with Forsdyke 2001: 339–41.

Strong evidence that Athenians linked good citizenship to individual self-interest comes from the corpus of Attic funeral orations, which were presented on behalf of hoplites who had died serving the city. From at least the mid-fifth century B.C., Athenians regularly held state funerals at public expense for the city's war dead; a significant feature of these was the delivery of a funeral oration (*epitaphios*) by a prominent individual elected by the *dēmos* (Th. 2.34).[35] These orations served as vehicles not only for praising the hoplites who had died fighting for Athens but also for promulgating civic ideology.

Although the Attic funeral orations often idealize the sacrifice of the city's hoplites, past and present, as a patriotic act inspired by love of country (Ziolkowski 1981: 110–12), they also insist that this self-sacrifice is a rational choice that is consistent with individual self-interest.[36] Athenians, they suggest, willingly risk death on the battlefield, because they have a vested interest in fighting to preserve and advance the democratic city in which they enjoy freedom and equality.[37] Those who perish, moreover, receive honors from the city in exchange for their self-sacrifice: burial at public expense; a funeral oration lauding them and the hoplites who have died before them; and fame in perpetuity through the city's annual ceremony and competitions commemorating the war dead.[38] While the city honors its dead collectively, each individual wins his share of praise at the same time: "Although they gave their lives in common, they took individually ageless praise" (Th. 2.43.2).[39] Athenian hoplites, knowing what benefits await those who die, bravely risk death, as they reckon by

[35] On the question of how often state funerals were held, see Loraux 1986: 363 n. 151.

[36] Cf. Balot (2004b: 415), who speaks of the "Athenians' rationalistic self-image" in connection with the democratic ideal of "rational courage."

[37] Democracy: Th. 2.37.1; Lys. 2.18; Pl. *Mx.* 238c; Dem. 60.26; Ziolkowski 1981: 108. Freedom: Th. 2.43.4; Lys. 2.14; Pl. *Mx.* 239a–b; cf. Lyc. 1.48–9; Demad. fr. 83.2; Hyp. 6.24; Ziolkowski 106–8. Equality: Th. 2.37.1; Lys. 2.56; Pl. *Mx.* 239a; Dem. 60.28; Gorg. 82 fr. 6.17–18 D-K; Ziolkowski 108–9.

[38] Honors and rewards: Th. 2.35, 46; Lys. 2.9, 80; Pl. *Mx.* 236d; Dem. 60.33; Ziolkowski 1981: 109–10. Annual ceremony and contests: Lys. 2.80, Pl. *Mx.* 249b3–6; Dem. 60.36; [Arist.] *Ath. Pol.* 58.1; Loraux 1986: 37–8.

[39] Consistent with this claim is the fact that the individual names of the dead were inscribed on tribal casualty lists – though without patronymic or demotic: see Loraux 1986: 23.

"a just calculation" (τῷ δικαίῳ λογισμῷ) that more is gained than lost through self-sacrifice (Dem. 60.32).[40] The Attic funeral orations thus pragmatically balance the call upon a citizen to consider what he can do for his country with assurances of how much his country can do for him, even when he is dead.[41] Consistent with this, when Thucydides' Pericles in his funeral oration invites his fellow citizens to become "lovers" (*erastai*) of their country (2.43.1; cf. Pl. *Lg.* 643e), he does so on the basis of the many benefits that this will bring them.[42]

That good citizens "give" to the city in expectation of "getting" something in return is vividly conveyed by the commonplace in Athenian civic discourse that a service performed for the city is a voluntary "loan" or "contribution" (*eranos*) that will be paid back.[43] Thus, in his funeral oration, Thucydides' Pericles characterizes the sacrifice of the city's hoplites as a "most noble contribution" (κάλλιστον δὲ ἔρανον), in return for which they obtain ageless fame (2.43.1–2; cf. Lyc. 1.143).[44] In keeping with this logic, a citizen's failure to contribute to the common pool could be viewed as grounds for depriving him of his "share" in the city and the benefits that came with this. Thus, in Aristophanes' *Lysistrata*, the female chorus leader contrasts her relation with the city to that of her male interlocutors:

I have a stake in the common fund (τοὐράνου): I contribute (εἰσφέρω) men to it. You wretched old men have no stake; you've squandered the fund (τὸν ἔρανον) that came to you from your grandfathers from the war with the

[40] For this calculus, see also Dem. 60.27; cf. Lys. 2.23; Hyp. 6.24; Isoc. 4.83.

[41] Contrast the idealism of John F. Kennedy's famous exhortation in his Inaugural Address (January 20, 1961), "And so, my fellow Americans, ask not what your country can do for you; ask what you can do for your country" (Bartlett 1980: 890: 12).

[42] For this reading of the *erastēs* metaphor, see Monoson 1994: 254, 267–8; cf. Balot 2001b: 510–12; McGlew 2002: 41–2; Wohl 2002: 55–62; Ludwig 2002.

[43] On reciprocity as central to the concept of the *eranos*, see Millett 1991: 154–5; cf. Monoson 1994: 267–8. The close association of the *eranos* with friendship (*philia*) (see Millett 1991: 156–7) made it a natural metaphor for the friendly pooling of resources by citizens; cf. the proverb "goods of friends are in common" (Pl. *R.* 424a; Arist. *Pol.* 1263a30).

[44] For a wealthy man's liturgy as an obligatory *eranos* owed to the fatherland just as to a father, see Dem. 10.40; for *eranos* as a metaphor for a son's debt to his father, see Millett 1991: 289 n. 11.

Persians, and now you don't pay your war taxes in return (οὐκ ἀντεισφέρετε τὰς εἰσφοράς) – indeed, we're positively in danger of ruin thanks to you.[45] (651–5)

While the speaker, despite her inferior civic status as a woman, has won a stake in the city due to her contribution of sons to the war effort (cf. 589–90), her male interlocutors have lost their stake because they take from the common fund without replenishing it.[46]

Further corroboration of the close link between good citizenship and individual self-interest in Athenian civic ideology is found in Thucydides' representation of political rhetoric in the Athenian Assembly. Thucydides' Pericles, for example, appeals to self-interest as the basis of good citizenship not only in his funeral oration, as noted earlier, but also in his two speeches to the Assembly in the *Histories*. He concludes his first speech, which urges Athenians not to shrink from war against Sparta and its allies, with a reminder that city and citizen alike stand to gain from war: "it is from the greatest dangers that the greatest honors accrue to both state and individual" (1.144.3; cf. 1.75.5; 2.46.1). In his final speech, which exhorts Athenians not to yield in the ongoing war, Pericles argues at length (2.60.2–5) that Athenians should give priority to the city's interests at this time, because its well-being is essential for individual prosperity: "For even though a man flourishes in his own personal affairs (τὸ καθ' ἑαυτὸν), yet if his country goes to ruin, he perishes with it all the same; but if he is in evil fortune and his country in good fortune, he is far more likely to come through safely" (2.60.3).[47]

45 *eranos* in this passage probably designates the pooled contributions of donors, rather than an individual contribution or the collective of contributors; cf. the use of *eranos* in reference to a shared meal to which all guests contribute (Hom. *Od.* 1.226, Aeschin. 3.251). Millett (1991: 153) does not seem to allow for this sense of the term in a financial context, when he states: "The word *eranos* could refer to either an individual contribution or the contributors collectively."

46 This speaker also portrays the city as nourishing *patris* (640–1, spoken together with the chorus of women), to which she "owes" (προυφείλω) good advice (648).

47 Although it is true that Pericles here "staunchly reasserts the priority of the unified public interests of the state over the diverse private interests of each individual Athenian" (Ober 1998: 89), he does so by appealing to individual self-interest: individuals will be best served in the long run by supporting their city. Note that Pericles prudently glosses over the fact that some individuals may suffer disproportionately in this process, as was the case for displaced farmers (Th. 2.14; cf. Foxhall 1993: 142–3).

Likewise, Thucydides' Nicias in the Sicilian debate invokes the idea that individual self-interest and good citizenship are compatible with each other. Although Nicias asserts that his opposition to the Sicilian expedition is not due to concern that it is contrary to his personal interests ("And yet from such an enterprise I for my part get honor, and have less dread than others about my life"), he hastens to add

> though I consider that he is quite as good a citizen who takes some forethought for his life and property; for such a man would, for his own sake (δι' ἑαυτὸν), be most eager that the affairs of the city should also prosper. (6.9.2)

Nicias appeals here not to exceptionally self-interested individuals but rather to Athenians at large, who – as Thucydides' Pericles also assumes – view their bond with the city as one based on mutual self-interest.[48]

While Thucydides' representation of Athenian political rhetoric confirms the centrality of self-interest in the bond between citizen and city under the democracy, his narrative calls attention to the fragility of this bond as plague (2.53) and the hardships of war (2.59) wear away at it. Although Thucydides' Pericles is able to persuade his fellow citizens that their personal interests coincide with those of the city, the *Histories* track the divergence of private and public interests after Pericles' death (Pouncey 1980: 39; Balot 2001a: 136–78). Personal interests come to threaten the city, as self-interested politicians, vying for power with one another, play to the greed of the *dēmos* (2.65.6–13); and members of the elite who come to view their interests as distinct from those of the *dēmos* league together to seize control of the city (411 B.C.) (8.63.4; cf. 8.48.1).[49]

Compare the similar pragmatism concerning individual self-interest in time of war exhibited by General George Washington (1778): "I do not mean to exclude altogether the Idea of Patriotism. I know it exists, and I know it has done much in the present Contest. But I will venture to asert, that a great and lasting War can never be supported on this principle alone. It must be aided by a prospect of Interest or some reward. For a time, it may, of itself push Men to Action; to bear much, to encounter difficulties; but it will not endure unassisted by Interest." (Quoted in Diggins 1984: 23; cf. Mansbridge 1990b: 7).

[48] Ober (1998: 108) suggests "This 'stake in society' argument seems to be an appeal to the less overtly public-spirited men obliquely alluded to in the Funeral Oration" (cf. 86). In my view, however, this is an appeal to mainstream Athenian civic values.

[49] Cf. Arist. *EN* 1167a27: "Concord is said to prevail in a state, when the citizens agree as to their interests . . . "

We need not embrace Thucydides' view of an Athens in decline after Pericles' death to appreciate that a bond of mutual self-interest between citizen and city can be difficult to maintain, especially in stressful times.[50] If citizens are drawn to support the city on the basis of mutual self-interest, when individuals perceive their interests to diverge from those of the city they may feel justified in pursuing these on their own or in collaboration with others. Arguably, in fact, there is something inherently risky in the city promoting good citizenship on the basis of mutual self-interest: to the extent that citizens viewed their relationship with the city in these pragmatic terms, this might lead some, through selfish calculation, to acts of bad rather than good citizenship.

Aristophanes is especially attuned to the precarious nature of the reciprocal relationship between citizen and state, and how selfish calculations on the part of individuals can upset this. Aristophanes' most striking exploration of this problem is found in *Ecclesiazusae* (*ca.* 392 B.C.). The city's women, in disgust at the failure of men to run the city properly, attend the Assembly disguised as men and win passage of a decree that puts the city in their hands (455–7); they then require that all things be shared in common, from private property to sexual assets, and that citizens dine together in the agora from their pooled supplies (590–729). While this caricature of Spartan-style communism makes for good comic fun, it also entails serious reflection on the nature and limitations of sharing and reciprocity among Athenian citizens.[51]

Of particular interest is the exchange between two citizens concerning whether to deliver property to the common pool (730–876).[52] One ("First Citizen"), honest but hopelessly naive, is on his way to deliver

[50] Even the Attic funeral orations occasionally acknowledge that individual selfishness is a threat to good citizenship: see Th. 2.40.1–2; 2.44; cf. Dem. 60.2; Ober 1998: 86.

[51] While Praxagora's scheme is not identical with Spartan arrangements (see Sommerstein 1998: 16), I doubt that an Athenian audience would miss the satire on their arch-rival's institutions (especially the common dining of the *syssitia*) and ideology. Dover (1972: 198–9; followed by Rothwell 1990: 7) overestimates Athenian receptiveness to state control of private property; on the attachment of the wealthy to their property, see Chapter 4.

[52] On the problem of their identities within the comedy, see Olson 1991b, who argues that the Neighbor is the First Citizen and the Second Citizen is an anonymous character.

his property to the city in compliance with the women's decree; his only concern is that, if he lingers, there may be no place left for his contribution (794–5). The other ("Second Citizen"), unscrupulous and cynical, holds back on contributing his share. He shrewdly waits to see if the fickle Assembly will rescind this directive (797–8; 812–22), and if others will actually comply: "Do you really believe that any single one of them who has any sense will bring his goods in? It's not our ancestral way" (777–8). While the cynical citizen refuses to contribute his share, he is more than ready to enjoy the common feasting. When a herald proclaims that the sumptuous dinner is in preparation (834; cf. 681–93), he sets forth to join the feast despite the protest of his interlocutor that he must first hand over his goods (855). The scene closes with the cynical Athenian reflecting: "I certainly need some scheme, by Zeus, to let me keep the property I've got, and also somehow share with these people in the communal meal that's being prepared" (872–4).

Although some scholars regard the cynical Athenian as but a momentary obstacle to the new order with which most citizens within the comedy cooperate (Sommerstein 1998: 20–1; Rothwell 1990: 7), his resistance is not so easily dismissed. His selfishness, in fact, is fully consistent with that attributed to Athenians at large by Praxagora earlier in the comedy: "you each look out for a way to gain a personal profit for yourselves, while the public interest gets kicked around . . . " (205–7; cf. 307–10, 380–2). His watchful stance of observing his fellow-citizens to make sure that they will contribute their fair shares before he contributes his (750–3; 769–70; 786–8; 859), moreover, seems perfectly rational in light of Praxagora's characterization of Athenian selfishness (cf. Dem. 14.15). To be sure, the cynical Athenian, who is utterly unscrupulous, is cast in an unfavorable light; but elsewhere Aristophanes allows unscrupulous figures legitimate observations (e.g., *Pl.* 907–19). His extended presence in this comedy's center calls attention, as Aristophanes does elsewhere, to the obstinate resistance of self-interested individuals to group enterprises on and off the comic stage (cf. Ober 1998: 148–9).

Although the city of Athens stopped well short of insisting that citizens embrace the sort of universal sharing and reciprocity found in the women's city in *Ecclesiazusae*, it called upon individuals to pool their resources, personal and financial, for the common good in carrying out their civic obligations; it encouraged this cooperation by assuring citizens that those who "give" to the city can expect to "get" something in return.[53] Aristophanes' cynical citizen highlights one way in which this ideology might fail in practice: an Athenian citizen might reject this reciprocal relationship altogether and seek to give nothing (i.e., evade his citizen obligations), while still enjoying the benefits of citizenship. As we shall see, Athenians appear to have been quite concerned about "free riders," to judge from their frequent allusion to shameless evasion of duties.[54]

Even those who accepted the basic terms of this reciprocal relationship, however, might fall short in their citizenship if they believed that, relative to other citizens, they were being asked to "give" too much or "got" too little in return for their efforts. Although individuals in any society may believe that they are being treated unfairly relative to others in the sphere of civic obligations, Athenians, as equal shareholders in their city, may have been especially sensitive in this regard; a citizen who felt that he was being asked to contribute more than his fair share or was receiving less than his fair proportion of civic goods might well feel justified in holding back on his contributions to the common pool. Athenians were, as we shall see, highly attuned to disparities in contributions between themselves and other citizens in both major areas of civic duty, military service and financial support of the city. They also appear to have been very concerned about whether, in return for their contributions, they were receiving their fair share of communal goods.[55] In either case, the perception of inequity could lead to resentment and justify, in the eyes of the disgruntled, underperformance or circumvention of citizen duties.

[53] Critics of the democracy exaggerate and protest this expectation that the individual should reap rewards from the community (see e.g., Isoc. 7.24–5; Pl. *R.* 565a). For elite complaints concerning demotic greed, see further in Chapter 4.

[54] On the term "free riders" in modern "rational choice" theory, see Mansbridge 1990b: 20; cf. Ober 1998: 133 n. 27.

[55] From the common man's perspective, for example, it might seem that politicians and other powerful persons took a disproportionate share of the city's bounty through embezzlement, extortion, and other corrupt practices: see Ar. *Eq.* 716–18, 1218–23; *V.* 666–85; Aeschin. 3.240, 250–1; cf. Pl. *R.* 565a.

CITIZENSHIP STRATEGIES: SELF-INTERESTED CITIZENSHIP

When Athenian civic ideology portrayed democratic citizenship as an exercise in enlightened self-interest, it did so in polemic opposition to the very real pull of narrow self-interests on citizens. In later chapters, we will consider in detail how basic concerns over property and personal well-being could lead citizens to fall short in performing their civic obligations. Before considering how the pursuit of self-interest could lead to acts of bad citizenship, however, it is important to appreciate that self-interest permeated the entire citizen enterprise. Strategic considerations based on self-interests came into play regularly in the practice of Athenian citizenship. While this is conspicuously true of bad citizenship, it is also evident across the broad spectrum of citizen behavior. Shrewdness and self-interest go hand-in-hand in Hellenic culture (cf. Détienne and Vernant 1978), and not least in the way Athenians approached their civic duties and represented their civic behavior to others.

Although the practice of shrewdness was problematic in the eyes of Athenians, it was an integral feature of social and civic life.[56] While politicians in the Assembly and litigants in the courts appealed to truthfulness and forthrightness as essential to social harmony and civic welfare, they often did so shrewdly to advance their personal ends; and in their competition with one another outside the public eye, politicians and litigants did their best, as far as we can tell, to outsmart and outmaneuver their rivals.[57] The apparent gap between publicly invoked ideal and personal practice (cf. Arist. *Rh.* 1399a) should not be taken

[56] On the lively discussion of deception and wiliness in Athenian sources and citizen ambivalence toward these, see Hesk 2000; cf. Christ 2003. While Athenians were naturally concerned about the threat these posed within the city (cf. Plu. *Sol.* 30), they – like other Greeks – were prepared to employ trickery against other states in time of war (Lyc. 1.83–9, X. *Eq. Mag.* 5.9; Krentz 2000; cf. Whitehead 1988). Although Athenians themselves enjoyed a reputation for shrewdness in antiquity (Hdt. 1.60.3; Plu. *Sol.* 30), they frequently accused their rivals, the Spartans, of duplicity and perfidy (see e.g., E. *Andr.* 445–53; Dover 1974: 84; Bradford 1994).

[57] For shrewdness in political rivalry, see e.g., Plu. *Per.* 9.2–3; cf. Ar. *Eq. passim*. On pre-trial maneuvering by potential litigants, see Scafuro 1997: 25–114; cf. Christ 1998a: 36–9.

simply as testimony to hypocrisy: while forthrightness was important for social harmony and the pursuit of common interests, shrewdness could be essential for individual self-preservation and advancement in a highly competitive society.

Just as Athenians were prepared to act shrewdly to achieve their legal and political ends, so too were they ready to do so when called upon to carry out their civic obligations. While some citizens may have carried out their duties more or less spontaneously, many were inclined to approach these self-consciously and prudently. Demosthenes takes this for granted in exhorting his fellow citizens:

> For you will notice, men of Athens, that whenever you have collectively formed some project and after this each individual has realized that it was his personal duty (ἑαυτῷ προσήκειν) to carry it out, nothing has ever escaped you; but whenever you have formed your project and after this have looked to one another to carry it out, each expecting to do nothing while his neighbor worked, then nothing has succeeded with you. (14.15; cf. 2.30; 4.7; Th. 1.141.7)

Although Demosthenes is all too prone to equate citizen hesitation toward his policies with shirking of civic duties (cf. 8.21–4; 9.74),[58] his portrayal of citizenship as a deliberate enterprise that involves self-conscious choices between alternatives is highly plausible as is his assessment of the temptation to hold back and allow others to carry the burden of civic duties (cf. Dem. 10.28; Lys. 20.23). While some Athenians might go so far as to seek means to avoid their obligations altogether, a citizen did not have to be an utter rascal to act in a canny manner; he might do so, for example, to avoid too frequent or onerous service. As we shall see, a wealthy man might choose to conceal his riches to avoid bearing what he viewed as more than his fair share of financial obligations; or a conscript might fabricate an excuse to avoid or postpone military service because he believed that he had already done his part by serving recently.

[58] For the many passages in which Demosthenes calls upon Athenians to rally against Philip of Macedon by increasing their contributions in money and service, see Yunis 1996: 258 n. 38; cf. Roisman 2005: 124 n. 60. On orators' rebukes to their audiences, see Ober 1989: 318–24; Yunis 1996: 257–68.

Although citizens' selfish interests naturally triggered the exercise of canniness in the sphere of civic duties, further impetus to act shrewdly, as we shall see, came from the perception that other citizens were already acting deviously to avoid carrying their fair share of civic obligations (cf. Ar. *Ec.* 769–72). An integral part of shrewdness in a Hellenic context is suspecting others of exercising cleverness at one's expense. Athenians, if not already inclined to suspect this was the case in the sphere of citizenship, were encouraged to do so by the frequent public airing of claims that individuals, named or unnamed, were successfully evading hoplite service or financial obligations. Furthermore, in a society in which social relations frequently entailed seeking and granting "favors," the public had good reason to suspect that the public officials who administered civic duties were susceptible to personal influence. Suspicion was natural, moreover, since it was very difficult for the public to know how widespread evasion was. Successful evaders in any society leave few tracks, and this was especially true in ancient Athens, where bureaucratic controls and record-keeping were limited.

Citizen wariness concerning the performance of civic obligations, if widespread, could lead to serious problems for a city, as Aristotle observes:

> . . . Base men try to get more than their share of benefits, but take less than their share of labors and liturgies (cf. Pl. *R.* 343d). And while each desires this for himself, he scrutinizes his neighbor to prevent him from doing likewise; for if they do not keep watch over one another, the common interests go to ruin. The result is civil strife, everybody trying to make others do what is right but refusing to do it themselves. (*EN* 1167b10)

Although Athens did not degenerate into Aristotle's discordant society, mutual distrust and wariness were probably important factors behind canny citizen behavior and documented problems with the administration of civic duties.[59] As we shall see, for example, mutual distrust

[59] Sagan (1991: 88) underestimates Athenian cynicism and mutual wariness, in generalizing: "Optimism about human nature is essential to the democratic spirit. By overcoming the paranoid position of basic mistrust, democracy substitutes a basic trust of one's neighbor, of the citizen one does not know, of one's political opponent. Democracy is impossible unless many people trust each other, reflecting an optimistic view of what a large number of humans are capable of."

among the wealthy, who feared being saddled with the liturgies avoided by their peers, had a profound effect on their behavior as citizens.

While Athenians acted cannily in connection with specific civic duties, they also did so as they developed broader citizenship strategies that served their personal ends. A wide range of options was available. At one extreme, an ambitious (*philotimos*) individual who planned to pursue a political career might choose to volunteer for civic duties, military or financial, so as to be able to exploit his good citizenship later as grounds for attaining a position of civic prominence. At the opposite extreme, an unscrupulous (*ponēros*) individual might do everything possible to avoid the personal risks and costs of civic duties. A less extreme option – and probably an attractive one – was to get by doing as little as possible, while enjoying the benefits of citizenship.[60] Although Athenians did not speak of "citizenship strategies" *per se*, they were well aware of these different options, to judge from the frequency with which they appear in public discourse; it was up to each citizen to choose the model that best suited his concerns and goals.[61]

An important facet of shrewd citizenship was careful crafting of one's public image. Effective self-fashioning could affect not only whether an individual was called upon for service at a particular time but also what the ramifications would be of his citizenship, good or bad. Successful self-presentation made it possible for a good citizen to capitalize upon his services to the city and for a bad citizen to avoid or reduce any negative consequences for falling short of citizen ideals.

Greeks were intensely conscious of how important self-fashioning through speech and behavior was for an individual's defense or pursuit of his self-interests.[62] Athens' marked "performance culture" (see

[60] The inactive citizen (the *apragmōn*) could be castigated on this basis (see Th. 2.40.2; cf. E. fr. 787). One did not have to be a disillusioned member of the Athenian elite to choose this course, *pace* Carter 1986: 27. On non-participation in political life as a real option for Athenians, see Shaw 1991: 202–3; cf. Sinclair 1988: 191–6.

[61] On the diversity of individual values and goals among Athenians, see further in Chapter 4.

[62] The Homeric Odysseus, who fashions his speech and behavior to gain the upper hand over others (e.g., *Od.* 13.291–5), is paradigmatic. Self-fashioning extends to control over "body language," including gait, bearing, facial expression, and gestures: see X. *Mem.* 3.10.5; cf. Lateiner 1995; Hesk 2000: 219–27; Worman 2002. For expressions of anxiety

Goldhill 1999) may have intensified this consciousness among Athenians. Athenian public institutions cultivated performance and invited reflection on it in a variety of ways. While this was conspicuously the case with the Athenian sponsorship of tragedy and comedy as a part of annual civic rituals (cf. Gorg. 82 fr. 23 D–K), performance art extended to the Athenian Assembly and lawcourts, where speakers sought through rhetoric to win over large audiences by presenting carefully fashioned *personae* and by unmasking their allegedly duplicitous rivals (Ober and Strauss 1990; Hesk 2000: 202–41). Athenians learned to be adept social actors off the public stage too, for example, as players in disputes and vendettas, where posturing could be an effective means to intimidate and prevail over a rival (cf. Scafuro 1997: 7–10, 25–114).

Although scholars have explored many aspects of "performance" in Athenian civic life, they have not fully appreciated the performative dimensions of citizen behavior in connection with civic duties. That citizens are "actors" in this sphere is most explicit on the stage, especially in Aristophanic comedy, where individuals frequently posture concerning their citizenship.[63] While these caricatures onstage are clearly inspired by citizen behavior offstage, in his *Frogs* Aristophanes comically asserts that life may sometimes imitate art: his Aeschylus rebukes Euripides for his frequent parading of beggar-kings on stage because this inspires wealthy men to don rags to dodge the trierarchy (1065–6). Although Athenians' "performance" as citizens may at times have been colored by what they viewed in the Theater of Dionysus, the circumstances in which they acted as citizens made it natural for them to fashion images of themselves to serve their diverse ends.

Posturing, as we shall see, could play an important part in specific strategies for evading or postponing service. For example, wealthy Athenians – even without instruction from Euripides – often sought to control the public's impression of their level of wealth to protect their fortunes from civic obligations. Similarly, Athenians who were called

over the difficulty of "reading" people, see e.g., E. *Med.* 516–19; *Hipp.* 925–31; Isoc. 20.14.

[63] This is true, for example, of military men (*Ach.* 572–625, 676–702; cf. *Pax* 1172–90). Tragedy also explores the performative dimensions of citizenship, for example, through the draft-evading ruses of Odysseus and Achilles (see Chapter 2).

up to serve as hoplites might through effective self-presentation to the generals, who administered conscription, win exemption from service. This is not to say, however, that it was always easy to dupe others through posturing of this sort. In a society attuned to self-fashioning and misrepresentation, individuals were often ready to unmask pretenders and expose their duplicity. Wealthy Athenians who were seeking release from liturgies had a strong incentive to expose their shirking peers; and the generals may often have been on the lookout for individuals who were fabricating excuses or feigning disabilities to evade conscription.

Posturing also figured prominently in citizens' representations of themselves and their citizenship, bad or good, after the fact, as we shall see. Because those who dodged or poorly performed their duties naturally sought to avoid incurring rebuke or punishment, they veiled their shortcomings from the public or, if this was not possible, put the best face on these.[64] Those who fell short of citizen ideals on the battlefield, for example, had good reason to deny or minimize their humiliation in the immediate aftermath of battle and upon returning home to Athens. Athenians who carried out their civic duties for their part were drawn, in representing their contributions, to amplify these to get the greatest personal benefit from them. Self-celebration was essential to staking a claim to honor and prestige within a competitive community. This was conspicuously the case when wealthy Athenians set up choregic monuments to celebrate the dithyrambic victories their money had helped to purchase or vaunted their generous performance of liturgies in the lawcourts or Assembly.

CIVIC RESPONSES: COMPULSION AND PERSUASION

Athenians were well aware of the threat to good citizenship posed by selfish and shrewd behavior and sought, institutionally and

[64] Cf. Plato's Glaucon (*R.* 361a–b): "For the height of injustice is to seem just without being so. To the perfectly unjust man, then, we must assign perfect injustice and withhold nothing of it, but we must allow him, while committing the greatest wrongs, to have secured for himself the greatest reputation for justice; and if he does happen to trip, we must concede to him the power to correct his mistakes by his ability to speak persuasively if any of his misdeeds come to light . . . "

ideologically, to ensure that this would not get out of hand. The manner in which Athenians mixed elements of compulsion and persuasion in this process reflected their shared democratic values. While later chapters will look closely at the interplay of these elements in connection with specific civic obligations, it is worth considering in advance how the democracy, through a combination of compulsion and persuasion, approached the general problem of eliciting good citizenship.

Athenians recognized that civic duties, if they were to be carried out promptly and properly, had to be compulsory. Although Athenian civic ideology represents good citizenship as voluntary and spontaneous, Athenians were cognizant of the fact that their duties were ultimately mandatory, as is evident from their frequent characterization of them as "orders" (τὰ προσταττόμενα) and "obligations" (τὰ δέοντα). As we shall see, Athenians charged state agents with assigning these duties to individuals, and established numerous legal mechanisms that could be used against those seeking to evade their obligations. These diverse measures, which take for granted that individuals, if left to their own devices, might evade their duties, almost certainly evolved not simply in anticipation of evasion, but in response to actual resistance on the part of individuals to civic duties.[65] The shrewdness with which some of this regulation was conceived suggests that, if shrewdness could facilitate circumvention of civic regulation, it could also be employed by the community to control shrewd, anti-social behavior.[66]

Athenians, however, were ambivalent concerning the use of compulsion against free individuals under their democracy, and not least in the sphere of civic duties. They were especially sensitive to the naked exercise of civic authority by state agents against democratic citizens (Dem. 22.47–56; cf. Christ 1998b). This sensitivity, along with considerations of cost and bureaucratic convenience, led the city to rely largely on private initiative to ensure that citizens would fulfill their civic duties.[67] Thus, for example, while the generals assigned citizens

[65] This is most readily documented in the sphere of financial obligations: see Chapter 4.

[66] The city was especially shrewd in its establishment of *antidosis*: see Chapter 4.

[67] Cf. how Xenophon's Simonides advises Hiero, "a ruler should delegate to others the task of punishing those who require to be coerced, and should reserve to himself the awarding of prizes" (*Hier.* 9.3). On volunteer prosecution and its place in democratic ideology, see Christ 1998a: 118–59.

to military service and led them in the field, the city relied upon private individuals for the public prosecution of draft evasion, desertion of the ranks, and cowardice. Similarly, while state agents were involved in administering liturgies and the war tax, the city relied upon wealthy citizens in a number of ways to police their peers and prevent them from evading their obligations. Although the city's considerable reliance on private individuals in the enforcement of compulsory civic duties may have helped defuse tensions concerning civic authority over citizens, as we shall see this also left individuals with considerable latitude for evading their obligations.

If compulsion, in various forms, had its role to play in encouraging compliance with civic obligations, Athenians preferred to elicit cooperation through persuasion. Athenians prided themselves on the role of free speech in their democratic society, and found in it a potent vehicle for winning over free men to good citizenship (cf. Dem. 60.25–6). A hallmark of Athenian democracy was the way it engendered public discourse in a range of civic contexts; this provided diverse opportunities for Athenians to articulate and promulgate civic norms, including what constituted good citizenship and its opposite. For example, public funeral orations for the state's war dead enshrined the patriotic principle of self-sacrifice for the city and, as observed above, argued on the basis of enlightened self-interest that this was a rational choice for democratic citizens. Furthermore, competing litigants in the Athenian courts invoked and exploited the notion that the city was divided into good citizens (themselves) and bad ones (their opponents), and called upon their audiences to praise and reward the former, and rebuke and punish the latter. Even Attic comedy and tragedy, which were performed before large audiences in the Theater of Dionysus, entered into this discussion of citizenship within their own idioms.

In preferring persuasion to compulsion in matters of citizenship, Athenians rejected the more authoritarian arrangement embraced by their Spartan rivals. In the Athenian view, the Spartans mistakenly sought to force good citizenship upon themselves through rigid regulations and laws (Th. 2.39; cf. Plu. *Cleom.* 9.1; Millender 2002). It was far better, in the Athenian view, for free men to embrace their civic duties willingly because of the close bond between them and their community that was based on a commonality of interests. This is not to say, however, that Athenians disregarded fear of the law as an inducement to good citizenship: the legal mechanisms that they established for pursuing bad citizens assumed the potential efficacy of this, and Athenians at times explicitly invoked fear of punishment as a real factor in citizens' decisions to carry out their obligations.[68]

While the Athenian preference for persuasion over compulsion reflects, first, democratic assumptions concerning the proper relation between city and individual, this was reinforced by optimism under the democracy concerning the power of persuasion to win over free and rational individuals to good citizenship (cf. Dem. 18.245; Balot 2004 b). Athenians would probably have agreed with Democritus' assessment of the relative efficacy of persuasion and compulsion as mechanisms for controlling social behavior:

> The man who employs exhortation and persuasion will clearly be better at engendering virtue (ἐπ' ἀρετὴν) than he who employs law and compulsion. For the man who is prevented by law from wrongdoing will probably do wrong in secret, whereas the man who is led towards duty (τὸ δέον) by persuasion will probably not do anything untoward either secretly or openly. Therefore the man who acts rightly through understanding and knowledge becomes at the same time brave and upright. (68 fr. 181 D–K)

Indeed, Athenians were critical of the Spartan reliance upon compulsion of citizens not only on ideological grounds but also practical ones: because Spartans were not won over to civic virtue by persuasion, they were believed to circumvent their city's laws stealthily at home and to flout them openly when abroad.[69]

[68] For fear of the city's laws as a motivator of good citizenship, see A. *Eu.* 696–9; Th. 2.37.3; Lys. 14.15; Aeschin. 3.175–6; Lyc. 1.130.

[69] Plato would appear to concur with Democritus' view of the practical limits of compulsion in shaping behavior: he observes that men living in timocratic states – of which Sparta is his prime example – turn to "enjoying their pleasures stealthily, and running away from the law as boys from a father, because they have not been educated by persuasion but by force" (*R.* 548a–b); cf. Arist. *Pol.* 1270b32. According to Plato, however, democracy errs in relying too little on compulsion: he criticizes democratic freedom – which he equates with "license to do whatever one wishes" (*R.* 557b) – because men accustomed to absolute freedom in their personal lives will not consent to "regulate their public and civil life by law" (*Lg.* 780a). Such men, he asserts, view even the performance of civic duties as a matter of free choice, and thus only serve their city when it suits them (Pl. *R.* 557e; cf. *Lg.* 955b–c).

Although Athenians tended to favor persuasion over compulsion in matters of citizenship, as we shall see the precise manner in which they balanced these varied with the specific duty involved and was subject to change over time. Notably, in the case of financial obligations, the city increasingly asserted its authority over the fortunes of the wealthy in the face of devious practices and evasion; compulsion loomed ever larger here over time. Notwithstanding the democratic ideal that good citizenship was voluntary, practical necessity sometimes prevailed over ideological preferences.

2

THE RELUCTANT CONSCRIPT

For war always hunts out young men. (S. fr. 554)

In time of war Athens required citizens who could afford armor and weapons to serve as hoplites, if called upon. At the time of the Peloponnesian War (431–404 B.C), some 18,000–24,000 men were eligible for service.[1] While most eligible citizens probably complied – if not always enthusiastically – with conscription, some evaded service. This chapter seeks to assess evasion of hoplite service in Athens both as a historical phenomenon and as an ideological problem for the city. In Athens, as in modern democracies, evasion of compulsory military service was a real temptation and possibility. Consistent with this is Attic tragedy's frequent treatment of evasion and tensions concerning compulsory service in connection with recruitment for the Trojan War and other martial endeavors. Tragedy, I will argue, provided an imaginative vehicle through which contemporary audiences might come to terms with the tensions surrounding compulsory military service and its evasion within a democratic society.[2]

[1] For this estimate of the number of Athenian hoplites, see Rhodes 1988: 274; cf. van Wees 2004: 241–3.

[2] I focus on evasion of hoplite service, because this is best attested in the sources. Evasion of cavalry service was also possible (Dem. 21.162–4; cf. Bugh 1988: 71–4), as was dodging of (sometimes) compulsory service as crew member in the Athenian fleet ([Dem.] 50.6–7; cf. Ar. *V.* 1114–21; Gabrielsen 1994: 107; Rosivach 2001). On draft evasion in modern states, see e.g., Chambers 1975: 182–94, 427–58; E. A. Cohen 1985: 108–9, 164–5; Forrest 1989; cf. Moskos and Chambers 1993. On evasion in second-century B.C. Italy, see J. K. Evans 1988.

The first section of this chapter will make the case for taking draft evasion seriously as a problem for the Athenian democracy. The second section will explore tragedy's intriguing engagement with evasion and tensions surrounding compulsory military service.

DRAFT EVASION AND COMPULSORY MILITARY SERVICE

Modern scholarship rarely addresses draft evasion in Athens or elsewhere in the Greek world. This may reflect the assumption that the martial orientation of Greek society and the high premium it placed on honor made evasion unlikely. Thus W. K. Pritchett (1971: 1.27) asserts, "There is little evidence for the existence of anything like the modern desire to avoid military service at all costs. I doubt that the ordinary soldier had any general philosophy about war, or that he even imagined any alternative."[3] The evidence for Athens suggests, on the contrary, that Athenians were well aware of draft evasion (*astrateia*) as an alternative to service, and that individuals had many possible reasons to dodge the draft and numerous opportunities to succeed in this.

Draft evasion crops up regularly in public discourse in Athens. For example, litigants regularly seek to rouse the public's ire against their opponents by attributing *astrateia* to them.[4] Whether the specific charges are true or false, these claims exploit and reinforce the public's suspicions that evasion may be all too common. For example, the younger Alcibiades' prosecutors assert that if his evasion goes unpunished, others who are inclined to seek safety over risk (Lys. 14.14, 15.8) will be all too ready to follow his base example (14.12, 45, 15.9).[5] Although this image of a society on the brink of crisis is manipulative and likely false, it effectively plays upon Athenian cynicism concerning human motivation and behavior.[6] Consistent with this exploitation of

[3] Cf. Hanson 1989: 223 ("There were no conscientious objectors in the Greek city-state in the great age of hoplite battle . . . "), and Sekunda 1992: 347 ("It is probable that few citizens [sc. in Athens] would avoid military service").

[4] See e.g., Lys. 6.46; 21.20; 30.26; Isoc. 18.47–8; Is. 4.27–9; 5.46; Dem. 54.44; Lyc. 1.147. For such charges in the crossfire between Aeschines and Demosthenes, see below, note 37.

[5] On the "consequentialist topos," see Lanni 2004: 166–8.

[6] On litigants' manipulation of Athenian anxieties over the preservation of social order, see Roisman 2005: 192–9.

popular concerns is the way some litigants make a positive virtue out of the fact that they have *not* shirked hoplite service. Thus, Lysias' client Mantitheus asserts:

When you made your alliance with the Boeotians and we had to go to the relief of Haliartus (395 B.C.), I had been enrolled by Orthobulus in the cavalry. I saw that everyone thought that, whereas the cavalry were assured of safety, the infantry would have to face danger; so, while others mounted on horseback illegally without having passed the mandatory review (*dokimasia*), I went up to Orthobulus and told him to strike me off the cavalry list, as I thought it shameful, while the majority were to face danger, to take the field having provided for my own security. (16.13; cf. 20.23).

While Mantitheus explicitly contrasts his behavior with that of shirkers,[7] the same contrast may be implicit when other speakers vaunt their outstanding military records (e.g., Is. 7.41; Aeschin. 2.167–9; cf. Dem. 21.95): a record of willing and frequent service is boastworthy precisely because not all men could make this claim.[8]

Attic comedy treats draft dodging in terms very similar to those found in forensic oratory. For example, comic writers regularly attack individuals, especially those who were politically active, for evading conscription.[9] Aristophanes – like Athenian litigants – suggests, however, that the phenomenon is more widespread than this. His chorus in *Wasps* (422 B.C.), which consists of jurors with stingers, asserts:

There are drones sitting among us; they have no stinger, and they stay at home and eat up our crop of tribute without toiling for it; and that is very galling for us, if some draft-dodger (ἀστράτευτος) gulps down our pay, when he's never had an oar or a spear or a blister in his hand on behalf of this country. No, I think that in future any citizen whatever who doesn't have his stinger should not be paid three obols. (1114–21; cf. *Ra.* 1014–17)

[7] Mantitheus is also navigating around negative perceptions of the cavalry that arose in connection with their support of the Thirty in 404/3 (see Bugh 1988: 129–30, 140–1).

[8] For a survey of claims in oratory concerning military service, see Burckhardt 1996: 154–256; Roisman 2005: 105–29.

[9] The evidence is collected below in note 37.

The chorus suggests that these deficient citizens, whom they cast as effeminate (they lack "stingers," i.e., phalluses: cf. Henderson 1991: 122), are plentiful.[10]

Although no extant comedy focuses exclusively on draft dodging, Aristophanes' contemporary Eupolis wrote a comedy entitled *Astrateutoi* (*The Draft-Dodgers*).[11] While little survives of this comedy, it apparently effeminized draft-evaders, to judge from the alternate title attested for it, *Androgunoi* (*The Womenly Men*) (cf. fr. 46). Given Old Comedy's fondness for cross-dressing, the title characters may have sought to dodge the draft by dressing as women; Euripides, as we shall see, presented this tactic on the tragic stage in depicting Achilles' ruse to evade service in the Trojan War. Draft dodging may also have figured prominently in Theopompus' *Stratiōtides* (*The Lady Soldiers*) (*ca.* 400 B.C.), in which the city's women apparently take over the male task of soldiering. The rationale for this inversion of normal gender roles was probably the alleged deficiencies of Athenian men – as in Aristophanes' *Lysistrata* and *Ecclesiazusae* – including their penchant for draft evasion.[12]

The relative frequency with which public discourse speaks of draft evasion suggests that the topic was of some concern to Athenians. While Athenians had no way of knowing the precise scope of *astrateia* in their city, a realistic assessment of motives and opportunities for evasion suggests that Athenians had some reason to be concerned about it.

Motives

Athenians had many reasons to comply with conscription. In Athens, as elsewhere in the Greek world, it was deemed honorable to serve the city in war and to die on its behalf. Furthermore, it was only

[10] For the draft-evader as effeminate, see also Ar. *Nu.* 685–93 (on Amynias); cf. D.S. 12.16.1–2.

[11] On this comedy, see Storey 2003: 74–81.

[12] Sommerstein (1998: 9–10) suspects that a man who seeks to dodge the draft may be behind the plan to make women soldiers (cf. fr. 57). Henderson (2000: 142) believes that the women may have shared duty with their husbands (cf. fr. 56, with Loomis 1998: 47).

human for some individuals to be optimistic about their prospects of survival: as Euripides' Theban herald observes, "When a war comes to be voted on by the people, no one reckons on his own death" (*Supp.* 481–2; cf. Th. 1.141.5). If a man survived a campaign, he could lay claim to personal glory for any successes won; if he died on the battlefield, the state undertook through annual ceremonies for the war dead to ensure his manly courage would be remembered along with that of other Athenians who had died while serving it (cf. Loraux 1986). Moreover, military service could provide an outlet for adventurism and yield profit through wages and plunder (cf. Th. 6.24.3). Common interests were also sometimes conspicuously at stake, for example, when Athenians confronted an invasion of their land or sought to keep their lucrative fifth-century empire intact.[13] These various inducements were sufficiently strong, in fact, to prompt some Athenians to volunteer for service (Plu. *Per.* 18.2; cf. Ar. *Av.* 1364–9).[14] The vast majority of hoplites serving on Athenian campaigns, however, were probably conscripts. Thus, for example, while Athenians at large were enthusiastic concerning the planned expedition to Sicily in 415 B.C. (Th. 6.24), those serving were conscripted in the normal way (6.26.2, 6.31.3).[15]

[13] On the attractions of war for both individual and group in ancient Greece, see van Wees 2004: 19–43.

[14] On hoplite volunteers, see Kromayer and Veith 1928: 48; Pritchett 1974: 2.110–12; Andrewes 1981: 2. Some may have volunteered, however, because they reckoned that conscription was imminent and they would have a greater claim to honor as volunteers (D.S. 11.84.4; cf. X. *Eq. Mag.* 1.11–12).

[15] van Wees (2004: 56–7, with 268 n. 28; cf. 2001: 59–60) believes that "working-class hoplites made up more than half of Athens' heavy infantry" and served voluntarily, i.e., were not subject to conscription. This makes too much in my view of Th. 6.43, which lists under the general rubric of hoplites heading to Sicily those serving by conscription (ἐκ καταλόγου) and *thetes* serving as marines (*epibatai*) (cf. Th. 8.24.2); the latter, as men armed like hoplites, could conveniently be grouped with the former (they do not fit into the categories of archers, slingers, and light-armed troops that follow), but this need not imply a two-track system for hoplites proper, in which wealthier hoplites were compelled to serve, while less wealthy ones had a choice in the matter. If half of all Athenian hoplites were in fact volunteers, moreover, it is odd that our sources, which speak frequently of conscription (Christ 2001 collects the evidence), make no mention of a two-track system. For further challenges to van Wees' hypothesis, see Gabrielsen 2002: 86–9, 92–8; cf. Rosivach 2002.

Despite the undeniable inducements to comply with conscription, many factors could make conscripts reluctant to serve. First, conscripts had not necessarily voted in support of the campaign on which they were called to serve. While all 30,000 or more Athenian citizens were eligible to participate in the Assembly, in practice probably no more than about 6,000 attended any particular meeting (Hansen 1991: 130–2) and a majority vote of these could set a campaign in motion; thus the vote of a few thousand Athenians could initiate conscription from the citizen body at large, and there was no guarantee that they were representative of the larger group (cf. [X.] *Ath. Pol.* 2.17).[16] What one man viewed as reasonable grounds for launching a campaign, another might regard as trivial ones.

Cynicism concerning a campaign might arise from the belief that public speakers (*rhētores*) or generals who were pursuing their own interests had duped the Assembly into supporting it. Euripides' Theseus thus rebukes Adrastus for leading the failed Argive expedition of the Seven against Thebes:

> You were led astray by young men who enjoy being honored and who multiply wars without justice to the hurt of the citizens. One wants to be general, another to get power into his hands to commit wanton abuse, another seeks profit and does not consider whether the majority is at all harmed by being so treated. (*Supp.* 232–7)[17]

Suspicions of powerful individuals could be amplified by the perception – so often voiced in Aristophanes – that while average citizens bear the greatest risks in war, the power elite reap the greatest benefits (e.g., *V.* 666–85).

Whether or not an individual had doubts concerning a military campaign, his personal interests naturally came into play as he evaluated whether to comply with conscription. While some Athenians were no doubt "risk-takers" (cf. Th. 1.70.3) who were eager to join in any military campaign, others were surely more reluctant to endure

[16] Meier (1990: 151) overlooks this in positing of the Assembly that "there was at least a fairly close approximation between those who made the policy and those whom it affected."

[17] For similar concerns about the motivations of advocates of war, see Th. 6.15.2; Aeschin. 2.79, 177; 3.82; cf. Roisman 2005: 115, with n. 32.

hardship and risk life for uncertain benefits.[18] In particular, a conscript had to weigh his obligation to serve the city against his responsibilities to and concerns over his household (*oikos*). In his absence, his property interests might suffer (Cox 1998: 155–61), or his wife might take a lover – as Clytemnestra did while Agamemnon was at Troy. If he died, moreover, his family would suffer hardship, emotional and physical. Aged parents would lose his financial support, and while his sons would receive maintenance at public expense until they reached manhood (Th. 2.46.1; Pl. *Mx.* 249a), this may only have been sufficient for subsistence (Ar. *Th.* 443–8; Loraux 1986: 26).

A major obstacle to appreciating the reluctance of some conscripts to serve is the assumption that considerations of honor would dictate compliance. First, this overestimates the primacy of honor in a Hellenic context: Greeks diverged widely from one another in the extent to which they pursued honor over other goods (Arist. *EN* 1095a22). Second, this underestimates the pull of self-interest on individuals, even those drawn to act honorably: thus, as noted earlier, Aristotle cynically observes that "all men, or most men, wish what is noble but choose what is profitable" (*EN* 1163a1). A man's concern over self-preservation, whether for his own sake or that of his household, could well take precedence over concerns that evasion might diminish his stock of honor.[19] In fact, an Athenian might not view compliance with conscription as essential to his honor. For example, if he had already served on campaign recently, he could feel that he had already done his fair part for the city and that others should now take their turn (cf. Lys. 9.4, 15). A man might believe, moreover, that his honor was not at great risk as his offense was unlikely to be brought before the public. It was far from certain, as we shall see, that he would be prosecuted for draft dodging in the city's courts.

[18] Raaflaub (2001) provides a good overview of how civic institutions and ideology could produce in Athenians a martial orientation, and concludes: "These constant reminders of their community's civic ideology conditioned the Athenian citizens from youth on to accept war as inevitable and even desirable" (339). In my view, however, this conditioning was only partly successful, as draft evasion attests.

[19] Similarly, when wealthy men were called upon by the city to carry out liturgies and to pay the war tax, they balanced their "love of honor" (*philotimia*) against their concrete self-interests: see Chapter 4.

Opportunities

If Athenians had many possible reasons for seeking to evade military service, how difficult was it for them to succeed in this? While there were institutional obstacles to evasion, Athenians had more latitude here than is commonly appreciated. A brief look at how conscription was carried out reveals a number of ways for a reluctant conscript to dodge or postpone service.[20]

For much of the classical period, the generals conscripted hoplites selectively (Christ 2001: 398–409). Whenever the Assembly voted to initiate a campaign, the generals called for the demes to submit lists of eligible hoplites; there was apparently no permanent, central roster before the mid-fourth century B.C. (Hansen 1985: 83). The generals, assisted by the tribal taxiarchs, were free to exercise their discretion in choosing which individuals on these lists should serve; once they had made their selections, they posted a written roster (*katalogos*) for each tribe (e.g., Ar. *Pax* 1179–84). Conscription by *katalogos* was cumbersome and subject to criticism as inequitable, for example, because one individual might be required to serve more frequently than another (cf. Lys. 9.4; X. *Mem.* 3.4.1). Probably considerations of efficiency and equity led to the abandonment of this arrangement and the introduction of conscription by age groups by at least 366 B.C. (Aeschin. 2.167–8, with Christ 2001: 412–16). Under the new system all eligible hoplites from ages 18 through 59 were listed by age group on permanent rosters displayed in the Agora; to initiate conscription for a campaign, the generals had only to announce which age groups were to appear ([Arist.] *Ath. Pol.* 53.4, 7).[21]

[20] For a detailed reconstruction of conscription with additional ancient sources, see Christ 2001.

[21] van Wees (2004: 103–4, with 279 nn. 7 and 8) believes that Athenians sometimes also conscripted select tribes for partial mobilization of their forces, citing *IG* I² 1085 = *ML* 51 = Fornara 101 (446 B.C.) and D. S. 18.10.2 (referring to 323 B.C.). The former, however, only attests to the deployment of Athenians by tribe (speaking of three tribes on an expedition to Megara) not to conscription carried out on this basis; other tribal contingents may have been active elsewhere at the same time. The latter explicitly mentions conscription by age group as the means by which *all* Athenian troops were selected and then speaks of the deployment of three tribes to guard Attica and of the remaining seven to operate abroad (see Christ 2001: 413 n. 56); there is no mention of conscription of selected tribes (*contra* van Wees 103). van Wees (104) is too ready to read the Athenian evidence in terms of Spartan practice (see esp. X. *HG* 6.4.17).

While both systems probably succeeded in mustering the approximate number of hoplites needed for a given expedition – at least we do not hear of expeditions canceled due to insufficient numbers – this should not be taken as proof that evasion was minimal. Because most expeditions did not require a full levy, the generals could call up more conscripts than they actually needed and thus ensure sufficient numbers. This would allow for the fact that many individuals would win exemptions legitimately or fraudulently and that some would fail to appear for muster.

Perhaps the best way to avoid service was through manipulation of exemptions. Under both methods of conscription, individuals were allowed to present claims of exemption after the initial call-up and before the time of muster.[22] The burden was on the individual to make his claim in person before the generals at their office in or near the Agora (Lys. 9.4); under special circumstances, for example illness, this claim could presumably be lodged by a conscript's representative (cf. Aeschin. 2.94–5; Dem. 19.124). Among the exempt were men under 18 or over 59 years of age; those who could not afford armor; the ill or disabled; officeholders; tax collectors; chorus members; performers of liturgies, including the *chorēgia* and trierarchy; and those already serving in the cavalry. The generals could presumably grant release from service on other grounds too, for example, personal hardship. Citizens traveling or living abroad were probably exempt *de facto* from service, as they could not be expected to hear of their conscription in time to comply.[23] While in some cases release was probably more or

[22] On exemptions, see Hansen 1985: 16–21; Sekunda 1992: 346–8; Christ 2001: 404–7.

[23]
- Men under 18 or over 59: [Arist.] *Ath. Pol.* 53.4; cf. Plu. *Phoc.* 24.4.
- Those who could not afford armor: cf. Lucian *Tim.* 51.
- The ill or disabled: Plu. *Phoc.* 10.2; cf. Lys. 14.14–15; Baldwin 1967.
- Officeholders: Lyc. 1.37.
- Tax collectors: [Dem.] 59.27; cf. Dem. 21.166.
- Chorus members: Dem. 21.15; 39.16; MacDowell 1982 [1989].
- *Chorēgoi*: Dem. 21.103, with MacDowell 1990: 9.
- Trierarchs: Dem. 21.166, with MacDowell 1990: 385.
- Cavalrymen: Lys. 16.13; cf. 14.14.
- Those with personal hardship: Plu. *Nic.* 13.7–8; *Alc.* 17.5–6.
- Men absent abroad: Sekunda (1992: 347–8) discusses cleruchs, mercenaries, exiles, and traders under this rubric. While the rules governing absence abroad are not known, it was very likely grounds for exemption from military service just as it was from

less automatic – for example, when a conscript was an officeholder – in others the generals could exercise discretion, notably, in judging claims based on disability, illness, or personal hardship.

Almost any exemption could be abused. For example, a man could falsely claim that he could not afford the requisite equipment, which was expensive at least in the fifth century (Hansen 1985: 49).[24] In Athens, public knowledge of a man's wealth was often limited (Gabrielsen 1986), and claims of financial difficulties therefore hard to disprove. The generals, however, were likely to cite prior service as hoplite by the conscript or his father as sufficient evidence of his qualification, and to place the burden on him to demonstrate that he could not afford to serve. Likewise, claims of personal hardship may have required evidence of dramatic events, for example, an individual's home burning down (cf. Plu. *Nic.* 13.7–8; *Alc.* 17.5–6). With these and other claims of exemption, the generals had to evaluate shrewdly whether individuals were legitimately exempt or cannily manipulating the system.[25]

Exemptions based on physical disability or illness were perhaps most susceptible to abuse in Athens, as they are in modern systems of conscription. Indeed, two factors made it easier to fake such claims in Athens. First, physical complaints were especially hard to refute

other civic obligations ([Arist.] *Ath. Pol.* 53.5; cf. Dem. 14.16). Moreno (2003: 97; cf. Meiggs 1972: 121) cites Th. 7.57.2 as evidence that cleruchs were "marshaled in the Athenian army in groups designated as, e.g., 'Hestiaeans', 'Lemnians', "Imbrians', etc.," but these groups appear to have been distinct from the Athenian forces (ξυνεστράτευσαν) and the individuals in them were probably not conscripted through the *katalogoi* posted in Athens.

Individuals just back from a hoplite campaign could seek exemption, but the generals might deny this: see Lys. 9.4, 15, with MacDowell 1994 and Christ 2001: 406–7.

[24] In this way, he could avoid service altogether or be reassigned to serve as a light-armed soldier (*psilos*), which might be less risky than serving as hoplite (cf. Lys. 14.14).

[25] Dem. 21.15 suggests that interested parties could challenge an individual's claim to exemption. A possible strategy for the generals to adopt under questionable circumstances was to allow the exemption only if the claimant could provide a substitute. Cf. how, when Aeschines claimed he was too sick to serve on an embassy to which he had been named, the Council sent his brother in his place (Dem. 19.124; cf. Aeschin. 2.94–5). As far as we know, however, conscripted hoplites in Athens were not routinely allowed to provide substitutes as was common, for example, in the American Civil War (see Chambers 1975: 171–81; E. A. Cohen 1985: 138–40, 145–6).

given the state of medical knowledge. Second, false claims had an air of plausibility because many individuals did have physical problems that warranted exemption, perhaps some twenty percent of Athenian men (Hansen 1985: 17–20).[26] The generals had good reason to take such claims seriously, as corporate survival depended on the physical ability of each individual to hold his place in the hoplite ranks: no one would want to be stationed next to a substantially disabled person.[27]

Acute illness could be faked to evade service: as a Greek proverb puts it, "Illness provides cowards with a holiday" (νόσος δειλοῖσιν ἑορτή) (Ant. Soph. 87 fr. 57 D-K; cf. Arist. *EN* 1150b10; Plu. *Alex.* 41.9).[28] A feigned injury might also do the trick: Aristogeiton was said to have appeared for muster leaning on a staff and with both legs bandaged (Plu. *Phoc.* 10.2).[29] Long-term disability could also be pretended, for example, poor eyesight (cf. Ar. *Ra.* 190–2; Hdt. 7.229), which must have been common in an age without corrective lenses. A few individuals may have been so bold as to feign mental disability: the Athenian astrologer Meton was said to have copied Odysseus' famed ploy for dodging service in the Trojan War to avoid participating in the Sicilian expedition (Ael. *VH* 13.12; cf. Plu. *Nic.* 13.7–8, *Alc.* 17.5–6.). This dodge, however, was surely not easy to carry off, as Odysseus discovered when his feigned madness was put to the test.

Wealthy men in particular had the resources and connections to avoid service through travel, or even by taking up residence abroad (Isoc. 18.47–8; Lys. 16.3–5; Lyc. 1.43; cf. Lys. 31.5–14; Is. 4.27–8). Only after the city's defeat at Chaeronea (338 B.C.) were citizens prohibited by law from leaving the city or sending their families abroad (Lyc. 1.53; Aeschin. 3.252; cf. Lys. 30.27–9). It was impracticable for the city to track down and notify conscripts who were absent from

[26] Lys. 24 suggests that similar difficulties were involved in reviewing claims for the stipend given to disabled citizens who were indigent and unable to work; on this stipend, see [Arist.] *Ath. Pol.* 49.4.

[27] A partially disabled person, however, might still be able to participate in hoplite battle: see Plu. *Mor.* 217c, 234e; cf. 210f.

[28] For alleged faking of illness in other civic contexts, see Dem. 58.43; 19.124 (but cf. Aeschin. 2.94–5); Plu. *Dem.* 25.5.

[29] Plutarch misses the fact that this is likely a ruse, which Phocion sees through.

the city, and those who later returned to the city could plausibly claim ignorance of the fact that they had been conscripted.[30]

A more subtle way to manipulate the rules was to exploit exemptions based on officeholding or other service to the city. Some one thousand Athenians each year could claim exemption from military service as officeholders, whether as magistrates or members of the Council of 500 (Hansen 1985: 17). By putting himself forward for offices based on election or lottery (see Hansen 1991: 230–1), an individual could actively seek the fringe benefit of exemption that accompanied office. Thus, for example, Aristophanes' Dikaiopolis complains of young men who dodge their military duties by gaining election as ambassadors, while grey-headed men serve in the ranks (*Ach.* 598–609).[31] Similarly, Aeschines complains of public speakers stirring up war, "yet when war comes never touching arms themselves, but instead getting into office as auditors (*exetastai*) and naval commissioners (*apostoleis*)" (2.177). Although any citizen could seek exemption from hoplite service on the basis of officeholding, wealthy men had other ways as well to win exemptions through civic activities: they could contract to collect taxes for the city or volunteer to perform liturgies (cf. Dem. 21.160–6).

More flagrant manipulation of such exemptions was, however, possible. While it would have been difficult for an individual to win exemption by a false claim that he was an officeholder or serving the city in some other way because such claims would be fairly easy to refute, he could abuse an originally valid exemption by using it after it had expired. This may have been common among chorus members, who received a temporary release from service while involved in a choral production; the temptation to extend the period of release may have been great, especially if an individual thought he might soon

[30] I am not persuaded by Sekunda (1992: 348) that Athenians abroad "made considerable efforts to join the army, even if they could have avoided conscription had they so wished"; Sekunda draws this inference from Xenophon's efforts in 362 B.C. to send his sons to Athens to join in the expedition supporting Sparta (D.L. 2.53), but this is more likely evidence of Xenophon's philolaconism than of typical behavior of Athenians abroad.

[31] The jibe at Ar. *Nu.* 685–93 concerning Amynias' evasion of military service may stem from his service on an embassy (see MacDowell 1971: 139); cf. Aeschin. 3.159, 253 (characterizing Demosthenes' mission abroad after Chaeronea as desertion).

be recruited for a chorus in a different festival (Dem. 39.16–17, with MacDowell, 1982 [1989]: 71–2; cf. Dem. 21.58–60).[32]

An individual could dodge the draft not only by unilaterally abusing legitimate exemptions but also through personal influence with the generals who were responsible for the conscription lists. We must not underestimate the ability of powerful individuals in Athens to have favors of this sort granted them in exchange for services or "gifts."[33] This was especially easy when conscription was carried out by *katalogos*, because the generals enjoyed broad discretion in compiling lists under this system. If a general wished to grant such a favor, he could arrange for an individual's name to be left off the list in the first place or erase it from the posted list. It was apparently routine for the generals and their staff to modify the posted lists as they granted exemptions and there was little to prevent them from removing names as favors at this time too.[34] The process of editing the lists could appear arbitrary: thus Aristophanes' chorus in *Peace* protests that the taxiarchs "enter some of our names on the lists and erase others haphazardly, two or three times" (1180–1).

If the generals wished to be more subtle in their favoritism, they could help wealthy individuals, who were especially likely to enjoy influence with them, not to dodge service altogether but rather to transfer from hoplite service to cavalry service and thus gain exemption from the former (Lys. 14.14, 15.5–6; cf. Ar. *Eq.* 1369–72; X. *Mem.* 3.4.1). This was doubly advantageous to those transferring because

[32] The poets whose works were being performed by choruses were probably also temporarily exempt from military service (cf. the likely exemption of *chorēgoi*: Dem. 21.103, with MacDowell 1990: 9) and thus might, like choristers, be tempted to evade service after their exemption expired; note the snipe against the military service of the dithyrambic poet Cinesias in Lys. 21.20. While Stephanus brought a successful indictment for evasion (*graphē astrateias*) against the poet Xenocleides ([Dem.] 59.27), his suit arose in connection with Xenocleides' claim to exemption as tax collector, not as a poet involved in a dramatic festival.

[33] On Athenian toleration of what we might view as bribery, see Wankel 1982; MacDowell 1983; Harvey 1985; Strauss 1985; C. Taylor 2001a, b. Many generals appear to have been ready to exploit their office for profit: see Pritchett 1974: 2.126–32.

[34] During the period when one general was selected from each tribe (see Hamel 1998a: 85–7), each general probably supervised the list for his own tribe and thus was in a good position to grant favors to fellow tribesmen. Under conscription by *katalogos* a demarch could also grant favors, because he could keep an individual's name off the deme's list of eligible hoplites that he sent to the generals (see Christ 2001: 401).

call-up for active cavalry duty was probably less frequent than that for hoplite service (Th. 3.16.1) and service as cavalryman safer than that as hoplite (Lys. 14.7, 14.14, 16.13; cf. X. *An.* 3.2.19).[35] While a possible check on such transfers was that a cavalryman had to pass a review (*dokimasia*) proving that he was qualified to serve, this does not appear to have hindered some dodgers. Enemies of the younger Alcibiades indicted him for dodging hoplite service, alleging that he obtained a transfer to the cavalry though he had never passed the review (Lys. 14.8, 15.8; cf. 16.13); the same generals who had allowed him to do so, however, appeared at trial to speak on his behalf (15.1–6).

Public speakers (*rhētores*) were in a particularly good position to use their personal influence with generals – especially those whom they had helped to win election – to avoid military service or at least to choose when and how they would serve. Because *rhētores* often held no formal office in Athens, they could not claim the exemption from military service granted to regular officeholders.[36] They might well wish to stay at home, however, for the same reasons as other citizens and sometimes, in addition, to maintain their political influence within the city (Dem. 19.124). In this case there may be a grain of truth to frequent attacks on them as draft-dodgers in the sources: they were targets of such attacks not merely because they were involved in public life but because they sometimes evaded conscription.[37]

[35] Members of the cavalry were apparently exempt from hoplite service as long as they were listed on the cavalry *katalogos*, that is, not only when they were on active duty (Lys. 15.7). Special permission was required for a cavalryman to serve temporarily as hoplite (Lys. 16.13). The Athenian state had a compelling interest in ensuring that its relatively few cavalrymen, who had special skills and who received a long-term state loan (*katastasis*) to purchase mounts (Bugh 1988: 56–8), did not perish as hoplites.

[36] Note, however, the assertion of Aeschines (2.177) that public speakers who agitate for war can avoid military service when war comes by becoming officeholders.

[37] Among the targets of such allegations and insinuations are: Aeschines (Dem. 19.113; cf. Aeschin. 2.167–9); Amynias (Ar. *Nu.* 685–93); Aristogeiton (Plu. *Phoc.* 10.2); Cleon (Ar. *Eq.* 442–4; cf. 368); Cleonymus (Ar. *Eq.* 1369–72); Demosthenes (Aeschin. 3.148); Peisander (X. *Smp.* 2.14; cf. Ar. *Av.* 1556–8; Eup. fr. 35). Ar. *Eq.* 442–4 caricatures how *rhētores* level charges of evasion against one another; cf. 368; Dem. 21.110. Cf. the prominent discussion in American politics of how former-President W. J. Clinton and President G. W. Bush avoided service in the Vietnam War through political connections (see e.g., *NYT* Feb. 15, 2004, Section 4, Page 1, Col. 3). A general's record of service could also be attacked: see e.g., X. *Mem.* 3.4.1 attacking Antisthenes (see Sommerstein 1998: 173) for never serving as hoplite and for undistinguished cavalry service.

The dodges discussed above entail engagement with the city's conscription system, if only to manipulate it. A more bold evader could, however, seek to avoid the system altogether by failing to appear at muster. This was probably relatively common in the Greek world. Thus Polybius, as a Greek observer of Roman practices, is impressed that in the Roman army, "all of those on the roll appear without fail, because those who have been sworn in are allowed no excuse at all except adverse omens or absolute impossibility" (6.26.4); here, as elsewhere in this excursus (e.g., 6.36–8), Polybius is likely contrasting Greek laxness in military matters with Roman strictness. Earlier testimony to the routine nature of non-appearance for service in a Greek setting is provided by Xenophon, who takes for granted that civic authority must regularly deal with men delaying when called to arms. His Hiero asserts that a tyrant is far more likely than a private citizen to incur hatred, in part because he must personally exercise authority over men who are slow to appear for service (*Hier.* 8.8–9); Hiero's interlocutor, Simonides, accepts this as a routine civic problem and proposes that "with the prospect of reward there would be more dispatch in starting for the appointed place" (9.7). While Xenophon does not mention Athens, his commonsense solutions to civic problems here may be inspired, like his *Poroi*, by the situation in his native Athens. More specific evidence of the problem in Athens crops up in an anecdote in Diodorus Siculus (1st c. B.C.) concerning the general Myronides in 457 B.C.: when some of the hoplites he had conscripted for an expedition to Boeotia did not present themselves at muster, he set forth with those who had appeared on the grounds that men who intentionally come late for an expedition would prove useless in battle anyway (11.81.4–5).[38]

A conscript who failed to appear for service might face prosecution later before a court of hoplites from the campaign that he had dodged (Lys. 14.5, 15, 17; cf. Dem. 39.17); the generals presided over such courts (Lys. 15.1–2), which also had jurisdiction over suits concerning offenses on campaign, including desertion of the ranks (*lipotaxion*) and

[38] On "delayers," see also Hdt. 7.230; E. *Heracl.* 700–1, 722–3; Lys. 3.45; cf. Pl. *Grg.* 447a, with Dodds 1959: 188.

cowardice (Lys. 14.5).[39] These courts were apparently convened as needed at some interval after hoplites had returned from a campaign; citizen-soldiers returning from abroad were unlikely to tolerate delaying their reunions with their families to accommodate immediate court proceedings, and time had to be allowed in any case for prosecutors to initiate their actions (cf. Dem. 21.103) and defendants to prepare their cases.[40]

The legal action most likely to be used against draft evaders was a public indictment for failure to serve, the *graphē astrateias* (see Lipsius 1908: 2.452–5; cf. Hamel 1998b). Several prosecutions of this type are attested: one against the younger Alcibiades, the outcome of which is unknown (Lys. 14, 15);[41] one against the poet Xenocleides, brought successfully by Stephanus ([Dem.] 59.27); and two against individuals involved with choruses, Sannion and Aristides, both of whom were convicted (Dem. 21.58–60, with MacDowell 1990: 279–81). Boeotus, a chorister, was probably also indicted through this *graphē*, but the case may have been dropped because court business was suspended at the time due to shortage of funds to pay jurors (Dem. 39.16–17, with MacDowell 1982 [1989]: 72).

Although these episodes attest that draft-dodgers faced some risk of prosecution and conviction, prosecution was far from certain.[42] Prosecution for any public offense in Athens was uncertain, because it depended on a willing prosecutor stepping forward (Christ 1998a:

[39] Dem. 39.17 suggests that taxiarchs could receive charges and "bring them into court" (εἰσάγειν). This may mean that under some circumstances taxiarchs presided over the court (Carey and Reid 1985: 180; but cf. Harrison 1971: 2.32–3, with 33 n. 1); if so they were probably acting under the ultimate authority of the generals.

[40] While one might speak loosely of these courts as "military courts," they were not part of a separate military justice system. To judge from Lys. 14 and 15, litigants within these courts resemble those in Athens' other courts in the ways they invoke laws, witness testimony, and deploy rhetorical conventions.

[41] Although Lysias 14 and 15 are prosecution speeches from the same trial (both are synegorial: see Rubinstein 2000: 27), the manuscripts label the former a prosecution for *lipotaxion* and the latter one for *astrateia*. I am persuaded by Hamel (1998b: 362–76; cf. Hansen 2003) that the action initiating the trial is one for *astrateia*, though the prosecutors tendentiously conflate this charge with that of *lipotaxion*.

[42] [X.] *Ath. Pol.* 3.5 (Bowersock) speaks vaguely of the frequency of such suits: "Now and again they have to judge suits involving evasion" (διὰ χρόνου <δὲ> διαδικάσαι δεῖ ἀστρατείας: ἀστρατείας Brodaeus).

118–59). The fact that a prosecutor of a public suit was subject to a thousand-drachma fine and partial disfranchisement (*atimia*) if he failed to pursue a suit that he had initiated or won less than one-fifth of the votes at trial must have been a deterrent to taking on public prosecutions for purely civic-minded reasons. The most likely volunteer prosecutor was a well-off individual who could risk the large fine and whose self-interest was served by punishing an offender.[43] While the generals had the power to "bind," that is, imprison, offenders before trial (Lys. 9.5–6), they were not, as far as we know, required to seek out offenders or to prosecute them. Moreover, if generals were complicit in the dodging – as the prosecutors of the younger Alcibiades claimed (Lys. 15.1–6) – prosecution by them was naturally out of the question.[44] Prosecution for draft evasion probably depended, therefore, on the initiative of powerful, interested parties, including personal enemies (Lys. 14.2, 15.12; cf. Dem. 21.59) and political rivals ([Dem.] 59.27, with Kapparis 1999: 222; cf. Ar. *Eq.* 442–4, 368). Prominent individuals with wealthy enemies and rivals may have been the most likely targets for prosecution, and enforcement was thus in effect selective (Lys. 14.12, 15.9; cf. X. *Eq. Mag.* 1.10).[45]

If a draft-dodger was so unfortunate as to be prosecuted, conviction may have been likely before a court of hoplites who had served on the campaign that he had dodged. Such a jury would probably be unsympathetic to excuses offered for non-service and furthermore might be inclined to view the punishment doled out to draft-evaders

43 On the statutory penalty for dropped or unsuccessful public prosecutions, see Christ 1998a: 29; on the sociology of Athenian litigation, see Christ 1998a: 32–4, and 2002: 4–5.

44 The fact that the generals presided over the courts in such cases may mean that they did not normally act as prosecutors; but cf. MacDowell 1978: 237.

45 In my view, therefore, it was the sociology of Athenian litigation that could make elite citizens more accountable than average citizens for draft evasion, rather than disparate standards for rich and poor as Roisman (2005: 124–9; 213) argues (e.g., 124: "the orations suggest that there was considerably more sympathy for men of lower social status and means who opted out of serving than for men of higher social status and means who did the same"). I am not aware of any evidence for this in connection with evasion of hoplite service. While it is true, as Roisman observes (125–7), that speakers could present the desertion of poor rowers as more understandable than the dereliction of wealthy trierarchs ([Dem.] 50.22–3; Dem. 51.11), I take these statements more as jabs at wealthy opponents than as evidence for a double standard concerning military service.

as a necessary and symmetrical complement to the rewards due to them for complying (cf. Lyc. 1.73; Pl. *Lg.* 943a–c). If convicted, a draft-dodger was punished with *atimia* (And. 1.74; Dem. 24.103; [Dem.] 59.27; Aeschin. 3.175–6; cf. Dem. 21.58–60).[46] While this was a serious penalty, it fell well short of the death penalty, which Sparta may have imposed on dodgers (Lyc. 1.129),[47] and would have weighed most heavily on individuals wishing to lead an active civic life – perhaps not a high priority for many draft-dodgers. It is not clear, moreover, how much of a disability *atimia* was in practice: Demosthenes asserts that Sannion and Aristides continued to participate in choral productions notwithstanding their convictions for evasion of military service (21.58–60).[48] While such defiance may have been risky, prosecution for violation of the rules governing *atimia*, as for *astrateia*, depended on a volunteer prosecutor stepping forward (cf. Hansen 1976: 94–5).

This analysis suggests that, while the safest way to avoid service in Athens was to manipulate exemptions, a conscript could also simply not appear at muster and take his chances on prosecution and punishment. Although this carried risks, to some at least these may have seemed remote in comparison to the patent risks of going on campaign.

The fact that Athenians did not methodically seek out and prosecute all draft-evaders through, for example, a state prosecutor and did not

[46] Unconvicted draft-dodgers and men who cast away their shields on the battlefield were apparently subject to partial *atimia*, in that they were prohibited from speaking in the Assembly and could be prosecuted through the procedure of "review of orators" (*dokimasia rhētorōn*) if they violated this rule (Aeschin. 1.28–32); if convicted, such individuals suffered full *atimia* (Aeschin. 1.134; cf. Dem. 19.257, 284) (see MacDowell 2005; cf. Wallace 1998a).

[47] Lycurgus asserts that the Spartans "passed a law, covering all not willing to risk danger for their fatherland, which expressly stated that they should be put to death" (1.129); the fact that he then produces a copy of the law (the text is not preserved) lends some credence to his claim (thus MacDowell 1986a: 70). While this law could be construed as a measure against cowardice in battle (*ibid.*), there is good evidence that Spartans punished this with disfranchisement and humiliation (see Chapter 3); the law invoked by Lycurgus may apply instead to those who failed to serve in the first place.

[48] MacDowell (1982 [1989]: 77) notes the apparent lenience. Speakers make much of the restrictions entailed by *atimia* when it serves their rhetorical purposes: see esp. [Dem.] 59.27.

always enforce *atimia* against those convicted is consistent with the democratic ideal that the city errs on the side of lenience when it comes to its own citizens (Dem. 22.51; 24.24). In the sensitive area of conscription – and also, as we shall see, in that of taxation – where compulsion to serve the city was potentially in conflict with ideals of personal freedom, Athenians were apparently uncomfortable with the rigid exercise of public authority against private individuals.

Plato regards this democratic moderation toward regulating citizen behavior as evidence of the laxness of democratic regimes: in giving free rein to personal freedom, they in fact exalt personal license at the expense of state authority (*R.* 557b; *Lg.* 780b). Plato thus includes in his tirade against democracy, in which his native Athens cannot be far from his mind, the charge that there is "no compulsion . . . to make war when the rest are at war" (*R.* 557e; cf. 561d–e; *Lg.* 955b–c; Plu. *Pyrrh.* 16.2). While Plato exaggerates the ability of citizens in a democracy like Athens to choose whether to undertake military service, there is a kernel of truth behind this caricature: the city, in keeping with democratic values, stopped short of rigidly forcing its free citizens to comply with conscription.

Athenians preferred to encourage patriotic behavior through persuasion rather than to force it upon free persons through the exercise of civic authority. They rejected the alternative model of Sparta, where law was *despotēs* (Hdt. 7.104.4–5, with Millender 2002) and the compulsory nature of military service manifest (Lyc. 1.129–30; cf. Th. 2.39.4).[49] Perhaps the most important vehicle for eliciting patriotism and, along with it, voluntary compliance with conscription was the *epitaphios* – the funeral oration given periodically to commemorate the city's war dead. The surviving speeches idealize the bond between city and citizen to inspire Athenians to sacrifice themselves willingly in time of war.

Although the ideology-laden Attic funeral orations suppress overt mention of conscription and, not surprisingly, evasion of it, the way

[49] Even more so did Athenians reject the naked compulsion that Persian despots exercised in conscripting their subjects (Hdt. 4.84, 7.38–9, 7.108; cf. 5.27; contrast 7.99), who were forced to fight to perpetuate their own servitude (Lys. 2.41; Isoc. 4.124; cf. Hp. *Aer.* 16).

they carefully navigate around the fact that the city's war-dead were regularly conscripts can be taken as indirect evidence of the tensions surrounding conscription in a free society.[50] These speeches emphasize the zeal (*prothumia*) with which Athenians serve their city, and present this as natural for free men who are fighting to preserve their freedom.[51] They are, however, consistently vague about the original circumstances under which the city's dead hoplites came to serve, preferring instead to focus on the moment of their heroism on the battlefield where they chose freely the courageous course of self-sacrifice.[52] To be sure, the funeral orations stop short of characterizing the city's hoplites as "volunteers" (*ethelontai*), that is, non-conscripts. But they foster the impression that Athenians, because of their innate courage, are uniformly willing to risk their lives (Th. 2.39.4: ἐθέλομεν κινδυνεύειν; cf. 2.42.4; Hyp. 6.15) and thus, one might infer, freely choose to serve. Consistent with this is how the funeral orations translate the compulsion of conscription, which is backed up by civic authority, into a sense of obligation that citizens feel: what compels the city's hoplites to serve is not so much their obligation to do so under the city's laws but rather their free judgment that it is necessary to fight for freedom (Pl. *Mx.* 239b) and to embrace their duties (Th. 2.43.1; cf. Gorg. 82 fr. 6.17f. D–K).[53]

While draft evasion never constituted a crisis in Athens as far as we can tell, the survey above suggests that it presented the city with a serious and persistent challenge. On the one hand, *astrateia* posed practical problems for the city in its efforts to carry out conscription; on the other hand it posed ideological problems as a deviation from the model citizen behavior advanced in the *epitaphioi* and elsewhere.

[50] On the suppression of communal tensions in the Attic funeral orations, see Loraux 1986 and Ober 1998: 86–9.

[51] *prothumia*: Dem. 60.18; Th. 2.36.4; cf. 1.70.6, 74.1–2, 75.1; Lys. 2.22. Fighting for freedom: Lys. 2.14; Pl. *Mx.* 239a–b; cf. Lyc. 1.48–9; Demad. fr. 83.2; Hyp. 6.24; Hdt. 5.78; Hp. *Aer.* 16; Ziolkowski 1981: 106–8.

[52] Free choice: Th. 2.39.4, 42.4, 43.1; Lys. 2.62, 79; Dem. 60.1, 25–6, 27–8, 37; Hyp. 6.15, 40; cf. Isoc. 4.83; Dem. 18.96–7, 205; Lyc. 1.49, 86, 143; Ziolkowski 1981: 112–13; Millender 2002: 50.

[53] Fear of the city's laws, however, does have its place within Athenian democratic ideology: see esp. Lys. 14.15 and Aeschin. 3.175–6 (both citing this as inducement to serve the city honorably in war); cf. A. *Eu.* 696–9; Th. 2.37.3; Lyc. 1.130.

Tragedy provided the Athenian public with a vehicle for addressing on an imaginative level draft evasion and, more generally, the problematic nature of compulsory military service in a democratic society. An awareness of tragedy's intimate connection with contemporary experience can help enrich our understanding of both tragedy and its historic context.[54]

CONSCRIPTION AND DRAFT EVASION THROUGH A TRAGIC LENS

Conscription in Athens, as we have seen, could pit individual and *oikos* against the state; involve the exercise of compulsion on otherwise free individuals; and inspire shrewdness on the part of evaders and ingenuity on the part of the state's agents. It is no coincidence that these very elements crop up prominently on the tragic stage in Athens. Tragedians regularly drew on myths involving what can be labeled a "recruiting motif": an individual is called on to serve the community in war; the call is met initially with hesitation and sometimes evasion; the community's agents must exercise persuasion, force, or deception to achieve its goals; in the end, the community prevails. Neither the ubiquity of this motif nor its relevance to the Athenian experience of conscription is fully appreciated. The tensions surrounding contemporary conscription intrigued tragedians, and this is reflected in the myths that they chose to present onstage and the terms in which they treated these. While tragedians remain true to their medium in not forcing their mythical material into a transparently contemporary framework and tend to explore rather than resolve contemporary tensions on the stage, their interests and perspectives are grounded in Athenian experience.

Tragedians construct a world onstage that mirrors the situation in Athens, where men did not always wish to serve and sometimes took evasive action. Euripides' *Heraclidae* provides a glimpse of this. As troops gather for battle against the oppressors of Heracles' children, Iolaus,

[54] For skepticism concerning tragedy as political discourse, see Griffin 1998. The following analysis suggests that Griffin (44) is mistaken in minimizing tragedy's engagement with Athens' military institutions. For further challenges to Griffin, see Seaford 2000; Goldhill 2000: 34–41; Gregory 2002; cf. Wilson 2000: 46–7.

who is himself a willing soldier despite his advanced years, speaks out without provocation against evasion: "This home watch (οἰκούρημα) of mine is a disgraceful thing: some men are joining in battle, while others by cowardice (δειλίᾳ) stay behind" (700–1).[55] Although Iolaus needs no prodding, Euripides makes the servant bringing him his armor urge him to avoid the appearance of evasion: "For the contest is near and Ares hates delayers (μέλλοντας) most of all" (722–3). While these allusions to evasion are hardly integral to their immediate context, they become meaningful if we take them as a reflection of the world offstage, in which evasion was a real alternative to service and the decision to serve a conscious rejection of this option.[56]

Although many myths could serve tragedians as vehicles for reflecting on compulsory service and evasion of it, some especially invited this. One such tale was that of the prophet Amphiaraus, who unwillingly joined the ill-fated campaign of the Seven against Thebes. Because Amphiaraus knew that he would die if he participated in the expedition, which his brother-in-law, Adrastus, was organizing, he was reluctant to join it; his wife, Eriphyle, however, compelled him to go, betraying him in exchange for a golden necklace. How exactly Eriphyle compelled this reluctant recruit to participate is variously explained (Gantz 1993: 2.506–8; Bond 1963: 84, with nn. 1 and 2). According to one version of the myth, Amphiaraus had gone into hiding and Eriphyle betrayed him by revealing his location to the authorities (esp. Hyg. *Fab.* 73).[57] Sophocles may have capitalized on the comic potential of this version in his satyr play *Amphiaraus*, by making satyrs join in the search for the draft-dodging prophet or by having them aid him as look-outs at his hiding place (fr. 113, with

[55] For οἰκουρός as a term of derision for draft-evaders in Athens, see Din. 1.82; cf. A. *A.* 1223–5, 1625–7; Hermipp. fr. 46. Note too how Iolaus is characterized in contemporary Athenian terms as a "hoplite" (694); on tragedy's "anachronistic reading of epic warfare," see Pritchard 1998: 50.

[56] Cf. Iolaus' words concerning his "good citizenship" at the opening of the tragedy: while it was possible for him to live a quiet life, he chose to share in Heracles' many labors (1–8). I am not persuaded by Mendelsohn (2002: 78–85) that Iolaus is "apolitical" at the tragedy's opening.

[57] M. Davies (1989: 29) suggests that this episode may have been treated in the Cyclic *Thebais*. Cf. Achilles' concealment on Skyros to avoid conscription for the Trojan War (Euripides' treatment of this myth is discussed below in the text).

Scheurer and Kansteiner 1999: 240–1). According to another version, however, Eriphyle compelled her husband to participate in another way: Amphiaraus and Adrastus had sworn an oath after a past quarrel to submit any subsequent disagreements between them to Eriphyle and to abide by her arbitration; when Amphiaraus resisted joining Adrastus' expedition, the dispute was therefore submitted to Eriphyle and she, bribed by Polyneices, ruled against her husband and thus forced him to serve (esp. Apollod. *Bibl.* 3.6.2). While we cannot be sure which of these two versions Euripides follows in his *Hypsipylē*, at one point his Amphiaraus speaks directly of the constraint operating upon him: "For I must serve . . . " (χρὴ γὰρ στρατεύειν μ') (fr. 1.V.15 Bond). It is unfortunate that so little remains of tragic treatments of Amphiaraus, as the sinister circumstances of his conscription may have provided tragedians with an opportunity to probe the dark side of compulsory service.[58]

Much better attested is the way tragedians explored tensions concerning compulsory service and evasion of it through the mythology of the Trojan War, which provided especially rich material for this. Tragedians' interest in conscription and evasion is apparent in their treatment not only of the initial mustering for the war but also of the expedition's later phases and its aftermath.

According to tradition, Tyndareus bound Helen's suitors by oath to defend the marital rights of whichever suitor prevailed; thus when Paris ran off to Troy with Helen, the unsuccessful suitors were obliged to join her husband, Menelaus, in the expedition to retrieve her

[58] Carcinus II (?) (70 F 1c) and Cleophon (?) (77 F 2) wrote tragedies titled *Amphiaraus*; Aristophanes, Plato, Apollodorus Carystius, and Philippides wrote comedies with this title (Radt 1977: 4.152).

Compulsion figures prominently in the next phase of this story too, as "Amphiaraus ordered his sons to kill their mother when they came of age and to march against Thebes" (Apollod. *Bibl.* 3.6.2); in this version Amphiaraus, himself compelled under unhappy circumstances to march against Thebes, forces his sons to do the same. A different version makes Eriphyle – this time bribed by a robe – persuade her sons to join in the expedition of the Epigoni (Apollod. *Bibl.* 3.7.2; cf. Gantz 1993: 2.525). We do not know which of these two versions Aeschylus might have used in his *Epigoni*, or Sophocles in his *Epigoni* and *Eriphyle* (which may be different names for the same tragedy); cf. Lloyd-Jones 1996: 72–3. Some authors make Amphiaraus' sons subject to compulsory military service as takers of the Oath of Tyndareus (Hes. *Ehoiai* frr. 196–204; cf. Apollod. *Bibl.* 3.10.8–9; Gantz 1993: 2.565–6).

(cf. Gantz 1993: 2.564–7). Tragedians treat the Oath of Tyndareus as the basis for the conscription of many Greek heroes who joined the expedition to Troy, because it made service a necessity (ἀνάγκη) (S. *Ph.* 72–4; cf. fr. 144; E. *IA* 395) for them – as contemporary conscription did for Athenians (Is. 10.20; cf. Dem. 2.30) – and gave recruiters grounds for compelling them, if necessary, to participate. There is, however, something potentially dark about this mythical foil for contemporary conscription. As Euripides' Agamemnon points out, the Oath was shrewdly imposed (πυκνῇ φρενί: *IA* 67) on the distracted suitors under duress (ὅρκους . . . κατηναγκασμένους: 395). The problematic nature of compulsion in this context is emblematic of the tensions surrounding it, whenever it crops up in recruiting stories in tragedy.

After Helen's flight with Paris, Menelaus traveled around Greece to gather heroes, including Odysseus, to join him in an expedition to Troy (cf. Gantz 1993: 2.580). While almost nothing survives of Sophocles' *Odysseus Mainomenos* (*Odysseus Gone Mad*), the title suggests that this tragedy treated Odysseus' attempt to dodge service by feigning madness (cf. Procl. *Chr.* 119–21 Severyns [*Cypria*]). Sophocles alludes to this myth, and perhaps also to his presumably earlier treatment of it, in his *Philoctetes* (409 B.C.): Philoctetes disparages Odysseus on the grounds that he served only when "put under the yoke by trickery and necessity" (κλοπῇ τε κἀνάγκῃ ζυγείς) (1025); earlier Odysseus himself alludes to the compulsion (ἐξ ἀνάγκης) upon him to serve because he was bound by the Oath (72–4). In *Odysseus Mainomenos*, the recruiting mission probably included Palamedes, whom most ancient sources credit with the stratagem that forces Odysseus to abandon his ruse. While different versions of Palamedes' ruse are attested, most involve a threat to the life of Odysseus' infant son, Telemachus, that tricks Odysseus into dropping his ruse (e.g., Procl. *Chr.* 119–21 Severyns [*Cypria*]; Gantz 1993: 2.580). The contest of wits involved here recurs in other recruiting stories, as we shall see.

Despite Odysseus' initial resistance, by most accounts he came to be one of the war's most enthusiastic supporters. Aeschylus' Agamemnon succinctly summarizes the reversal: "Only Odysseus – even though he sailed unwillingly – carried his harness readily once yoked to me" (*A.* 841–2). Odysseus' turnabout is nowhere more evident in tragedy than in his frequent role as recruiter, both at the war's onset in the quest to recruit Achilles and near its conclusion in the missions to fetch Neoptolemus and Philoctetes. In each case, Odysseus' shrewdness, which was once used to resist conscription, is now put to use on behalf of the war effort against reluctant recruits.

Euripides may well have caught the paradox of reluctant recruit turned recruiter in his *Skyrioi* – perhaps one of his earlier tragedies (Webster 1967: 4, 86) – which treated the myth that Odysseus helped hunt down Achilles on the island of Skyros so as to recruit him for the expedition to Troy (cf. Gantz 1993: 2.580–2). Euripides' prologue, which was quite possibly spoken by Thetis (Webster 1967: 96), probably provided the essential background: Thetis, knowing that Achilles would die if he went to Troy, dressed him as a girl and placed him on Skyros with the king, Lycomedes, who did not know his identity and brought him up with his orphan daughter, Deidameia (*Hyp.* 11–20, in Austin 1968: 95–6). As the tragedy opens, however, Achilles has raped Deidameia, who is now pregnant (*Hyp.* 20–2) with the future Neoptolemus; Lycomedes discovers her condition (frr. 682–4), but does not know who is responsible. Meanwhile, Odysseus (fr. 683a N^2 Suppl. *apud* Plu. *Mor.* 34d, 72e), accompanied by Diomedes, appears on the scene to recruit Achilles in accordance with an oracle bidding the Achaeans not to make their expedition without him (*Hyp.* 22–6).[59] Odysseus presumably exposes Achilles' identity by a ruse, perhaps that described by later mythographers: Odysseus places on display for the women of Lycomedes' court not only feminine baubles but manly weapons; an accomplice (Diomedes?) then sounds a war-trumpet in the distance as if invaders are approaching. Achilles snatches up the weapons, ready for battle, and is thus found out (esp. Hyg. *Fab.* 96). When Odysseus exposes Achilles' identity, he both solves the mystery of Deidameia's pregnancy and paves the way for his attempt to recruit Achilles.[60]

[59] The embassy probably set out from Aulis, where the Achaeans had already gathered: the hypothesis speaks of "those around Agamemnon" (οἱ δὲ περὶ τ[ὸν Ἀγαμέ]-/μνον[α]) sending it.

[60] The partially preserved hypothesis and fragments do not provide any support for Webster's conjecture (1967: 96–7) that the mystery of Deidameia's pregnancy has already been solved before the recruiting mission arrives.

While Achilles' taking up of arms in response to Odysseus' ruse can be construed as a precursor of his armed participation in the expedition, his recruitment is still incomplete at this point. The Achilles of this tragedy was apparently under no compulsion to join the expedition: he must have been beardless to carry off his disguise and therefore was presumably too young to have been one of Helen's suitors and party to the Oath of Tyndareus.[61] Thus, Odysseus must seek to persuade him to join the expedition. It is probably in this context that Odysseus sarcastically rebukes Achilles:

> Do you, son of the best father among the Hellenes, spend your time carding wool and thus extinguish the bright light of your ancestry? (fr. 683a N² Suppl.)

It is natural, given Achilles' cross-dressing, that Odysseus should seek to shame him by highlighting how far the feminine role he has assumed lies from the manly role he should adopt.[62] In invoking Achilles' father, Odysseus pointedly suggests that Achilles should embrace his masculine example rather than yield to the fears of his mother, who had induced him to hide in this way. In the end, Achilles' manly nature presumably prevails, just as it did in his impregnation of Deidameia, and he willingly leaves behind the sheltered feminine sphere to set off on the manly enterprise of war.

Just as the recruitment of Odysseus and that of Achilles are necessary preliminaries to the Trojan expedition, so too is the recruitment of Iphigeneia as sacrificial victim at Aulis, where the Achaeans muster (cf. Gantz 1993: 2.582–8). The manner in which Iphigeneia is induced to appear at this muster encourages equation of her situation with that of male recruits. In Euripides' *Iphigeneia among the Taurians*, Iphigeneia reports that Odysseus was sent by the Achaeans to Argos to fetch her and lured her to Aulis with the false promise of marriage to Achilles (24–5, 361–71, 852).[63] Odysseus' role as devious recruiter

[61] By contrast, E. *Hel.* 98–9 makes Achilles one of Helen's suitors. On the problem of Achilles and the Oath of Tyndareus, see Gantz 1993: 2.564–5.

[62] Webster (1967: 97) suggests that E. frr. 880 and 885, which are preserved without assignation to a particular tragedy, also belong to this context.

[63] Sophocles' *Iphigeneia* may have focused on this mission (cf. Lloyd-Jones 1996: 3.139); fr. 305 indicates that Odysseus was in on the ruse.

here is similar to the one he plays in fetching Achilles from Skyros in Euripides' *Skyrioi* and Philoctetes from Lemnos in the various tragic treatments of this story (see below). As in their dramas involving male conscripts, moreover, tragedians treating the Iphigeneia story are especially interested in whether she is enlisted by force or willingly.[64] Most commonly, tragedians depict her as an unwilling victim, lured from the female sphere for sacrifice at the muster of men (e.g., A. *A.* 228–47; E. *El.* 1020–3; *IT* 359–71). Euripides' *Iphigeneia at Aulis*, however, makes Iphigeneia, though initially reluctant, a willing volunteer once she realizes that her death will serve the common good (1386–7). Her turnabout is analogous to that of male recruits like Achilles who hesitate at first but then accept the call to serve.[65]

Sophocles' *Achaiōn Sullogos* (*The Gathering of Achaeans*) was probably set at the initial mustering of the troops at Aulis. This provides the most plausible context for fr. 144: "But you on your chair who hold the tablets with the writing, mark off (νεμ') any who swore but is not present!"[66] When the speaker refers to swearing, he is presumably alluding to the Oath of Tyndareus; his order to identify any of those who swore the Oath but are absent suggests that some conscripts may be missing.[67] The procedure portrayed here sounds very much like that employed at an Athenian muster: the taxiarchs, who assisted the

[64] Tragedians regularly explore this tension when they present scenarios involving human sacrifice on behalf of the community (cf. Wilkins 1990; Mendelsohn 2002: 89–104). The martial context of these scenarios and the often explicit link between the individual sacrifice involved and the situation of hoplites risking their lives for the city (E. *Ph.* 997–1005; *Heracl.* 500–6; *Erec.* fr. 360.22–37; cf. Lyc. 1.101; Dem. 60.29) suggest that they invite reflection on the tensions involved in compulsory military service.

[65] Note how Aeschylus' Agamemnon views Iphigeneia's sacrifice as a test of *his* willingness to serve: "How can I become a deserter of the fleet (λιπόναυς) and fail my allies?" (*A.* 212–13).

[66] νεμ' could also mean "read off" (Hsch. s.v. νέμω = ν290).

[67] Some scholars believe that Sophocles' Ἀχαιῶν Σύλλογος is identical with his Σύνδειπνοι (discussed below in the text), because Athenaeus (1.17c) gives the latter the title Ἀχαιῶν Σύνδειπνον; on the debate, see Radt 1977: 4.163, 425, and Lloyd-Jones 1996: 3.280–1. I doubt, however, that these titles refer to the same tragedy. First, fr. 144 fits the situation of an initial muster at Aulis better than a later review of the troops in Tenedos, the likely setting of Σύνδειπνοι. Second, σύλλογος is the normal word for muster (E. *IA* 825; cf. 514; fr. 727c12 K in Collard, Cropp, and Lee, eds., 1997; Th. 4.77; X. *Cyr.* 6.2.11; Christensen and Hansen 1983) and not a very likely synonym for σύνδειπνον.

generals, checked off conscripts against their lists and made a special notation next to the names of no-shows (Poll. 8.115). This projection of Athenian-style procedure onto the mythical past gave an Athenian audience further impetus, if needed, to equate their experience of conscription with that portrayed onstage.

After the Achaeans finally leave Aulis, they confront another obstacle at Tenedos on their way to Troy when Achilles threatens to return home because Agamemnon fails to invite him (Arist. *Rh.* 1401b16–21) or invites him late to a feast of the leading Achaeans (Procl. *Chr.* 144–7 Severyns [*Cypria*]) (cf. Gantz 1993: 2.588–9). Sophocles explored this situation in his *Sundeipnoi* (*Those Who Dine Together*); it is not clear whether this was a tragedy or a satyr play (Heynen and Krumeich 1999: 396–8). The situation anticipates Achilles' later withdrawal from battle at Troy due to his conflict with Agamemnon, as recounted in the *Iliad* (cf. A. *Myrm.*); Sophocles' use of Odysseus as intermediary between the two also encourages equation of these two episodes (fr. 566; cf. Hom. *Il.* 9.225–306). At the same time, however, the situation may look back to the familiar story that Achilles was reluctant to join the expedition in the first place. Sophocles' Odysseus, like Euripides' Odysseus in *Skyrioi* (fr. 683a N^2 Suppl., quoted above), goads the young hero to act in a manly and honorable way:

> ODYS.: Are you afraid already at the sight of the buildings of Troy?
> ACH.: (*expresses anger and says that he is leaving*)
> ODYS.: I know what you wish to flee from! Is it not from ill-repute? (οὐ τὸ μὴ κλύειν κακῶς;) But Hector is near! Is it not honorable (καλόν) that you remain?[68] (fr. 566 *apud* Plu. *Mor.* 74a)

Ultimately, Achilles presumably accedes to the demands of manliness and heroism – as in Euripides' *Skyrioi* – and rejoins the Achaean expedition.[69]

Near the end of the war, the Achaeans initiate a new round of recruiting, this time targeting Philoctetes and Neoptolemus. In treating

[68] I follow Lloyd-Jones' punctuation (1996: 3.284).

[69] Elsewhere Achilles is cast as an eager supporter of the expedition and impatient with those who delay it: see E. *Tel.* fr. 727c10–23 K in Collard, Cropp, and Lee, eds., 1997; cf. *IA* 818. On Achilles in tragedy, see Michelakis 2002.

these episodes, tragedians suggest that they mirror the recruiting tales set at the war's opening. At the same time, however, the special situations of the recruits provide tragedians with fresh material for exploring tensions concerning conscription and resistance to it.

When the Trojan seer Helenus is captured by Odysseus, he prophesies that the Achaeans cannot take Troy without Philoctetes and his bow (cf. Procl. *Chr.* 211–13 Severyns [*Little Iliad*]; Gantz 1993: 2.635). The Achaeans, therefore, send a mission to fetch Philoctetes back from Lemnos, where they had abandoned him on their way to Troy due to his malodorous wound from a snake bite (Hom. *Il.* 2.721–5; Procl. *Chr.* 144–6 Severyns [*Cypria*]). Aeschylus, Euripides, and Sophocles each devoted a tragedy to the tale; while little remains of Aeschylus' tragedy, enough survives of Euripides' play to suggest how it diverged from Sophocles' extant *Philoctetes*.[70]

Euripides' *Philoctetes* (431 B.C.) has been characterized as an exploration of politics and politicians (Olson 1991a: 278–83), and of patriotism (Müller 1990 [1993]: 250–2). In addition, it constitutes a striking treatment of the recruiting motif that invites reflection on the behavior and motivations of both recruiter and recruit. First, the story of how Odysseus comes to take on the recruiting mission, which he relates in the prologue (D.Chr. *Or.* 52.11–13), can itself be viewed as an abbreviated tale of recruitment, in which Odysseus, though initially reluctant, ultimately embraces the role of recruiter. When Helenus prophesied that Troy could not be taken without Philoctetes and his bow (*Or.* 59.2; cf. 52.13), the Achaean leaders asked Odysseus to fetch him, but at first he was not willing to do this (59.3). The basis for Odysseus' refusal to serve was that he did not know how he could persuade Philoctetes to rejoin the Achaeans because Odysseus was responsible for stranding him on Lemnos; indeed, he feared that Philoctetes would kill him on sight (59.3). Odysseus' hesitation to act as recruiter was, however, overcome by Athena, who exhorted him in a dream to take

[70] Dio Chrysostom (*Or.* 52.2) views the tension between coercion and volition as central in all three treatments. Philocles (24 F 1 Snell) and Theodektes (72 F 5b Snell) also each wrote a *Philoctetes*, as did Achaios – but his tragedy was probably set in Troy (20 F 37 Snell); cf. Olson 1991a: 270 n. 5.

courage and go, as she would disguise him so that Philoctetes would not recognize him (59.3, 59.5; cf. 52.13). Yielding to this divine urging and emboldened by the security assured him (59.3), Odysseus sets out on his mission, accompanied by Diomedes (52.14). In so doing, he serves his fellow Achaeans and himself, as success on the mission will help him preserve and advance his personal prestige (frr. 788–9).[71]

Euripides adds a further element of interest to the recruiting tale that he inherited by making the Trojans send a competing recruiting mission, because they too have heard a prophecy from Helenus concerning Philoctetes, according to which Troy will be safe with Heracles' bow in their possession (*Hyp.* 254–8, in Austin 1968: 100; cf. D.Chr. *Or.* 59.4). This enables Euripides to stage a debate (cf. 52.13, 11) between the Trojan mission, which urges Philoctetes to join them, and Odysseus, who does his best to prevent this from happening while still maintaining his disguise (Olson 1991a: 275; Müller 1990 [1993]: 246–7). This debate, besides its immediate purposes within the tragedy, invites reflection on honorable and dishonorable inducements to enlist for military service. The Trojans try to bribe Philoctetes to turn traitor against his fellow Greeks by promising him profit (*kerdos*) (fr. 794; cf. D.Chr. *Or.* 59.4) and even offering him the kingship of Troy (*Or.* 52.13). Odysseus, in rebuttal, presumably calls attention to the sordid nature of the Trojan proposal and the disgrace of betraying Greeks to barbarians, especially because only some of the Greeks had harmed Philoctetes (fr. 796).

After Philoctetes rejects the Trojan embassy and it has departed, Odysseus probably steals his bow while he is sleeping and finally reveals his identity to Philoctetes when he awakes (cf. Olson 1991a: 277). Although Odysseus may attempt to persuade Philoctetes to join him willingly (e.g., frr. 798–9), any such efforts fail. The fragmented hypothesis of the tragedy suggests that someone compelled Philoctetes to accompany him to the ship (ἀναγκάζει [πρὸς τὴν ν]αῦν συνακ[ο]λουθεῖν: 265–6);[72] Odysseus, in possession of the bow,

[71] On Odysseus' characterization of his pursuit of honor (*timē*), see Olson 1991a: 279–81 and Müller 1990 [1993]: 243.

[72] For other possible restorations, see Müller 1997: 49–51.

probably forced Philoctetes to embark (Olson 1991a: 277; cf. Müller 1990 [1993]: 250).[73] If this reconstruction is correct, Euripides' depiction of recruitment is bleak, as it is justified in the end not so much by principle as the superior power of recruiter over recruit (cf. Olson 1991a: 282; Müller 1990 [1993]: 251). While the reluctant recruiter Odysseus is recruited, according to his prologue, due to the divine intervention of Athena, Euripides – unlike Sophocles in his *Philoctetes* – apparently does not introduce a *deus ex machina* at his tragedy's conclusion to prod Philoctetes along into accepting his role as recruit.

Sophocles' greatest innovation in his *Philoctetes* (409 B.C.) is the introduction of Neoptolemus as Odysseus' partner in the mission to fetch Philoctetes and his bow from Lemnos.[74] This deviates from the tradition that Neoptolemus joined the Achaeans only after Philoctetes had come to Troy (Procl. *Chr.* 211–18 Severyns [*Little Iliad*]). As scholars have often noted, this allows Sophocles to explore how Neoptolemus, who is on the verge of manhood, responds to the ethical issues that are raised by the mission. This innovation, however, also highlights the recruiting motif by making Neoptolemus, who is himself a recent recruit, a recruiter collaborating with Odysseus.

Sophocles deftly weaves the recruiting motif into his tragedy, inviting his audience to compare the current mission to fetch Philoctetes with other recruiting missions conducted by the Achaeans. While scholars have argued that this mission recalls the embassy to Achilles in Book 9 of the *Iliad*,[75] the more immediate parallels, which Sophocles invokes explicitly, are to the recruitment of Neoptolemus and that of Odysseus; Sophocles' interest in these parallels comes as no surprise because he had treated each of these recruiting episodes in a tragedy likely antedating his late *Philoctetes*, *Skyrioi* (see below), and

[73] This may help explain why D.Chr. *Or.* 52.16 asserts that Sophocles' Odysseus is much more gentle (πρᾳότερον) than Euripides' Odysseus, i.e., because the latter forces Philoctetes to comply.

[74] Although there is some confusion over whether Philoctetes' bow alone is required (68, 113, 1055–60) or Philoctetes *and* his bow (839–42; cf. 610–13, 985, 1296) (see Hesk 2000: 192–4), Philoctetes' presence is presumably obligatory and is thus ensured by the *deus ex machina* at the play's conclusion.

[75] See Bowie 1997: 59–60 (with earlier bibliography).

Odysseus Mainomenos, respectively. Odysseus refers to Neoptolemus' recent recruitment near the tragedy's opening (72–3), and Neoptolemus repeatedly speaks of it – most extensively in his deceptive account to Philoctetes of how he came to abhor those who had recruited him (343–53; cf. 114, 969–70).[76] Odysseus, in referring to Neoptolemus' recruitment, contrasts the young man's willingness to serve with his own reluctance to join the expedition at its outset (72–4). Later, when Odysseus seeks to conclude the current recruiting mission by using force, Philoctetes rebukes him by recalling the radically different circumstances under which the two of them had originally joined the expedition: while Philoctetes had sailed willingly, Odysseus joined only when "put under the yoke by trickery and necessity" (1025–7). By alluding to the recruiting missions to fetch Odysseus and Neoptolemus and to the original circumstances of Philoctetes' joining the Achaeans, Sophocles encourages his audience to view the current quest after Philoctetes also as a recruiting mission.[77]

The special circumstances of Philoctetes' (re-)recruitment, however, allow Sophocles to explore the extreme case of whether an individual wronged by the community should nonetheless support it in its martial endeavors.[78] To judge from the tragedy's conclusion, Sophocles endorses the claims of the community on the individual, at least under the parameters of his story.[79] When Heracles appears *deus ex machina* and exhorts Philoctetes to join in the expedition (1409–44), he puts a divine stamp on what the representatives of the Achaean community have been seeking all along.[80] Philoctetes' service is thus in the end "necessary" in the view not only of his fellow Achaeans but also of the

[76] Note how Neoptolemus (379) weaves the charge of evasion into his deceptive account, claiming that Odysseus refused to turn over Achilles' arms to him on the grounds that he had evaded service.

[77] While this tragedy focuses on the problematic recruitment of Philoctetes, it is simultaneously about Neoptolemus' reconsideration of his recent recruitment: see esp. 969–70; cf. 1368–9.

[78] This prompts Bowie (1997: 56–61) to argue that this tragedy encourages reflection on Alcibiades' troubled relations with Athens.

[79] On the heated debate over the conclusion, see Goldhill 1990: 121 and Hesk 2000: 188–99.

[80] On Heracles' intervention as a natural conclusion to the tragedy rather than a jarring intrusion, see Schein 2001.

gods themselves.[81] Lest this exhortation appear to come at Philoctetes' personal cost, Heracles confirms that Philoctetes' cooperation is very much in his self-interest because his sickness will be cured at Troy (1423–4) and he will win great glory there (1425–9). In light of these diverse considerations, Philoctetes accedes and agrees to join the expedition (1445–7).

An important feature of this relatively happy resolution of the difficulties surrounding Philoctetes' recruitment is Sophocles' characterization of his decision to serve as a free one. A major question throughout the tragedy is what means the community may legitimately employ to achieve its ends in recruiting Philoctetes. At one extreme is the position of Odysseus, who advocates the use of any means, including deception (e.g., 80, 111, 133) and physical force (981–98; cf. 592–4), to ensure Philoctetes' participation. Neoptolemus, by contrast, initially goes along with Odysseus' scheme to dupe Philoctetes out of his bow despite misgivings (87–8, 95), but ultimately rejects the use of trickery (esp. 1226–7); his attempts to use persuasion rather than force to gain Philoctetes' willing (1332, 1343; cf. 1392) participation are, however, unsuccessful (1263–1408). The resulting impasse is resolved by the appearance of Heracles, who urges but does not force Philoctetes to cooperate; his successful use of persuasion rather than coercion can be taken as confirmation that Neoptolemus' methods as recruiter are preferable to those of Odysseus. While the pressures on Philoctetes to go on the expedition are remarkable, the decision is his: he chooses not to disobey Heracles' words (1447; cf. Hom. *Il.* 1.220) and goes off to Troy with no cause to complain (1465), conveyed by not only "mighty Fate" and "the all-powerful god" (i.e., Zeus: cf. 1415) but also the "advice of friends" (1466–8).[82] In the end Sophocles' Philoctetes, like Athens' ideal hoplites in the Attic funeral orations, freely chooses to do what is necessary, and in so doing benefits himself and his community. Although Sophocles, true to the tragic genre, diverges from civic ideology in acknowledging and exploring

[81] The Achaean claim that this is necessary (δεῖ: 915, 1339–40; ἀνάγκη: 922–3, 1339–40) and the will of Zeus (989–90; cf. 1373) is corroborated by Heracles, who invokes both necessity (χρεών: 1439) and Zeus' plans (1415).

[82] Neoptolemus (1448) also responds to Heracles' words as if he is free to accept or reject them.

the conflict between individual and community that precedes this resolution, there is optimism and arguably even patriotism in his suggestion that such tensions can and should be overcome for the greater good.[83]

Sophocles apparently treated the story of Neoptolemus' recruitment in his lost *Skyrioi*; we do not know if, as in his *Philoctetes*, he deviated from tradition in making the recruitment of Neoptolemus precede that of Philoctetes.[84] If Sophocles had his *Skyrioi* in mind when composing his late *Philoctetes*, the latter may provide some clues to the basic features of the former.[85] In this case, the basis of the recruiting mission to Skyros would be the prophecy that Neoptolemus must join the Achaean forces for them to take Troy (*Ph.* 69, 114–15, 1334–5, 1433–5; cf. 60–1, 343–53). The heroes sent to fetch Neoptolemus from Lycomedes' court, where he was being raised (*Ph.* 243), would be Odysseus and Phoenix (*Ph.* 343–4; cf. Hom. *Od.* 11.508–9; Gantz 1993: 2.639–40).[86]

In this tragedy, as in other recruiting dramas, the central question was probably whether the targeted recruit would consent to military service. If Neoptolemus was eager to participate in the expedition from the start, as Lloyd-Jones (1996: 3.277) suggests (cf. Philostr. min. *Im.* 1b, 2f; Q.S. 7.170–4), there would have been little tension in the drama. It is preferable, therefore, to suppose that Neoptolemus – like his father, Achilles, as a young man in the same locale under similar circumstances (cf. E. *Skyrioi*) – required some persuading before he agreed to embark

[83] In my view, therefore, Sophocles not only brings these tensions to the fore (thus Goldhill 1990: 123–4) but also offers some resolution of them. It is not surprising that Sophocles, who had served as general in 441/0 B.C. (Androtion *FGrH* 324 F 38), should advance this perspective on military service.

[84] Although some scholars have thought that this tragedy, like Euripides' *Skyrioi*, focused on Achilles' recruitment, fr. 557 strongly suggests that it treated Neoptolemus' recruitment: see Radt 1977: 4.418–19 and Lloyd-Jones 1996: 3.276–7.

[85] Webster (1970: 6) speculates that Sophocles' *Skyrioi* and *Philoctetes* may have been part of the same connected trilogy, along with his *Philoctetes at Troy*.

[86] Although in Sophocles' *Philoctetes* this detail comes from Neoptolemus' deceptive account to Philoctetes, Neoptolemus has no reason to lie about the identity of his recruiters. This recruiting mission would evoke not only the one to recruit Achilles from Skyros, in which Odysseus participates (cf. E. *Skyrioi*), but also the embassy in Book 9 of the *Iliad* to persuade Achilles to rejoin battle, in which both Odysseus and Phoenix participate.

(cf. S. *Ph.* 114, 343–53).[87] Neoptolemus' grandfather, Lycomedes, and his mother, Deidameia, probably opposed his going (fr. 555b; cf. fr. 555; Apollod. *Epit.* 5.11; Philostr. min. *Im.* 1b, 2f; Q.S. 6.81–2, 7.235–393), having lost Achilles already to the war (cf. fr. 557). One of them may have declared, "For war always hunts out young men" (φιλεῖ γὰρ ἄνδρας πόλεμος ἀγρεύειν νέους) (fr. 554), as a dark assessment not only of the current efforts to recruit Neoptolemus but also of those aimed earlier at Achilles (cf. Q.S. 7.242–52).[88] In opposition to this familial resistance, Odysseus and Phoenix presumably invoked the prophecy that Neoptolemus was essential to the taking of Troy and emphasized the glory he would win by participating (cf. S. *Ph.* 343–53). In addition, they may have sought to win over Neoptolemus by promising him rewards, including his father's armor (cf. Procl. *Chr.* 217–18 Severyns [*Little Iliad*]; S. *Ph.* 58, 349, 378, 1363; Q.S. 7.193–212) and perhaps also marriage to Hermione, daughter of Menelaus and Helen (cf. E. *Andr.* 968–70; Q.S. 6.84–92, 7.213–18).[89] Neoptolemus, like his father before him, presumably joined the expedition despite the concerns of his family.

Just as the recruitment of Philoctetes and Neoptolemus late in the war recalls the recruitment of heroes at the expedition's inception, so too the sacrifice of Polyxena after the fall of Troy (Procl. *Chr.* 277–8 Severyns [*Sack of Ilium*]; cf. Gantz 1993: 2.658–9) recalls Iphigeneia's sacrifice at the outset (cf. Anderson 1997: 60–1). In Euripides' *Hecuba*, when the Greeks are on the verge of sailing home from Troy, Achilles' ghost appears over his tomb and demands that Polyxena be sacrificed to him as a prize of honor (*geras*) (35–44). Polyxena's sacrifice, like that of Iphigeneia, could be construed as the culmination of a perverse recruitment carried out by Odysseus as agent of the Achaeans (130–40; cf. *IT* 24–5). Euripides, however, explicitly links her sacrifice to

[87] On the many correlations between Neoptolemus and Achilles in early Greek myth, see Anderson 1997: 38–48.

[88] Alternatively, this may have been spoken by one of the recruiters in justification (γάρ) of the mission.

[89] Cf. how Homer's Odysseus offers Achilles diverse rewards, including a profitable marriage, to return to battle (*Il.* 9.262–99).

the recruiting motif in a different way, when Odysseus seeks to justify to Hecuba why her daughter must die:

> It is exactly here that most cities get into trouble, when a man who is both valiant and eager to serve (πρόθυμος) wins no greater prize of valor than his inferiors. Achilles is worthy of honor in our eyes, lady, since he died gloriously on behalf of the land of Greece. Is it not a disgrace then if we treat him as our friend while he lives but after he is dead treat him so no longer? What then will someone say if occasion arises for another mustering (ἄθροισις) of the army and fight against the enemy? Will we fight or will we save our skins (φιλοψυχήσομεν) since we see that those who die receive no honor? (306–16)

In this remarkable passage, Odysseus imagines that Greeks will evade service the next time the need to mobilize arises, if they see a glorious soldier like Achilles going unrewarded. While Odysseus' hypothetical scenario looks to the future, his words call to mind the difficulties surrounding recruitment at the mustering of the Greek forces ten years earlier for the Trojan expedition. Indeed, as a reluctant recruit himself on that earlier occasion according to tradition, Odysseus is an ironically appropriate commentator on potential difficulties in future recruiting.

The recruiting motif continues to crop up in interesting ways in tragedians' treatment of the aftermath of the Trojan War. Thus, for example, in Euripides' *Helen*, when Menelaus looks back to the launching of the expedition to Troy, he asserts that he "led not as tyrant, not by force (πρὸς βίαν), but as commander of willing young men of Hellas" (395–6). This happy view of the expedition (cf. E. *Andr.* 682–3; contrast *Or.* 647–8), however, overlooks the fact that, according to tradition, many of the Greek heroes who participated did so because they were bound by the Oath of Tyndareus and some had gone so far as to try to evade service.

Agamemnon's unhappy homecoming provides tragedians with a further opportunity to reflect on the call to service through the negative example of Clytemnestra's lover, Aegisthus, who failed to serve in the Trojan War. Aeschylus, for example, derides Aegisthus as a cowardly and effeminate "stay-at-home" (οἰκουρός) (*A.* 1223–5, 1625–7; cf. 808–9; Hom. *Od.* 3.262–4) – a term Athenians applied derisively to those evading service (Din. 1.82; cf. E. *Heracl.* 700–1). For Agamemnon, the conquering warrior, to be slain surreptitiously with the connivance of this evader renders his demise all the more ignoble.

In Euripides' *Orestes* (408 B.C.), the Messenger reports how a farmer stood up at Orestes' trial to condemn Clytemnestra's affair with the stay-at-home Aegisthus as a crime against not only Agamemnon and his household but the *polis* at large. This plain-speaking man asserted that Orestes deserved a crown from the city for avenging his father (923–4) and

> killing a wicked and godless woman, who kept (ἀφῄρει) men from taking up arms and marching out to war, leaving behind their homes, in fear that those left behind would destroy their households, corrupting their wives. (925–9)

Notably, according to the Messenger's account, the farmer did not speak vaguely of the danger to future recruitment posed by the seduction of a soldier's wife, but rather of actual harm to the city during the Trojan War: men were conscious of the affair between Clytemnestra and Aegisthus, and this *continued* to keep them (note the imperfect ἀφῄρει) from joining in the war effort.[90] This passage is remarkable in suggesting that difficulties surrounding recruitment for the Trojan War extended to the populace at large – that is, they were not limited to famous figures – and in characterizing recruitment as a problem throughout the war, not just at isolated points. This passage provides a striking instance of Euripidean realism in its attention to the behavior of "average men" in war time, as voiced by an average farmer, and to the problematic nature of conducting recruitment in a long war – not unlike the ongoing Peloponnesian War (cf. Willink 1986: 236).

An important feature of the tragic recruiting stories surveyed above is that they treat recruitment as a source of conflict between not only individual and community but also *oikos* and *polis*. In so doing, they realistically acknowledge and explore the ambivalence of households toward the conscription of their beloved and vital members.

[90] There is no need to take this imperfect, as Willink (1986: 236) does, as one of uncompleted action.

Repeatedly on the tragic stage representatives of the *oikos* seek to protect young men from military service. As we have seen, in Euripides' *Skyrioi* Thetis seeks to shield Achilles from service by hiding him at Lycomedes' court, and in Sophocles' *Skyrioi* Neoptolemus' mother and grandfather probably seek to dissuade him from going to Troy. The author of the *Rhesus* posits similar familial resistance in the case of Rhesus: his mother, a Muse, who knew that her son would die if he went off to support the Trojans (934–5), laments over her dead son, "you set out with me seeking to dissuade you and with your father pleading forcibly (βιαίως)" (896–901).[91] The fact that the young men in all three of these situations defy parents and join the community in war can be construed as confirmation not only of the inevitability of youthful rebellion against parental authority but also of the priority of community over *oikos* in time of war.[92]

While in all three of these cases women play a prominent part in seeking to keep their sons from going off to war,[93] Euripides sometimes upsets this common gender stereotype (cf. Ar. *Ec.* 233–4) by making women ardent advocates of the priority of the *polis* over the *oikos* in time of war.[94] Thus, in Euripides' *Erechtheus* Praxithea declares, "our very reason for bearing children is to safeguard the gods' altars and our fatherland" (fr. 360.14–15; cf. *IA* 1386–7; Ar. *Lys.* 651), and insists that mothers must be ready to sacrifice their children for the city:

If our family included a crop of male children instead of females, and the flame of war was gripping our city, would I refuse to send them out to battle for fear of their deaths? No, give me sons who would not only fight but stand out among the men and not be mere figures raised in the city to

[91] The similarity of this situation to that of Thetis and Achilles is made explicit when the Muse links her loss of Rhesus with Thetis' imminent loss of Achilles (976–7) (cf. Hom. *Il.* 11.330–2).

[92] Cf. how in Euripides' *Phoenissae* (999–1005) Menoeceus defies his father, Creon, who seeks to send his son out of the land rather than sacrifice him to save Thebes from the Seven.

[93] Note, however, the presence of male dissuaders as well in two of the three cases surveyed in the previous paragraph; cf. Creon's role as dissuader in E. *Ph.* 962–76. For paternal efforts to protect sons from military service, see e.g., Hom. *Il.* 11.330–2; Hdt. 4.84; 7.38–9; cf. 1.87.4.

[94] According to tradition, Spartan women regularly played this role: see e.g., Plu. *Mor.* 240f–242b.

no use. When mothers' tears send sons on their way, they make many men into women (ἐθήλυν') as they set out for battle. I detest women who choose life rather than what is noble for their sons or exhort them to cowardice (κακά). (fr. 360.22–31)

Praxithea's subordination of the *oikos* to the community is fully consistent with the ideals of the Attic funeral orations (e.g., Th. 2.44.3).[95] Praxithea's daughters, in keeping with their mother's patriotic values, offer themselves as sacrificial victims to save the city and thus willingly undertake the female equivalent of male sacrifice on the battlefield (cf. Lyc. 1.101; Dem. 60.29); how far Euripides supported or undercut this patriotic self-sacrifice in the rest of this tragedy is, however, open to debate (cf. Cropp, in Collard, Cropp, and Lee, eds., 1997: 154–5).

A similar inversion of feminine resistance to military service is found in Euripides' *Suppliant Women*, where Aethra urges her son, Theseus, to face the Thebans in battle to force them to release for burial those who had perished in the unsuccessful expedition of the Seven. While the Attic funeral orations present this episode as unambiguous evidence of the willingness of Athenian hoplites to defend the weak against their oppressors (Lys. 2.7–10; Pl. *Mx.* 239b; Dem. 60.8), Euripides lends the episode interest and tension by making Theseus initially reluctant to get involved in others' problems.[96] When the mothers of the Seven and Adrastus, king of Argos, supplicate him, Theseus rebukes the Seven and their supporters for having embarked on a foolhardy expedition: when he contrasts bravery with good counsel (161–2), he not only criticizes the disastrous expedition but also provides an explanation for his own reluctance to become involved. While Theseus' reluctance is due to prudence rather than cowardice,[97] Aethra urges her son to be

[95] Loraux (1998: 13) views Praxithea as "an extremist of civic motherhood, an 'Athenian' more than a mother . . . and more Spartan than Athenian."

[96] On this as an evocation of the contemporary discussion of ἀπραγμοσύνη see Michelini 1994: 226–30.

[97] While Theseus' exercise of prudence is not necessarily inconsistent with Athenian ideals (see e.g., Th. 2.40.2–3; cf. E. *Ph.* 745–7), the line between prudence and cowardice can be a thin one; the Theban herald clearly crosses it in advising Theseus, "The man inactive in season is wise. In my view bravery (τἀνδρεῖον) really amounts to discretion (ἡ προμηθία)" (509–10).

bold on behalf of these wronged persons (304–5) because others will construe Theseus' hesitation as cowardly evasion of toil for the city:

> Someone will say that in fear you stood aside out of physical cowardice (ἀνανδρίᾳ χερῶν), although you could have won for the city a crown of glory. They will say that you struggled against a wild boar, a trivial labor, but where you ought to have struggled through in the face of enemy helmets and spear points, you were found to be a coward (δειλὸς) . . . your country flourishes in its toils. (314–23)

In pressing her son to seize this opportunity to serve the city, Aethra sets aside a mother's natural concerns for her son (cf. 510) in favor of the ideology of toil and sacrifice enshrined in the Attic funeral orations.[98] Theseus, inspired by her words, accepts the challenge before him: "I cannot refuse toils. What will my enemies say about me when you, who bore me and would naturally be worried about me, are the first to urge me to undertake this toil" (342–5). Theseus, the initially reluctant recruit, then – following a pattern we have seen elsewhere – himself becomes an eager recruiter: "When I have persuaded the citizens of these things and have mustered (ἀθροίσας) a picked band of Athenian youth, I will come here" (355–7). Theseus encounters no trouble in mustering the Athenians: soon he reports that his army is undergoing review (κἀξετάζεται) (391) and that the city took up this toil "willingly and gladly" at his behest (393–4).

Although Theseus' initial reluctance to embrace the toil of war for his city is distinct from the draft evasion of an Odysseus or Achilles, it raises doubts concerning his commitment to his city and his courage, as his mother pointedly reminds him. When Adrastus in his funeral oration characterizes courage as something that can be taught (913–14), his words have a special relevance to Theseus, who learns, with his mother's help, not to shun risk and toil on behalf of his city. Like Achilles in Euripides' *Skyrioi*, this young man needs to be educated in manly valor for the good of his reputation and that of the community. Theseus' conversion into a zealous hoplite on behalf of Athens can be taken as confirmation of Athenian civic ideals and, in light of

[98] On the gender dynamics involved in making Aethra her son's instructor in civic virtue, see Mendelsohn 2002: 161–79; cf. Foley 2001: 272–300.

Theseus' status as an archetypal young Athenian, as a model for the city's ephebes.

The best explanation for the prominence of the recruiting motif in Attic tragedy is that this had contemporary resonances for tragedians and their audiences as they experienced compulsory military service and evasion of it in their society. A possible objection to this hypothesis is that most of the myths involved can be traced back to Homer or the Epic Cycle and therefore need bear no specific relation to classical Athens (cf. Griffin 1998: 48, 56). The antiquity of these basic themes and the fact that they are part of a common Hellenic heritage, however, only suggest that Athenians were not the first or the only Hellenes to grapple with the problems surrounding compulsory military service.[99] The fact that Athenian tragedians so frequently drew on this shared body of material suggests that these tales were especially intriguing to them and their audiences.

The emphasis that tragedians place on the interplay of compulsion and persuasion in their treatments of these myths may help explain much of their special appeal to Athenians. While freedom-loving Greeks within other city-states may sometimes have been troubled by the community's use of compulsion against individuals in conscription, Athenians were especially sensitive to this. As citizens of a democratic polity in which personal freedoms were especially valued, Athenians were not entirely comfortable with the exercise of compulsion on free and autonomous individuals. We have seen how the *epitaphioi* reflect this uneasiness with their suppression of conscription and emphasis on voluntarism. Viewed against this backdrop, tragedy's mythical recruiting scenarios provided Athenians with a safe vehicle for reflecting on the problematic nature of compulsory military service in their own society.[100]

[99] Note how conscription crops up at Hom. *Il.* 13.663–70, 23.296–9, and 24.396–400. Rhodes (2003) argues that Athenian tragedy frequently addresses concerns that are not narrowly Athenian, but those of "*polis*-dwelling Greeks in general" (104, abstract; cf. 119).

[100] Cf. the general observation of Meier 1993: 215: "It was to the great advantage of tragedy that it could rehearse contemporary questions in the distant shape of myth."

While it is sufficient to my thesis to demonstrate that tragedians reflect contemporary concerns over conscription and its evasion in treating the recruiting motif, it is natural to ask to what extent they challenge or confirm Athenian civic ideology, which advocates the willing sacrifice of individual for the city.[101] In general, tragedians appear to support rather than undercut the principle that individuals should serve the community in time of war. They show consistently how the community prevails in inducing individuals to participate; the fact that no individual in tragedy – as far as we know – ultimately escapes this "necessity" suggests a certain inevitability about the submission of individual to community. This may indicate that in the view of tragedians civic necessity, like necessity in general in Greek thinking, is impossible to resist. This may be true, however, not only because of the superior power of the community over its members and the threat of coercion that it wields, but also because of the ethical imperative that a man should support his friends and community. In serving the community, the individual does "what he is bound to do" (τὰ δέοντα, cf. Th. 2.43.1) in light both of the community's authority over him and what is right and honorable. He should choose to comply therefore with what is in any case obligatory.

If tragedians ultimately endorse military service on behalf of the community, however, they diverge from Athenian civic ideology in airing and exploring tensions over recruitment. If compliance with conscription is a necessity, it may be a grim one with devastating costs for individuals and their households. The manner in which individuals are induced to participate, moreover, is a matter of concern to tragedians, not least when Odysseus, the wily manipulator and erstwhile draft-dodger, acts as the community's recruiter. None of this, however, appears to call into question the basic principle that individuals are bound to support their communities in war. While tragedians invite reflection on the tensions of civic life, they stop well short of stirring up resistance to obligatory service.[102]

[101] On the problem of tragedy and Athenian ideology, see Saïd 1998; Heath 1999: 151–9; Goldhill 2000; Rhodes 2003.

[102] Cf. Pelling 1997b: 235: "Part of civic ideology, in fact, was to feel worried about civic ideology, in the right place and the right setting. And the tragic theatre was the right place."

Athenians, like the citizens of modern democracies, had many reasons for seeking to evade compulsory military service and many ways to succeed in this. To judge from the frequent appearance of the subject in Attic oratory and comedy, the public was well aware of draft evasion and the threat it might pose to the city. Tragedians were attuned to contemporary concerns about evasion and, more generally, to the problematic nature of compulsory military service in a democratic society. Both the frequency with which they brought onstage mythological recruiting scenarios and the terms in which they present these point to their engagement with contemporary experience. If societal tensions over conscription and its evasion were largely unresolvable, tragedians gave their fellow citizens opportunities to reflect on and come to terms with these through the myths they brought before them.

3

THE COWARDLY HOPLITE

> I will not bring shame on my sacred arms nor will I abandon the man beside me, wherever I may stand in line. I will defend the sacred and holy and will pass on my fatherland not smaller but greater and better insofar as I am able and with the help of others.
>
> (The Ephebic Oath: Tod II.204.6–11 = Rhodes and Osborne 88.1.6–11)

When Athenian conscripts appeared for hoplite service and went out on campaign, they fulfilled a fundamental obligation of their citizenship. This duty carried with it, however, a further one, namely, to serve honorably and above all to refrain from cowardly behavior. While Athenian hoplites were probably as courageous as any in the Greek world to judge from their military successes,[1] the relatively abundant source material from Athens allows us to probe anxieties and tensions there concerning citizen deportment on campaign. This chapter seeks to break new ground by studying this neglected aspect of the Athenian experience and, in particular, by exploring the interplay between actual behaviors on military campaign – including those that might invite the charge of cowardice – and their representation both on location and after the fact in Athens. Only by considering Athenian

[1] On the difficulties inherent in assessing a people's courage, see Balot 2004b: 408, with n. 7 ("... Greek or Athenian claims to superior courage are not only historically unverifiable, but also inherently ideological"); 2004c: 83–4; cf. Hanson 2001: 8, 10. As many scholars have observed, there was a close link between Athenian ideals of courage/manliness and Athens' imperialism: see Cartledge 1998: 56–61; Wohl 2002: 176; Balot 2004c: 85–6; cf. Raaflaub 2001.

concerns about cowardice within this broad framework can we fully appreciate their historical and cultural significance.[2]

Although Athenians often linked draft evasion and cowardice on campaign as kindred breaches of good citizenship (e.g., Lys. 14.5–7; Aeschin. 3.175–6; cf. Lyc. 1.77), these differed from one another in fundamental respects. First, cowardice was a more nebulous category than draft evasion. While the charge of draft evasion, as we have seen, was subject to manipulation by hostile parties, the nature of the offense alleged was fairly straightforward. By contrast, what constituted cowardice was much less clear, except in egregious cases – for example, if a man dropped his shield and spear in mid-battle and fled the field on his own. Notwithstanding the Athenian tendency to characterize courage and cowardice as stark alternatives, a wide range of behaviors between these two extremes was possible.[3] Where an individual placed an act on this spectrum, moreover, depended very much on his perceptions and assumptions.[4] An appreciation of the highly subjective and contestable nature of cowardice is, as we shall see, critical to understanding both citizen behavior on campaign and civic discourse in Athens concerning this type of bad citizenship.

Second, while Athenians often characterized both draft evasion and cowardice as alternatives to good citizenship that individuals *chose*, this was not always the case with cowardice. A man's decision to evade the draft was normally a conscious and deliberate one, as we have seen, that involved strategic calculations and plans to ensure success;

[2] In general, scholars have been much more interested in Athenian courage than cowardice (see below, notes 4 and 7); to the extent that cowardice has received attention, this has focused largely on its representation within particular genres (Storey 1989 [comedy]; Roisman 2005: 105–29 [oratory]). Hanson (1989: 96–104) discusses cowardice briefly in connection with the Greek hoplite experience, but does not pursue Athenian dimensions of this on or off the battlefield.

[3] For courage and cowardice presented as stark alternatives, see e.g., E. *Hec.* 400–2; Ar. *Th.* 832–9; *Ec.* 678–80; Lyc. 1.74; Arist. *EN* 1116a20.

[4] See Arist. *EN* 1108b24–5 ("a coward calls a brave man rash and a rash man calls him a coward") and Pl. *La.* 197b (Nicias observes: "So you see, the acts that you and most people call courageous, I call rash, and it is the prudent acts which I speak of that are courageous"); cf. Wissmann 1997. On the problem of defining courage, see Plato's *Laches* and Arist. *EN* 1115a–1117b; Smoes 1995; Hobbs 2000: 76–112; Miller 2000: 1–14 and *passim*; Balot 2001b; 2004b; 2004c; Deslauriers 2003; Roisman 2005: 109, 111, 188–92.

while a conscript might well be influenced by his fear of death or injury as he considered whether to evade service, he was able to weigh these threats from afar and in relative calm. By contrast, cowardice – especially on the battlefield itself – was often a spontaneous response to imminent risk; fear and inexperience could have an enormous impact on this. To the extent that cowardice could be a largely involuntary response, it presented the city with a special challenge as it sought to elicit unwavering courage from its hoplites.[5] Although compulsory military training for young men as part of the *ephēbeia* could seek to steel future hoplites for battle,[6] and state funeral orations for the war dead could work to encourage citizen resolve in the face of the enemy, the hardships of campaign and the grisly reality of battle could overwhelm individual and group and lead to conspicuous lapses in valor.

Because the Athenian discussion of cowardice as a violation of citizen norms is especially given to hyperbole, distortion, and ideological manipulation, it is useful to begin by looking closely at the hoplite experience itself and how cowardice figured within this both as a reality and as an idea. Having explored cowardice in this context, we will turn to consider how, at a remove from the campaign and battlefield, Athenian institutions addressed and in some cases overlooked this sensitive matter and the role of public discourse in this process.

5 On the involuntary aspect of cowardice, see Gorg. 82 fr. 11.16 D–K; and Arist. *EN* 1119a27–31: "the possession of a cowardly character would seem to be more voluntary than particular manifestations of cowardice: for cowardliness in itself is not painful, but particular accesses of cowardice are so painful as to make a man beside himself, and cause him to throw away his arms or otherwise behave in an unseemly manner; so that cowardly actions actually seem to be done under compulsion." In Aristotle's view, courage is produced by habituation and training: see *EN* 1103b18; 1104b3. The Attic funeral orations suppress the potentially involuntary nature of cowardice in representing the rejection of cowardice as a rational choice: see below in the text.

6 Although an ephebic system of some sort was likely in place already in the late-fifth century B.C., the *ephēbeia* was reformed in the early-fourth century; the new arrangement may have innovated in extending service to two years and in modifying the form of training during this period (cf. Ober 1985: 90–5). For arguments in favor of an early *ephēbeia*, see esp. Pélékidis 1962: 71–9 and Reinmuth 1971: 123–38. For a survey of scholarship on the *ephēbeia*, see Raaflaub 1996: 157, with 172 nn. 148–9.

COWARDICE ON CAMPAIGN

Athenians, like other Greeks, were drawn to an ideal of manliness (*andreia*) based above all on courage in battle on behalf of the community.[7] Intimately connected with the pursuit of this ideal was the rejection of behavior that could be deemed cowardly. As a practical matter, in fact, it was more important for an Athenian hoplite to shun cowardice or the appearance of it than to win distinction for courage: while a hoplite who merely fell short of ideal valor ran little risk of public consequences, one who fell markedly below minimal standards of hoplite behavior could face rebuke, ridicule, and even prosecution as we shall see. Consistent with this is the way the Ephebic Oath, sworn by young Athenian men who were preparing for military service, gives priority to shunning shameful behavior: "I will *not* bring shame on my sacred arms *nor* will I abandon the man beside me, wherever I may stand in line." (Tod II.204.6–8 = Rhodes and Osborne 88.1.6–8).[8]

The double imperative of shunning cowardice and embracing courage profoundly affected how hoplites behaved individually and collectively on campaign. While behavior in battle was especially subject to scrutiny in these terms, the contest (*agōn*) for preserving and enhancing manly reputation was ongoing during a campaign; it entailed both fending off present and potential attacks on reputation and actively asserting manliness, often at the expense of others.[9] This competition shaped how hoplites acted before, during, and after battle, and how they represented their behavior to others at all these points;

[7] See e.g., Arist. *EN* 1115a30–2: "What form of death then is a test of courage? Presumably that which is the noblest. Now the noblest form of death is death in battle, for it is encountered in the midst of the greatest and most noble of dangers." On *andreia* in Hellenic and Athenian culture, see Rosen and Sluiter 2003a, b; Bassi 2003; Roisman 2005; cf. Winkler 1990: 45–70; Salkever 1991; Loraux 1995: 63–100.

[8] On shame as a constraint on behavior in Hellenic culture, see Cairns 1993: 27–47; Williams 1993: 75–102, 219–23; Elster 2002: 2–5; Roisman 2005: 64–83.

[9] In the hyper-masculine world of the campaign, manly competition could threaten military order: just as Athenians at home sometimes got drunk, traded insults, engaged in fist-fights, and fought over sexual interests, so too on campaign they engaged in this sort of behavior (Dem. 54.3–5; cf. X. *An.* 5.8.4). On the problem of military discipline, see note 16.

while public reckonings of manliness were not entirely negotiable, they could depend to a high degree on how those involved presented themselves and their actions.[10]

Notwithstanding these pressures on hoplites to compete successfully in the ongoing contest of bravery, as a practical matter individuals differed widely in their ability and desire to live up to civic ideals of manliness and to avoid appearing cowardly (X. *Mem.* 3.9.1).[11] A man's temperament, physical condition (Pl. *Prt.* 326b–c), and prior military experience could all affect his ability to hold up on campaign and stand firm on the battlefield; likewise, his attitudes toward a specific campaign or general could make him more or less likely to act in accordance with citizen norms and ideals. Groups of hoplites, moreover, sometimes fled the field prematurely in panic; and regularly, when the battle turned against them, hoplite forces turned and fled the field with little thought for honor in the face of imminent death. In these diverse circumstances, it was critical for hoplites to deflect, as much as possible, any blame that might attach to their shortfall in courage.

In what follows, we will consider how concerns over cowardice and courage crop up in various ways throughout a military campaign and shape behavior and self-presentation on the part of average hoplites and the officers and generals leading them.[12] While this is a less tangible feature of the Greek hoplite experience than the physical ordeal of campaign and battle itself, this is fundamental to understanding it. If hoplites on campaign were participants in a military contest for victory or defeat, they were simultaneously involved in an ongoing contest for

[10] While the negotiability of military courage is particularly salient in Attic oratory (Roisman 2005: 111, 188–92), in my view this negotiability played a significant role in behavior and self-presentation on campaign as well. Balot (2004b: 407 n. 3) is correct, in my view, to argue that there are limits to the negotiability of courage in Athens and to reject the more extreme view that *andreia* is simply a "matter of what Athenians say" (Bassi 2003: 56).

[11] Pritchett (1994: 130) exaggerates in asserting, "The ancient soldier aspired to a hero's role in a way quite foreign to the modern. One cannot ignore the social context of the times in which every male citizen saw service in war."

[12] In this survey I rely primarily on Athenian sources. Whereas many elements of the hoplite experience are common to all Hellenes participating in hoplite warfare, Athens' institutions shaped precisely how its hoplites competed for honor on campaign and at home.

individual and group reputation that had both immediate and future implications for them.[13]

Muster

When Athenian hoplites responded to the call to serve by gathering at the point of muster, they took a first step toward staking a claim to courage in the eyes of the community and distancing themselves from the reproach of cowardice. While those who evaded service likely did so for a wide range of reasons not limited to cowardice, it was natural for compliant hoplites to categorize those who failed to appear as "stay-at-homes" and "cowards" (see Chapter 2); the individual names of no-shows may, in fact, have been read out at muster (cf. Poll. 8.115; S. fr. 144).[14] By contrast, the act of appearing for service could be construed as evidence in advance of the valor a hoplite would display on the battlefield. Consider, for example, an anecdote that Diodorus Siculus (1st c. B.C.) relates concerning the Athenian general Myronides at a muster of his troops (457 B.C.):

> When the appointed time arrived and some of the soldiers had not come to the specified place of muster, he took those who had reported and began to lead them into Boeotia. And when certain of his officers and friends said that he should wait for the tardy men, Myronides, who was not only an intelligent general but a man of action, replied that he would not do so; for, he declared, men who of their own choice are late for the departure will in battle also behave ignobly and cowardly and therefore not withstand dangers on behalf of their fatherland, whereas the men who presented themselves ready for service on the appointed day gave clear evidence that they would not desert the ranks in war. And this is what actually took place; for leading

[13] Krentz (2002; cf. van Wees 2004: 115–50) argues persuasively that scholars should not press too far the view of classical hoplite battle as a ritualized contest (*agōn*) with a myriad of formal rules and conventions.

[14] The names of no-shows may also have been posted on notice boards attached to the base of the Eponymoi (the statues of the ten eponymous heroes of the tribes in the Agora), as were the initial lists of draftees under conscription by *katalogos* (Ar. *Av.* 450; *Pax* 1183–4; Christ 2001: 403). For the public posting here of the names of those who fell short as citizens, see Is. 5.38; cf. Pl. *Lg.* 762b–d. Announcements of prosecutions, including those for military offenses, were also posted here (Dem. 21.103, with MacDowell 1990: 326).

forth soldiers who were few in number but the best in courage, he drew them up in Boeotia against a vastly superior force and utterly defeated his opponents. (11.81.5–6; cf. Plu. *Mor.* 185f6–186a3)

This laudatory anecdote, regardless of its historicity, gives a plausible glimpse of how hoplites entered a contest of manly reputation even before they left the city on campaign. This was true not only for the rank-and-file hoplites who presented themselves for service but also for their officers: the bravado attributed to the general Myronides on this occasion can be taken as a self-defining act by a prominent individual whose manliness would be subject to especially close scrutiny throughout the campaign.[15]

Desertion

Once on campaign, a hoplite had numerous opportunities to display cowardice or courage, and thus to lose or gain prestige even before contact was made with the enemy. One basic test of mettle was whether a hoplite remained with his comrades throughout the campaign. When desertion occurred, it was naturally construed as evidence of cowardice, which set the guilty party apart from those who courageously remained in the ranks. Consider, for example, how the Athenian general Phocion reportedly responded to the desertion of some of his hoplites in Euboea in 350 B.C.:

When disorderly and worthless rascals ran away from the camp and made their way home, Phocion bade his officers give no heed, for in the camp their lack of discipline would make them useless and harmful to the fighting men (τοῖς μαχομένοις), while at home consciousness of their own guilt would make them less likely to cry down their commander and would keep them entirely from bringing false charges (συκοφαντήσειν) against him. (Plu. *Phoc.* 12.3; cf. *Tim.* 25.5)

Just as draft evaders in the Myronides anecdote provide a negative foil both to compliant hoplites and their courageous general, deserters here

[15] The manliness of generals could come under scrutiny even before a campaign was initiated when they argued for or against launching a military expedition: see below in the text.

cast into relief the mettle both of the "fighting men" who stay in the ranks and of the general who confidently dismisses the significance of their flight for the success of his troops.

While most Athenian hoplites did not abandon their fellow troops, desertion among hoplites – as among rowers in the city's fleet ([Dem.] 50.14–16; Gabrielsen 1994: 113, 122–4) – may have been fairly common.[16] There were many reasons why a hoplite might decide to desert, including anger at an officer or general, campaign hardships, failure to receive pay, or desire to attend to personal or political affairs at home (cf. Lys. 13.7–12). The temptation to desert and the ability to succeed in this may have been especially great when hoplites were in close proximity to Athens (Plu. *Phoc.* 12.3; Lyc. 1.131). Although a deserter, if caught, might be rebuked or punished on the spot by his general (cf. Lys. 3.44–5) or even be prosecuted back in Athens – perhaps through a *graphē lipostratiou* (Poll. 6.151, 8.40; Hamel 1998b: 399–401) – punishment was not certain.[17] As the Phocion anecdote above suggests, it might be more prudent for a general to look the other way in such matters than to pursue them: generals often faced prosecution upon returning to Athens and disgruntled troops who remained in service might well join in legal proceedings against them, while deserters were not in a position to do so.

Endurance of Hardships

For the vast majority of hoplites who did not desert, the hardships of campaign provided an ongoing trial of manliness in advance of the ultimate test of this in battle. Plato's Alcibiades vividly illustrates this in

[16] Temporary absence from the ranks was probably quite frequent, for example, when hoplites went off in search of loot (X. *An.* 5.8.13). Generals were thought to enrich themselves on campaign (Lys. 28.7–8; Pritchett 1974: 2.126–32; 1991: 5.398–401) and average hoplites expected some license to reap profit on hostile terrain as well (e.g., X. *HG* 1.2.5; Pritchett 1971: 1.82–4; 1991: 5.375–98); the exercise of strict discipline on citizen troops was a highly sensitive matter and a degree of laxness likely prevailed here as elsewhere (X. *Mem.* 3.5.19–21; Pritchett 1974: 2.232–45; Hamel 1998a: 59–64; van Wees 2004: 108–13).

[17] The democratic politician Cleophon was condemned to death on a charge leveled by his oligarchic enemies that "he had not gone to the camp to sleep" (Lys. 13.12; cf. Pl. *Lg.* 762b–d; 943d); the charge may well have been desertion.

his account of Socrates' extraordinary endurance during the campaign to Potidaea (432 B.C.):

Well, first of all, he surpassed not me only but everyone else in bearing hardships (τοῖς πόνοις): whenever we were cut off in some place and were compelled, as often in campaigns, to go without food, the rest of us were nothing [sc. compared to him] in endurance . . . Furthermore, in his endurance of winter – in those parts the winters are awful – he was remarkable and not least so when once there came a frost about as awful as can be. We all preferred not to go outside, or if any of us did, we wrapped ourselves up with great care, and after putting on our shoes we muffled up our feet with felt and little fleeces. But he walked out in that weather, clad in just such a coat as he always used to wear, and he made his way more easily over the ice unshod than the rest of us did in our shoes. The soldiers looked askance at him, thinking that he despised them. (*Smp.* 219e–220b)

While this encomiastic narrative may exaggerate Socrates' ability to bear hardships, it provides a credible picture of how manly endurance was on display and under scrutiny on campaign. Although this anecdote emphasizes the distinction attained by a hoplite who surpasses others in enduring hardship, it also alludes to the uneasiness that this might elicit in fellow soldiers and rivals for honor: the hoplites who witness Socrates' wondrous endurance see in it implicit criticism of their relative softness.[18]

On the Brink of Battle

When battle loomed, the pressure on hoplites to suppress any signs of cowardice and display courage intensified. Verbal bravado in the face of danger was one way for a man to show his mettle, as in the famous case of the Spartan Dieneces at Thermopylae: when a Trachinian reported that, when the multitudinous Persians shot their arrows, these veiled

[18] Alcibiades presents Socrates' endurance on campaign as a precursor of his courage in battle at Potidaea, where he helped save Alcibiades' life and armor (*Smp.* 220d–e, quoted below in the text); Alcibiades proceeds to describe Socrates' courage at Delium as well (221a–c, quoted below in the text). Cf. Xenophon's anecdote (*An.* 3.4.46–9) concerning his own display of endurance to shame a complaining hoplite on the march. Eupolis' *Taxiarchoi* humorously portrays the soft Dionysus being trained for the hardships of the soldierly life: see e.g., fr. 272; Storey 2003: 246–60.

the sun, Dieneces was said to have replied: "Why, my Trachinian friend brings us good news. For if the Medes hide the sun, we shall fight them in the shade and not in the sun" (Hdt. 7.226).[19] In a culture that was highly attuned to "body language" (cf. Goldhill 1999: 4–5; Hesk 2000: 224), how a man carried himself in the tense prelude to battle could also affect his manly reputation. Homer's Idomeneus, for example, suggests how differently the coward and the brave man bear themselves when individuals are being selected to ambush the enemy:

> There the coward comes to light and the man of valor; for the color of the coward changes ever to another hue, nor is the spirit in his breast checked so that he sits still, but he shifts from knee to knee and rests on either foot, and his heart beats loudly in his breast as he imagines death and his teeth chatter; but the color of the brave man changes not, nor does he fear excessively when once he takes his place in the ambush of warriors, but he prays to mix immediately in woeful war.[20] (*Il.* 13.278–86)

If inadvertent body language could yield clues of cowardice in advance of battle (cf. Hanson 1989: 96), so too naturally could a deliberately assumed confident posture or look of equanimity before the gaze of fellow soldiers convey the impression of courage.

A general's courage was under especially close scrutiny as battle loomed, and his force's perceptions of this were a key factor in their morale (Hanson 1989: 107–16). A general's decision whether or not to engage with the enemy could itself affect his manly reputation: readiness to do so might be attributed to his courage, hesitation to his cowardice (cf. Plu. *Nic.* 16.8, 21.2–4; cf. Ar. *Av.* 638–9). Once the decision to engage was made, it was essential for a general to show no physical sign of fear,[21] and to convey confidence and courage through

[19] While Dieneces' bravado wins him a place in collective memory according to Herodotus ("This and other sayings of the same sort are recorded as having been the memorials of Dieneces the Lacedaimonian" [7.227]), the Trachinian whose words betray his pre-battle nervousness passes into oblivion unnamed.

[20] On Homer's exploration of fear in the *Iliad*, see Loraux 1995: 75–87 ("in the *Iliad* fear is more widespread than anything else, and only Zeus escapes it" [76]); cf. Wissmann 1997: 17–76.

[21] According to Plutarch (*Arat.* 29.5), detractors of the Achaean general Aratus claimed that he "always had cramps in the bowels when a battle was imminent," and "torpor and dizziness would seize him as soon as the trumpeter stood by to give the signal."

his words to his troops as he circulated among them or, as circumstances permitted, addressed them in larger groups in advance of battle (e.g., Th. 4.95).[22]

As hoplites lined up for battle, their position in the ranks could be read as a tentative prediction of their likely mettle in battle, and thus as a measure of relative manliness. The greatest prestige attached to those fighting in the front ranks, because they bore the highest risk of mortality and their courage was essential to group success.[23] Hoplites stationed further back in the ranks, who bore less risk, were in a relatively less prestigious position. It was natural to place inexperienced hoplites here as well as those believed to be less courageous; strategists, in fact, recommended placing cowards behind the front ranks and stationing some experienced troops behind them to discourage them from fleeing the battlefield (X. *Mem.* 3.1.8; *Cyr.* 6.3.25, 27; cf. Hom. *Il.* 4.297–309, with Wheeler 1991: 159 n. 40).

Because position in the ranks could be construed as a gauge of relative manliness, it is natural to ask how this arrangement came about on each occasion for Athenian forces. It seems likely that each tribe's taxiarch assigned the hoplites in his tribal contingents at least approximate positions in the ranks in advance of battle (cf. Lys. 16.15–16), considering experience, ability, and fortitude.[24] Although civic ideology lauded the uniform courage of Athenians in battle (see below), it would have been dangerous to rely too much on this in stationing hoplites within the ranks.[25] That a hoplite's placement was largely beyond his control is suggested by the way Athenians routinely speak

[22] Hansen (1993; 2001) doubts that generals were able to address their troops en masse in advance of battle as ancient historians often envision; Pritchett (1994: 27–109; 2002: 1–80) insists they were able to do so.

[23] See e.g., Tyrt. fr. 12.15–19; Pi. *I.* 7.35–6; Lys. 16.15; X. *Mem.* 3.1.10; *Lac.* 11.8; cf. Pritchett 1985: 4.85–9. Plutarch's Aristides (*Arist.* 12.1) argues polemically against this ("valor is not taken away from a man, nor is it given him, by his position in the line").

[24] Hanson (1989: 121–2) believes that "each time the phalanx marched out, men knew exactly their own assigned place within the formation." Lazenby (1991: 89) argues, however, that "it is difficult to believe that every man would have had a fixed position, and one suspects that before a battle there was a certain amount of jostling as men found themselves a place."

[25] Likewise, pragmatism prevailed in the Athenian practice of electing generals rather than selecting them by lot, which was the method employed for most other offices: to have done otherwise would have put the lives of hoplites at risk.

of position in the ranks as something assigned: a hoplite takes his place "wherever he is stationed" (Aeschin. 3.7; Dem. 15.32; Pl. *Ap.* 28d–e; cf. Plu. *Phoc.* 25.2). Individuals could, however, volunteer to serve in the front ranks, as Lysias' client Mantitheus boasts to have done (16.15, quoted below in the text). While average hoplites were under no positive obligation to step forward to serve in the front ranks, taxiarchs and generals were under pressure to do so to dispel any impression that they feared to take the risks that some under their command faced (X. *An.* 3.1.37; *Eq. Mag.* 2.6; cf. Ar. *Pax* 1172–90). As scholars have often noted, Athenian generals frequently exposed themselves to risk and died on the battlefield (e.g., Th. 2.79.7; 4.101.2; 5.10.9; 5.74.3; Hanson 1989: 112–15; Pritchett 1994: 130–8).

Battle

While many factors could affect how courageously hoplites performed in battle, morale was naturally a critical one (Hanson 1989: 117–25: Lazenby 1991: 104–7). Athenian hoplite forces, like those of other city-states, tended to enjoy a high degree of cohesion. Although hoplites were not entirely homogeneous socially – relative degrees of wealth were sometimes evident, for example, in the arms each bore (cf. Hanson 1989: 58–9) – the fact that they constituted an elite group within the city encouraged solidarity. Furthermore, because Athenian hoplites fought in the company of their fellow tribesmen, they often had ties of friendship and blood that bound them to their fellows in the ranks.[26] The conditions of hoplite battle strongly reinforced this sense of solidarity, because hoplites were directly dependent on one another within the densely packed ranks for protection (e.g., E. *HF* 191–2): each man's shield, which he held in his left hand, protected his neighbor's exposed right side.[27] In these circumstances not only did a sense of shame before peers encourage men to hold their places in

[26] Hanson (1989: 121–2), however, overstates – at least for an Athenian context – the degree of familiarity among hoplites in the ranks ("the relatives and friends who served in front, behind, and at their side"). Athens was not a "face-to-face" society and fellow tribesmen and even demesmen were not necessarily intimates (see E. E. Cohen 2000: 104–29).

[27] Krentz (2002: 35–7; cf. van Wees 2000b: 155–6; 2004: 166–87) argues that the hoplite phalanx developed this form only after the Persian Wars.

the ranks, but also self-interest, because individual and group survival were interlinked (X. *Mem.* 3.4.11; *Lac.* 9.1–2; cf. Hom. *Il.* 5.529–32; 15.561–4). Nonetheless, the pressures of battle could lead individuals and groups to fall far short of civic ideals.

Ancient battle narratives provide evidence of behavior ranging from glorious to ignoble on the part of Athenians and other Greeks in the diverse phases of battle. As opposing armies advanced to engage, tensions naturally ran high (X. *Eq. Mag.* 8.20; Hanson 1989: 96–104). Thucydides describes one common consequence of this:

> All armies are apt, on coming together, to thrust out their right wing too much; and both sides extend with their right beyond their opponents' left wing, because in his fear each man brings his uncovered side as close as possible to the shield of the man stationed on his right, thinking that the closer the shields are locked together the better is the protection. And it is the first man on the right wing who is primarily responsible for this, since he is always eager to withdraw from the enemy his own exposed side, and the rest, from a like fear, follow his example. (5.71.1; cf. Lazenby 1991: 91–2)

While this manifestation of collective nervousness was sufficiently routine that it was not likely to be viewed as cowardly, other forms of group behavior could be read as such. Hostile forces were on the lookout for physical signs of fear on the part of their rivals and poised to exploit these. Thus Thucydides' Brasidas, a Spartan general, observes of the Athenians before the battle at Amphipolis (421 B.C.): "These men will not stand before us; they show it by the motion of their spears and of their heads; men who do that never await their attackers" (5.10.5; cf. X. *HG* 3.2.17). At its extreme, group fear could lead to panic and premature flight; Athenians, like other Greeks, sometimes succumbed to their fears and fled the field (Th. 5.10.8; 5.72.4; cf. 7.80.3; Hanson 1989: 96–104, 161; Lazenby 1991: 91). As Gorgias puts it, fear can "cause oblivion of what custom judges honorable and of the advantage derived from victory" (82 fr. 11.16 D–K).

If opposing forces scrutinized one another for signs of weakness and cowardice as their lines approached, hoplites on each side were also conscious of how those around them in their own ranks were bearing up. Tell-tale signs of fear – including excessive sweating, chattering teeth, and incontinence (Hanson 1989: 100–2) – might be noticed by those nearby, and rumors of these come back to haunt a man after battle. While extreme fear might make an individual who was not hemmed in by his fellow hoplites wish to flee the ranks, the certainty of this shameful act being noticed was a strong deterrent to individual flight at this phase of battle. Singing of the paean by troops marching into battle could help fortify their spirits and dispel mounting fear (A. *Th.* 268–70; cf. Krentz 2002: 34)

Once the opposing lines clashed, there were many opportunities for acts of bravery or cowardice on the part of individual hoplites.[28] These opportunities varied, however, with a man's position in the ranks (cf. Hanson 1989: 84). Those in the first three ranks came into direct contact with the enemy; their courage was put directly to the test as they struggled to strike down their opponents and move forward into their ranks. While hoplites in the first ranks may have had little choice but to press on when those behind them began to push forward in what was termed the *ōthismos* ("the shoving"),[29] before this point in a battle they could choose to fight with more or less zeal; for example, a hoplite could aggressively thrust his spear forward into the opposing ranks, or adopt a more defensive posture by hiding behind his shield (X. *HG* 2.4.16; cf. Din. 1.82). The greatest test of courage for those behind the front ranks must have been how swiftly they stepped forward to fill the holes in the ranks that developed as those in front of them fell, and thereby entered the killing zone (cf. Lazenby 1991: 93–4).[30]

Although it was physically difficult, if not impossible, for most hoplites to flee the ranks outright in the thick of battle because they were surrounded by others, it may have been possible in some cases to move back within the ranks for less than honorable reasons. Because hoplites who were wounded seriously might sometimes be shuttled back through the ranks to safety (X. *HG* 6.4.13; Lazenby 1991: 96), an

[28] On the familiarity of cowardice, see e.g., Pl. *Grg.* 498a: Socrates.: "In war have you ever seen a coward?" Callicles: "Of course I have."

[29] Although some scholars believe that the *ōthismos* involved a literal pushing from behind of those in the front ranks (see Hanson 1989: 157–8; 172–5; Lazenby 1991: 97–100; Luginbill 1994), others question this (see Cawkwell 1989; Krentz 1994; Goldsworthy 1997; van Wees 2004: 184–5, 188–91).

[30] Thus while hoplite warfare could call for what Lendon (2005: 50–3) describes as "passive courage" because hoplites were expected to hold their place within the phalanx, it also demanded more active courage.

individual could perhaps pretend to have a more serious injury than he actually had to escape from battle, or eagerly lend help to a fallen comrade not only to assist him to safety but to get out of harm's way himself (cf. Thphr. *Char.* 25.5–6). It may also have been possible for individuals to move back in the ranks upon losing a spear or shield, as this would have been not only humane but also in the interest of group success, which depended upon fully armed hoplites pressing forward confidently (cf. Thphr. *Char.* 25.4). If this was common practice, however, little distinction could be made in the tumult of battle between a hoplite who had lost his equipment honorably and one who had done so shamefully.

While the Greek battlefield was witness to a myriad of acts ranging from the courageous to the cowardly, the hoplites engaged in battle must often have been oblivious to these. The Greek battlefield, like the modern one, was frequently a place of great confusion. As soon as the battle lines intermingled, order gave way to disorder and sometimes even chaos as hoplites struggled to survive wherever they found themselves; a cloud of dust might rise over the battlefield (campaigns were normally in the very dry summertime), and the din could be immense (Hanson 1989: 147–51; cf. Lazenby 1991: 95–7). Even under the best of circumstances, moreover, the helmets that hoplites wore severely limited their field of vision and hearing (Hanson 1989: 71).

Although scholars have appreciated how confused the Greek battlefield could be, they have not pursued the implications of this for determinations of cowardice and bravery. V. Hanson, for example, paints a vividly realistic picture of the chaos of battle (1989: 147–51), but in treating the question of unit spirit and morale, he asserts that "a man's moment of bravery or lapse into cowardice was manifest to all who fought in rows and files to his rear, front, and side" (119). This picture of high accountability, however, is difficult to reconcile with the very limited ability of helmeted hoplites to monitor the behavior of those around them in the mêlée of battle.[31]

[31] Hanson (119) cites Tyrt. fr. 11.11–16 in support of his position, but this passage makes no claims concerning the visibility of cowardly behavior in the heat of battle. Lendon (2005: 52–3) adopts a position similar to that of Hanson, but makes some allowance for the difficulty of assessing hoplite courage and cowardice in the heat of battle ("neither will seeing who stood or fled have been without its problems" [57]).

That accountability was considerably lower is suggested by numerous ancient sources. Thucydides, for example, remarks in his vivid narrative of the chaos surrounding the nighttime assault on Epipolae, that even in daylight "each man hardly knows anything except what is happening to himself" (7.44.1). Euripides' Orestes, reflecting on the problem of judging a man's nobility asks, "Who, as he stands facing a spear point, can bear testimony to the bravery of others?" (*El.* 377–8).[32] Euripides' Theseus elaborates this skeptical perspective:

> Can a man stand in battle as the spears fly thick and fast before his eyes and tell us clearly who was brave? I could not ask for such a report nor believe anyone who was so bold as to give it. When a man stands face to face with the enemy, he is barely able to see what he needs to see. (*Supp.* 850–6)

While Euripides is likely responding critically to literary as well as personal accounts of bravery (cf. Collard 1975: 2.321), his basic observation is consistent with what we hear of ancient battles in Thucydides and elsewhere.[33] We do not have to adopt a position of utter skepticism concerning the observation of acts of cowardice and courage in battle to appreciate the considerable difficulties involved. Conspicuous acts by individuals who were in the limelight (especially officers) and groups (e.g., tribal contingents) might well attract notice, but much inevitably was missed in the confusion of battle.[34]

Rout

When the tide of hoplite battle turned, one side typically retreated from the field (Hanson 1989: 177–84; van Wees 2004: 192). Although this was an embarrassment to those involved and to their city (Pl. *La.* 181b),

[32] On the debate over the authenticity of these lines, see Cropp 1988: 123.

[33] Lendon (2005: 52) assumes that E. *Supp.* 850–6 alludes critically to Homeric battle narratives, but Euripides is not this specific; note, in fact, how earlier in this tragedy Euripides' Messenger (650–730) freely mixes features of contemporary hoplite battle with those of Homeric warfare in his account of the battle between the Athenians and Thebans (see Pritchard 1998: 50–1). Lendon inconsistently takes *Supp.* 855–6 later (80, with 347 n. 4) as "perhaps alluding to" the Battle of Delium and the confusion of Athenian forces there (Th. 4.96.4).

[34] The fact that wealthy individuals – many of whom served as officers – often purchased distinctive armor (Plu. *Nic.* 28.5; *Alc.* 16.1–2; *Dem.* 20.2; Hanson 1989: 58–9; van Wees 2004: 52–4) made it easier for others to track their battlefield behavior.

retreat was not in itself deemed cowardly. As a practical matter, retreat was in the interest both of the hoplites whose lives were thus saved and of their city, because annihilation of an entire force would endanger its future military capacity. Athenian hoplites were routed on numerous occasions, for example, at Spartolus in 429 B.C. (Th. 2.79), Delium in 424 (4.96), Amphipolis in 422 (5.10), Epipolae in 414 (7.43–5; cf. Plu. *Nic.* 21.9), Ephesus in 409 (X. *HG* 1.2.7–9), Nemea River in 394 (4.2.9–23; Lys. 16.15), and Chaeronea in 338 (D.S. 16.86.4).

While retreat was common, how it was initiated and carried out could damage or enhance the reputations of those involved. The very nature of retreat, however, made assessments of individual and group behavior in it very difficult. If hoplite behavior was frequently beyond scrutiny in the thick of battle, all the more so was it as men scrambled to save their lives with the enemy in pursuit.

How a retreat was initiated was rich with implications for individual and group reputations. Ideally, the command to retreat would come from the general (Pl. *Lg.* 942a–b), who might signal a retreat through a herald or trumpeter, or by passing verbal orders to his officers (Krentz 1991: 116–18; cf. Pritchett 1994: 118–30). In such situations, the brunt of the blame or credit for the withdrawal might fall upon the general: his decision to retreat could be construed after the fact as an act of timidity or cowardice or, alternatively, as rational and humane in light of his troops' travails.[35]

In practice, however, retreats probably often began without an order from the general, when hoplites in the back ranks – who were in the best position to withdraw – perceived that the battle had turned badly against their side and started to back off or flee individually or in groups. This set off a chain reaction as those further forward became aware that their support was peeling away: as Xenophon observes, "it is very hard to find men willing to stay in place, when they see some of their own side in flight" (*HG* 7.5.24; cf. Hanson 1989: 160). In such situations the instinct for self-preservation won out over any respect

[35] Prudent withdrawal was not necessarily inconsistent with courage as commonly conceived: courage was one thing, rash and irrational risk-taking another. On the importance of exercising courage with prudence and forethought, see E. *Supp.* 161–2, 510; *Ph.* 745–7; Pl. *La.* 197b; Arist. *EN* 1107b; 1115a-b; cf. Th. 2.40.3; Gorg. 82 fr. 8 D–K; Balot 2004b.

for, or confidence in, hierarchy of command that citizen-soldiers had. To await an order from a general, in fact, might be foolish and deadly in the face of a rapidly developing rout: communication in a struggling hoplite force could be strained at best (e.g., Plu. *Dion* 30.7), and there was no guarantee that a general – who often fought in the front ranks, as noted above – was alive to give the order to retreat.

When retreat was more or less spontaneous, it must have been extremely difficult to pin blame on the individuals who had initiated it. Those leaving the ranks while others were fighting could be rebuked for abandoning the ranks (*lipotaxion*) and even face a legal charge on this basis back in Athens (Lys.14.5; see further below).[36] Hoplites, however, may often have been aware only that the retreat had begun in a certain part of their line and therefore have blamed the tribal contingent located there, without looking further for the responsible parties (cf. Lys. 16.15–16, discussed below). While Athenians seem to have been quite ready to blame and even prosecute their elected generals for military failures as we shall see, they apparently had little interest in ferreting out the average hoplites who may have initiated a rout.[37]

Manly reputations were at stake not only when a rout began but also as the ensuing retreat was carried out. Ideally, a certain order and decorum were to be maintained in retreat not only to preserve honor but life, because a chaotic retreat could lead to high casualties (Tyrt. fr. 11.10–14; Hanson 1989: 177–81). Consider, for example, how Plato's Alcibiades holds up Socrates as a model hoplite in the Athenian retreat at Delium (424 B.C.):

Let me tell you, gentlemen, what a notable figure he made when the army was retreating in flight from Delium. I happened to be there on horseback, while he marched under arms. The troops were scattering, and he was retreating along with Laches,[38] when I chanced to come up with them and, as soon as I saw them, bid them to have no fear, saying I would not abandon them.

[36] Cf. the exhortation of Tyrt. fr. 10.16: "do not start shameful flight or panic."

[37] Contrast the Roman practice of *decimatio*: if entire maniples deserted their posts on the battlefield, one-tenth of those involved, chosen at random, were brutally beaten, and the rest given reduced rations and placed in a vulnerable position outside the main camp (Plb. 6.38).

[38] Although Laches served often as general, at Delium he may only have been an officer (see Develin 1989: 133).

> Here, indeed, I had an even finer view of Socrates than at Potidaea – for personally I had less reason for fear, as I was mounted; I noticed, first, how far he outdid Laches in collectedness, and next I observed – to use a phrase of yours, Aristophanes – how there he stepped along, as he also does in our streets, "swaggering, with ever a sidelong glance [cf. *Nu.* 362]," turning a calm look on friend and foe alike, and convincing anyone even from afar that whoever touches this man will find he can put up a stout enough defense. The result was that both he and his comrade got away safely: for, as a rule, people will not lay a finger on those who show this disposition in war; it is men flying in headlong rout (προτροπάδην) that they pursue. (*Smp.* 221a–c)

Such composure in flight was, however, exceptional at Delium, as Alcibiades makes clear (cf. Th. 4.96.6–8; Pl. *La.* 181b), and in general disorderly flight was probably the norm for most routed forces (Hanson 1989: 181–4).[39]

For troops in flight, considerations of shame and honor often yielded to the instinct for self-preservation. It was in these situations in particular that behaviors that could be construed as cowardly were especially common. While a wound in the back was potentially an emblem of shame (cf. Tyrt. fr. 11.17–18; *adesp. tr.* fr. 450), swift-footed retreat with back turned could seem the best recourse, for example, when enemy cavalry entered the scene in pursuit of those fleeing (Th. 2.79; 4.96.8–9).[40] Likewise, although the abandonment of a shield could be viewed as shameful, retreating hoplites routinely dropped their shields when they became an encumbrance; shields were made primarily of wood and could be replaced at only slight expense (Hanson 1989: 63–5; cf. Hom. *Il.* 17.760–1).[41] Thus, for example, the defeated Athenians left their arms on the field at Epipolae (Th. 7.45; Plu. *Nic.* 21.9).

[39] Note that Socrates was also present at Amphipolis in 422 B.C. (Pl. *Ap.* 28e), where Athenian forces fled pell-mell in a rout (Th. 5.10.7–10).

[40] Ober (1996: 56; cf. Hanson 2000: 219) suggests that it was a convention of Greek warfare that "Pursuit of defeated and retreating opponents should be limited in duration." Krentz (2002: 30; cf. van Wees 2004: 135) argues convincingly, however, that "When they had the opportunity to do so safely, Greeks showed little hesitation in slaughtering their enemies."

[41] For the inflammatory charge that a hoplite has cast away his shield on the battlefield, see Lys. 10.1, 9, 28, and Aristophanes' repeated attacks on Cleonymus (see below, note 82). I doubt (*contra* Schwertfeger 1982) that shield-tossing (ῥιψασπία) was viewed as any less shameful in the Archaic age than in the Classical period. When Archilochus

Aristophanes quips concerning this common occurrence: "These men of ours, many of them have lost their family rod and the spearhead on the end of it, and many others on campaigns have thrown away the parasols from their shoulders!" (*Th.* 824–9).[42] In the confusion accompanying a rout there were probably few direct witnesses to a man's desperate acts of self-preservation among his fellow hoplites, and if he survived and any rebuked him for his loss of equipment, he could attribute this to necessity or accident rather than any lack of spirit.[43] The city, for its part, preferred not to look too closely at the behavior of average hoplites in a rout. For example, after the Athenian rout at Chaeronea (338 B.C.), it did not seek to reproach the large numbers who must have lost their shields in flight, but rather crowned Diotimus and Charidemus for their donations of shields in 338/7, which were probably intended to help replace these (Dem. 18.114, 117; *IG* II^2 1496.22–5, 28–39).[44]

In the immediate aftermath of defeat, however, routed hoplites were vulnerable to mutual recriminations (Dem. 3.17) and criticism. Interesting evidence of this is found in a speech presented by Lysias' client Mantitheus, in connection with his *dokimasia* to become a member of the Athenian Council sometime between 394 and 389 B.C. His representation of himself and his tribe in the rout suffered by the Athenians at Nemea River in 394 (X. *HG* 4.2.9–23) is of interest, as this sheds light on the tensions immediately after a rout and later back in Athens in speaking of it.

(7th c. B.C.) vaunts his alleged tossing of his shield (fr. 5; cf. Alc. fr. 428a; Anacr. fr. 381b), he humorously engages with cultural norms that view this as disgraceful.

42 For the commonplace representation of cowards as effeminate, see e.g., Ar. *Nu.* 672–80, with Sommerstein 1982: 197; Pl. *Lg.* 944d–e; D.S. 12.16.1–2.

43 For possible justifications for loss of a shield, see Pl. *Lg.* 943d–945a; X. *HG* 5.4.17; cf. Hanson 1989: 67.

44 On these donations, see Davies 1971: 164, 571–2, and Develin 1989: 343. On the likely spuriousness of Dem. 18.116, which claims to be the decree awarding the crowns, see Yunis 2001: 29–31. When the city bestowed panoplies on hoplites' orphans at age 18 (Pl. *Mx.* 249a6–b2; Aeschin. 3.154), this served a practical, as well as an ideological, function, because this ensured that orphans would be equipped to serve as hoplites: whereas surviving hoplites may frequently have passed their equipment on to their sons, the equipment of dead hoplites was often lost on the battlefield.

Mantitheus begins with a highly condensed account of the Athenian rout at Nemea River that is interesting both for what it mentions and what it omits:

> Then after that, gentlemen, there was the expedition to Corinth; and everyone knew in advance that it would be dangerous. Some were trying to shirk their duty (ἑτέρων ἀναδυομένων), but I contrived to have myself posted in the front rank for our battle with the enemy. Our tribe had the worst fortune and suffered the heaviest losses among its own men; I withdrew from the field later than the fine fellow of Steiria who has been reproaching everybody with cowardice (ὕστερος ἀνεχώρησα τοῦ σεμνοῦ Στειριῶς τοῦ πᾶσιν ἀνθρώποις δειλίαν ὠνειδικότος). (16.15)

Although Mantitheus does not directly address the circumstances of the rout, he does his best to present himself and his tribe in a favorable light.[45] He contrasts himself, first of all, with men among the forces who were prepared to "shirk their duty;" such men, if any, one may infer, were responsible for the rout, not those like the speaker who had boldly volunteered to be in the front rank. Mantitheus then turns to defend his tribe, with whom he was presumably stationed: it was due to bad fortune that they suffered "the heaviest losses"; while high casualties were common among fleeing troops (Hanson 1989: 183–4; Krentz 2002: 30–1), Mantitheus implies that his tribe suffered their losses honorably while fighting not from any cowardice in retreat.[46] Mantitheus, however, provides no specific information concerning his tribe's role in the flight or behavior in it; instead he turns once more to himself and insists that he withdrew from the field later than "the fine fellow of Steiria"; this is commonly taken as a reference to Thrasybulus, who may have been general on this campaign (Develin 1989: 208). Although Mantitheus does not specify where he was within the fleeing army, he suggests that his behavior should be assessed by his position relative to Thrasybulus in retreat; courage is a relative thing among

[45] Craik (1999: 626) goes so far as to suggest that Mantitheus here "makes claims so extravagant as to verge on the absurd."

[46] In light of Mantitheus' favorable portrayal of his tribe as well as himself, it is not quite right to say that he advances "monopolistic claims to courage and patriotism at the expense of other Athenians" (Roisman 2005: 112).

retreating troops, he implies, and the general's position in retreat a key reference point.[47]

Although it is not surprising to find a hoplite on the defensive in representing his role and that of his tribe within a rout, Mantitheus' allusion to Thrasybulus suggests another reason for this feature of his account. Apparently Thrasybulus had been "reproaching" his troops for cowardice in this situation: the perfect participle ὠνειδικότος indicates that this began at some point in the past – probably immediately after the rout – and continued up to the present back in Athens. This charge invites the recrimination on the part of the speaker that he at least was slower to withdraw than Thrasybulus. While Mantitheus asserts that Thrasybulus has been reproaching *all* with cowardice, his personal reply to this and his defense of his tribe's behavior may be because Thrasybulus had attacked them directly.

In any event, Thrasybulus' rebukes after the battle, whether against all his troops or Mantitheus' tribe in particular, may have prompted Mantitheus to take the extraordinary step, as he goes on to relate, of urging his tribe's taxiarch to volunteer their tribe (*taxis*) for a dangerous mission against the Spartans "without drawing lots" (16.16). Indeed, perhaps the best way to salvage individual and group reputation in the aftermath of a rout was to undertake acts of bravery. While some campaigns consisted of a single battle and thus provided but one conspicuous test of courage, in many cases subsequent military ventures within a campaign provided further opportunities for men to prove their mettle and to make up for any earlier shortfall in courage (Plu. *Alc.* 29.1–2; cf. X. *HG* 1.2.15).

Victory

While the members of a routed force had to do their best to defend their manly reputations in the face of defeat, a victorious force – after

[47] Cf. the words of a Confederate soldier who joined in flight at Sharpsburg: "It never entered my head to throw away gun or cartridge box; but, encumbered as I was, I endeavored to keep pace with my captain, who with his long legs and unencumbered would in a little while have far outstripped me but that he frequently turned towards the enemy, and, running backwards, managed not to come out ahead in this our anything but creditable race" (Durkin 1945: 46–7, quoted in Miller 2002: 28).

the initial exuberance of prevailing and the seizure of battlefield booty – had to take steps to ensure that others would recognize their achievement and honor them for this. How others would perceive their victory depended very much on their actions immediately after a battle.[48] From at least the 460s B.C., when hoplite forces routed their enemies, they staked their claim to victory and the prestige accompanying it by erecting battlefield trophies (Krentz 2002: 32, 34; cf. Pritchett 1974: 2.246–75). If the opposing side made a request to retrieve corpses after a battle, this was commonly construed by Hellenic custom to justify the erection of a trophy (Plu. *Nic.* 6.5; Pritchett 1985: 4.247–8). In the absence of such a request, the side that viewed itself as victorious could formalize its claim to victory by erecting a trophy; the assertive and potentially tendentious quality of this is apparent when both sides set up a trophy (Th. 4.134; X. *HG* 7.5.26). Although the erection of a battlefield trophy served the immediate purpose of conveying an assertion of victory to the opposing force (X. *HG* 7.2.4; Plu. *Arat.* 28), it also provided a basis for a victorious force and its general (cf. Plu. *Them.* 3; *Per.* 38) to seek honor upon returning home.

If the erection of a battlefield trophy reflected well on the entire victorious force, special awards of distinction (*aristeia*) – often in the form of a panoply – were sometimes bestowed after battle on hoplites who had displayed exceptional valor.[49] While many individuals might boast to have behaved heroically on the battlefield (X. *Hier.* 2.15–16), a force's general(s) apparently determined whether such awards should be given and to whom (Hamel 1998a: 67–70). Plato's Alcibiades provides a glimpse of this process in his praise of Socrates' valor at Potidaea:

If you care to hear of him in battle – for there also he must have his due – on the day of the fight in which I gained my prize for valor (*aristeia*) from our

[48] Cf. Balot's (2004b: 408) apt observation: "Courage is often the way that victors reinvent luck."

[49] On *aristeia*, see Pritchett 1974: 2.276–90; Hamel 1998a: 64–70; van Wees 2004: 194, with 302 nn. 50 and 51. There is some truth to Pritchett's generalization (1974: 2.290): "In a small way, the award of the aristeion reveals national psychology. The Greeks took the positive view and gave awards for deeds of valor. The Persians took the negative view and punished men when they did not fight well." As we shall see, however, Greeks differed from one another in the extent to which they used negative or positive stimuli to elicit valor; Spartans, in particular, relied heavily on the former.

generals, it was he, out of the whole army, who saved my life: I was wounded, and he would not abandon me, but helped me to save both my armor and myself. I lost no time, Socrates, in urging the generals to award the prize for valor to you; and here I think you will neither rebuke me nor say that I am lying. For when the generals, out of regard for my status, were inclined to award the prize to me, you outdid them in urging that I should have it rather than you. (*Smp.* 220d–e)

Whether or not we believe Alcibiades' claim about the grounds on which the generals gave the award to him rather than Socrates, there was a large element of subjectivity in determining who stood out most in courage. Because the Athenian evidence for this practice is sparse, we cannot be sure exactly how this institution operated among Athenian forces and how frequently awards were made.[50]

This survey points to some of the complex social dynamics of courage and cowardice in the hoplite experience. Throughout a campaign Athenian hoplites competed with each other and their enemy to appear courageous or at least not cowardly. The evaluation of martial valor, however, could be highly subjective, depending as it did on the personal assumptions and biases of the observer; it was, moreover, rendered difficult and sometimes impossible by the fog of war and confusion of battle. This gave considerable scope to the negotiation and contestation of assessments of valor and cowardice during a military campaign and, as we shall see, at home in Athens after a campaign.

COWARDICE ON THE HOME FRONT

While Athenian hoplites were hardly unique in the Greek world in seeking to protect and advance their manly reputations on campaign, the way that they viewed courage and cowardice was colored by their city's democratic institutions. It is to these institutions and the place of hoplite courage and cowardice within them that we now turn. We

[50] While Thucydides and Xenophon do not mention these awards, this may reflect more the nature of their war narratives (thus Pritchett 1974: 2.288) than the infrequency with which *aristeia* were bestowed in the late-fifth and early-fourth centuries B.C. I am persuaded by Hamel (1998a: 64, with 64–7) that "the chronological distribution of the known instances suggests that the practice of awarding *aristeia* was carried on by the Athenians throughout the classical period."

will consider first, how, as hoplites reentered the city after a military campaign, their courage or lack thereof might come before the public eye, and how the competition for reputation that began on campaign evolved in the presence of Athens' civic institutions. Next, we will examine how the democratic city responded to the problem of cowardice in particular, considering first the limited scope of legal prosecution for this offense and then the wider scope in public discourse for alleging cowardice, especially on the part of prominent persons.

The Hoplite's Homecoming

Hoplites returning home from campaign faced numerous difficulties. Some bore physical wounds, temporary or permanent; others were scarred emotionally, having witnessed the bloody reality of hoplite battle and having lost close friends or relatives. Many would find – like veterans of modern wars – that resuming life at home was difficult, as war had transformed them, or their domestic situations had changed in their absence; the stories of the troubled homecomings of Agamemnon and Odysseus after the Trojan War must have had deep resonances for returning hoplites.[51] Hoplites, however, also faced another challenge, namely, how to defend or enhance their reputations individually and collectively before the public. While this was an extension of the competition for reputation on campaign in which hoplites engaged, the terms of this contest were transformed as it was played out through the city's institutions. Naturally, the military success or failure of a hoplite force had broad implications for the negotiation of group and individual reputation on its return home.

Although a victorious force was in a good position to win acclaim upon its return, the public's bestowal of praise was not entirely automatic and the form that this took varied widely. It was incumbent on a force's general to take active steps to ensure that he and his troops would receive the honor due them. Even before a victorious force

[51] For possible connections between the Greek experience of war and its aftermath and that of modern veterans, see Shay 1994; 2002; Tritle 2000; Tatum 2003; but cf. van Wees 2004: 151.

returned to Athens, it was important that it lay the groundwork for a claim to public gratitude and honor. First, it was essential to erect a battlefield trophy (*tropaion*) at the point of the rout of the enemy: as noted earlier, this not only constituted an exclusive claim to victory on the spot but also provided a tangible basis for seeking honors back in Athens. Next, it was expedient to send a laudatory account of the success back to Athens, preferably through distinguished messengers. For example, the news of the Athenian victory at Tamynae (349/8 B.C.) was conveyed by Aeschines, who had received a crown on the scene for his valor, and a taxiarch from the successful force; when the *dēmos* voted Aeschines an additional crown (Aeschin. 2.169), this reflected well on the force that he represented. Finally, the manner in which hoplites returned to the city could affect how the public viewed them and their victory. While Athenians did not carry out formal triumphal processions as the Romans did, an Athenian force could draw attention to its victory as it returned to the city, for example, by conspicuously displaying captured shields and other spoils of war (cf. Plu. *Alc.* 32).

Once a victorious force had returned to Athens, its general could approach the Assembly to petition for public honors (Aeschin. 3.183–7; cf. Plu. *Cim.* 8.1). Like victorious athletes returning from the Panhellenic games (cf. Kurke 1991), successful generals and their forces had to take care not to arouse envy; the best strategy was to represent their victory as a communal one that enhanced the reputation not only of those who had won it but the community that they represented (Aeschin. 3.183–5; cf. Plu. *Cim.* 7–8.1). Depending on the nature of the victory and the persuasive skills of the petitioner, the Assembly might pass an honorary decree (Aeschin. 3.187); allow the victors to erect a monumental inscription (Aeschin. 3.183–5; cf. Plu. *Cim.* 7); or grant them permission to display in public space a commemorative painting (Aeschin. 3.186; Paus. 1.3.3–5; 1.15.1–3) or captured shields (Lys. 10.27–8; Paus. 1.15.4; Camp 1986: 71–2).[52]

[52] On private and public dedications of armor and weapons, see Pritchett 1979: 3.240–95; Jackson 1991. On different forms of war commemoration in Athens, see Tritle 2000: 146–7, 156–61, 165–72; Raaflaub 2001: 323–5; cf. Low 2002: 104, 110–15.

A general, in lobbying for rewards for his force, could also seek honors for himself. The granting of individual honors to generals, however, was a sensitive matter under the democracy, as Miltiades, who served as general at Marathon, learned. According to Plutarch,

> When [Miltiades] asked for a crown of olive merely, Sophanes the Decelean[53] rose up in the middle of the Assembly and protested. His speech was ungracious, but it pleased the people of that time. "When," he said, "you have fought out alone a victory over the barbarians, then seek to be honored alone." (*Cim.* 8.1)

Similarly, Aeschines asserts that the people refused to allow Miltiades to have his name written on the painting commemorating the battle of Marathon in the Stoa Poikilē in the Agora but did permit him to be portrayed in the front rank urging on his men (3.186; cf. 183).[54] Notwithstanding tensions surrounding honors to individual generals, Athenians seem to have granted these with some regularity, even in the form of statues set up in the Agora (Aeschin. 3.243; Lyc. 1.51; Paus. 1.3.2; Buckler 1972).[55]

Most returning hoplites, however, did not receive individual acclaim from the public for their role in victory, and therefore it was up to them to lay claim to the personal glory that they believed they deserved. In daily conversation, at symposia, and elsewhere, individuals could advance claims concerning their endurance and courage on

[53] On Sophanes, see below, note 57.

[54] Carey (2000: 228 n. 213) notes the anachronism: "Since Miltiades died in the early 480s and the Painted Portico belongs to the early 460s, he was in no position to make this request." For other passages that question singling out generals for honors, see And. 2.17–18; Dem. 23.196–8; 13.21–3; cf. E. *Andr.* 693–8; Roisman 2005: 122–4.

[55] Athenians bestowed honors on generals more freely in the fourth century than in the fifth century: see Sinclair 1988: 177–8 and Roisman 2005: 120. Statues of generals could be viewed as part of what Balot (2004b: 418) labels the Athenian "topography of courage," which included statues of the tyrannicides, Harmodius and Aristogeiton. Note also how the Athenian casualty lists identify generals and officers and sometimes set their names apart from those of the hoplites who served under them: see Bradeen 1969: 147; 1974: nos. 22 and 23; Loraux 1986: 359 n. 106; cf. Paus. 1.29.4, 11–12; Tritle 2000: 166. While Athenians may sometimes have rewarded successful generals with a special allotment of booty, the evidence for this is sketchy: see Pritchett 1971: 82–6; 1991: 399–400.

campaign (cf. Pl. *Smp.* 219e–220b, 220d–e, 221a–c), supporting these with displays of battle scars (X. *Mem.* 3.4.1; Plu. *Pel.* 2.3, cf. *Mor.* 187c) or booty seized from the enemy (cf. Hdt. 9.80–1).[56] Herodotus, in his epilogue on the battle of Marathon, records one veteran's remarkable story of courage and injury (cf. Tritle 2000: 159–60):

A wondrous thing happened there: an Athenian, Epizelus, son of Cuphagoras, who was in the thick of the fighting, and fighting bravely himself, lost the sight of his eyes. He was not struck on any part of his body or hit by a missile, but he continued blind from that day, all the rest of his life. But I heard that he used to tell the story of the matter thus: that he saw confronting him a huge hoplite whose beard covered all his shield. This apparition passed by Epizelus himself but killed his comrade beside him. That is what I understood Epizelus reported. (6.117)

If, as noted above, it could be difficult for hoplites on campaign to evaluate one another's claims concerning behavior in battle, it must have been all the more difficult for the Athenian public to assess these later.[57] Xenophon's Hiero cynically remarks:

For, as I am sure you know, when states defeat their foes in a battle, it is not easy to describe the pleasure they feel in the rout of the enemy, in the pursuit, in the slaughter of the enemy. How they exult at the deed! How they take upon themselves a radiant glory! How they rejoice believing that they have exalted their city! Each man pretends that he had a share in the plan and killed the most; and it is hard to find where they do not lie, claiming to have killed more than all that were really slain. So glorious it seems to them to have won a great victory. (*Hier.* 2.15–16)

[56] A private dedication in a temple could bolster claims: see e.g., Dem. 57.64; Pl. *Lg.* 943c; cf. X. *Eq.* 1.1. Loraux (1995: 87–90; cf. van Wees 2004: 148) underestimates the potential significance of battle scars in a Hellenic context ("I would willingly wager that for a fifth-century Greek, valor has no need of being written on the body" [90]) and goes too far in distinguishing Greek practices from Roman ones; on the displaying of wounds and scars in Rome, see Leigh 1995; R. J. Evans 1999.

[57] Cf. the alternative accounts that circulated concerning Sophanes' heroism in battle at Plataea, one holding that he literally anchored himself to the ground to face the enemy, the other that he had an anchor depicted on his shield, which he wielded aggressively against his opponents (Hdt. 9.74). On Sophanes' valor, see also Hdt. 6.92.3 and 9.75.

That Athenians were familiar with, and ready to be skeptical of, veterans' claims concerning battlefield bravery is suggested by the emergence of the "braggart soldier" as a stock buffoon in Attic comedy.[58]

Although Athenians were prepared to bestow honors collectively on victorious hoplites, they do not appear to have been eager to reproach routed hoplites as a group. While there was a well-established process through which victorious hoplites could receive due praise by appeal to the Assembly, there was no analogous one whereby the performance of defeated hoplites came conspicuously before the public eye. In fact, when a defeated force returned to Athens, it likely dispersed as soon as possible and members of it did not reconvene again as an identifiable group, unless briefly for trials concerning military offenses (see Chapter 2); if the members of this force served again as hoplites, this was as part of a newly constituted group of conscripts that bore no stigma of prior defeat.[59]

That Athenians did not choose to focus attention on, or inquire into, the collective behavior of routed hoplites can be explained, first, by the fact that this was an embarrassment not just for those immediately involved but also for the city itself (cf. Pl. *La.* 181b). Thus, if public speakers addressed these unhappy episodes at all, they attributed them to bad fortune (*tuchē*) (see below) rather than to a collective failure of nerve that would reflect negatively on Athens and its institutions. Second, as a practical matter, it would have been highly imprudent for a public speaker to criticize or rebuke an entire hoplite force, and thus risk alienating the large number of members of it and perhaps also the larger constituency of hoplites within the city who might identify with them. By contrast, the wealthy Athenian knights who

[58] On the gradual evolution of the type, see Nesselrath 1990: 325–9; cf. Pierce 1998: 136–9; Storey 2003: 78. Note also how Aristophanes satirizes the tired claims of "Marathon-fighters" (*Ach.* 692–702; *V.* 1060–90; cf. 235–9).

[59] A freshly defeated force that was still on campaign, however, might be stigmatized: "In Lampsacus, Alcibiades tried to organize the entire army into a single formation, but his soldiers did not want to serve in the same ranks as those who came with Thrasyllus on the grounds that they were unbeaten but those had come from a defeat. They all, however, spent the winter there fortifying Lampsacus" (X. *HG* 1.2.15; cf. Plu. *Alc.* 29.1–2).

constituted a much smaller group within the city and one viewed with a degree of hostility by average Athenians, were probably more vulnerable to criticism; the popular politician Cleon, in fact, is said to have accused the knights of desertion (κατηγόρησε γὰρ αὐτῶν ὡς λειποστρατούντων) (Theopomp. Hist. *FGrH* 115 F 93).[60]

Although groups of routed hoplites were immune from formal public scrutiny or censure, individuals could find themselves under pressure to defend their participation in a rout. In such circumstances, it was only natural for them to assert that others were responsible for what had transpired. As Demosthenes pointedly observes:

> In the dangers of battle no one among those fleeing blames himself, but rather his general, those near him, and everyone else rather than himself. But surely to those fleeing collectively the defeat is due; for he might have stood firm who now blames the others, and if each man had stood, they would have been victorious. (3.17)

A hoplite might simultaneously advance a positive image of his own behavior during the rout, by asserting that he had left the battlefield later (Lys. 16.15) or with greater dignity (cf. Pl. *Smp.* 221a–c) than others had. While participation in a rout could be a sensitive matter for a man's reputation,[61] there appears to have been little risk that an average hoplite would be singled out and subject to legal prosecution on the basis of cowardice in connection with a rout (see below).

Athenians appear to have focused attention after a rout not so much on deficiencies in hoplite performance, individual or group, as on shortcomings of the general(s) involved. If generals could receive a disproportionate share of praise and honor for their role in victories

[60] On this episode, see Bugh 1988: 111–14; on the charge of *lipostration*, see Hamel 1998b: 399–400. Cleon's accusation was probably a slander made before the public rather than the basis of a legal prosecution: while select members of the cavalry might be prosecuted on this grounds, it is unlikely that the entire cavalry could be named as defendants. On popular hostility towards the knights under the special circumstances of the early-fourth century B.C., see Low 2002; if Theopompus' testimony concerning Cleon's slander of the knights is accepted, Low (108; cf. Spence 1993: 220) is mistaken to view as a fourth-century innovation the allegation of cowardice as a characteristic of the cavalry.

[61] Gossip about a man's alleged role in a rout, for example, might bring shame on him. On gossip concerning bad citizenship in Athens, see Hunter 1994: 106–11.

(cf. E. *Andr.* 693–705), it may have seemed only fair to the public that they bear a greater share of blame and punishment for defeats (cf. Roisman 2005: 122). As has often been noted, Athenians were very receptive to legal prosecutions of unsuccessful generals.[62] While these prosecutions may often have centered upon a general's alleged incompetence or treason, questions concerning his personal courage could easily arise; the very fact that a general had survived while many of those under him had perished could be construed as evidence of his cowardice (cf. Lys. 2.58; Wheeler 1991: 151).[63] The frequency of indictments of unsuccessful generals may reflect, among other things, the need of Athenians to find an explanation for collective failure that would not call into question group courage.

If generals could serve as scapegoats for routs in their immediate aftermath, politically prominent individuals could find themselves the targets of allegations of cowardice years after a rout in which they had participated. These charges, as we shall see later in this chapter, are of considerable interest, both as a feature of competitive politics in Athens and as evidence of how the Athenian public reflected on civic courage and cowardice at a safe remove from the battlefield.

Legal Accountability for Cowardice?

Athenian law provided for public prosecution of cowardice and related offenses on campaign by any willing citizen (ὁ βουλόμενος). At least two actions were available: the *graphē lipotaxiou*, for prosecution of deserting the ranks; and a *graphē deilias*, for prosecution of cowardice.[64] Although the spheres of these actions seem to overlap, this is not

[62] See Pritchett 1974: 2.4–33; Hansen 1975; Roberts 1982: 174–80; Knox 1985; Sinclair 1988: 146–52; Hamel 1998a: 122–57.

[63] This may have figured in the condemnation to death of the general Lysicles after Chaeronea (D.S. 16.88.1–2 = Lyc. fr. 75 Sauppe). Cf. Paus. 1.29.11–12, claiming that Athenians did not list the general Nicias on the Athenian casualty lists for Sicily, because he voluntarily surrendered to the enemy. I doubt (*pace* Tritle 2000: 166–8) that an average soldier who died in battle faced much risk of being left off a casualty list due to doubts about his courage.

[64] There may also have been a separate action for prosecution of throwing away a shield (ῥιψασπία) in battle: see And. 1.74; cf. Pl. *Lg.* 942a5–945b2; Hamel 1998b: 361 n. 1.

unusual in Athenian law (cf. Todd 1993: 122). A single law concerning military offenses, with several provisions, may have set forth these actions along with the *graphē astrateias* for prosecution of draft evasion (Lys. 14.5; Aeschin. 3.175–6; cf. And. 1.74).[65] All three actions were to be brought before popular courts that were manned by Athenians who had served on the campaign in connection with which the alleged offense had occurred (Lys. 14.5); the board of generals convened these courts (15.1–2).

Although the ancient sources refer to the *graphē lipotaxiou* and *graphē deilias* a number of times, there is scant mention of actual prosecutions involving these. The only certain case of a *graphē lipotaxiou* is that initiated against Demosthenes by an agent of Meidias but dropped before trial (Dem. 21.103). No evidence has survived of a *graphē deilias* in action. By contrast, the *graphē astrateias* is fairly well attested with five cases surfacing in the record; while four of these came to trial, the remaining one may have been dropped (see Chapter 2).

This dearth of attested cases involving the *graphē lipotaxiou* and *graphē deilias* may reflect the actual infrequency of such suits. There is no reason to believe that the surviving corpus of Attic oratory – which preserves much of the information we have concerning lawsuits in Athens – is biased against preserving evidence of such cases; in fact, the corpus preserves an abundance of slanders concerning cowardice that might provide a springboard for allusion to notorious instances that had come before the courts. That cases of the *graphē deilias* were particularly uncommon is suggested by Aeschines:

> For Solon, the ancient lawgiver, thought it necessary to apply the same penalties to the coward (τὸν δειλὸν) as to the man who evaded conscription (τὸν ἀστράτευτον) or the man who deserted his post (τὸν λελοιπότα τὴν τάξιν). For there are such things as indictments for cowardice (δειλίας γραφαί). Some of you may indeed be surprised that there are indictments for inborn defects. There are. (3.175)

[65] On these actions and their spheres, see MacDowell 1962: 111; Carey 1989: 143–4; Hamel 1998b; Velho 2002: 241–2, 249–50. For interesting reflections on the similarly overlapping offenses delineated under "misbehavior before the enemy" in the United States' Uniform Code of Military Justice (10 USCS @ 899 (1997) Art. 99), see Miller 2002 (building on *ibid.* 2000: 92–105).

In insisting that these indictments really do exist and anticipating the surprise of some jurors at this, Aeschines assumes that cases involving this *graphē* are largely unfamiliar to his audience.[66]

That Athenians might be reluctant to bring actions alleging desertion of the ranks and cowardice would not be surprising in light of the risks involved for prosecutors. Public prosecutors were liable to a thousand-drachma fine and partial disfranchisement (*atimia*), if they failed to pursue a suit that they had initiated or won less than one-fifth of the votes cast at a trial. If, as suggested in Chapter 2, this prospect had a chilling effect on the prosecution of draft evasion, this might be even more the case for prosecution of desertion of the ranks and cowardice. A potential prosecutor of a *graphē astrateias* might convince himself that he would not incur the statutory penalties for unsuccessful prosecution: the offense of draft evasion was well defined; an individual's guilt might be easy to establish; and a jury composed of hoplites from the campaign in question was likely to convict those who had not shared the risks of campaign with them. By contrast, a potential prosecutor of a *graphē lipotaxiou* or *graphē deilias* might be less sanguine about his prospects: these offenses were less well defined than *astrateia*; an individual's guilt might be difficult to document, given the chaos of the battlefield; and the hoplites manning a jury might hesitate to hold one of their own number accountable for a momentary lapse especially when, as in a rout, others may also have behaved dishonorably. A further deterrent to bringing actions alleging martial shortcomings was that a prosecutor who failed to win his suit by any margin could find himself a defendant in a retaliatory slander suit; false assertions that a man had thrown away his arms on the battlefield, which might well arise in prosecutions for martial malfeasance, were grounds for initiating a slander suit (Lys. 10.9, 12; cf. van Wees 2004: 112).

When offenses on campaign were prosecuted, who was most likely to initiate them? The fact that Athenian generals convened the courts that adjudicated these cases may have kept them from acting as

[66] Note, however, that earlier passages that speak of *deilia* as a military offense (Lys. 14.5; Ar. *Eq*. 368; *Ach*. 1129) treat it as if it may be familiar. Aeschines (3.175) may be characterizing indictments for cowardice as unfamiliar because this allows him to pontificate about them.

prosecutors within them; even if a general could prosecute a hoplite who had served under him (cf. MacDowell 1978: 237), he might avoid doing so because his own performance as commander might come under fire at trial (cf. Plu. *Phoc.* 12.3). Wealthy Athenians may sometimes have had recourse to these actions in pursuit of their personal enmities, as Meidias apparently did when he employed an agent to bring a charge of deserting the ranks against Demosthenes (Dem. 21.103). Politically active individuals, who often undertook public prosecutions, may sometimes have found these actions to be useful against their political rivals, because a guilty verdict carried *atimia* with it (And. 1.74; Dem. 15.32; cf. Aeschin. 3.176) and thus prevented an opponent from addressing the public in the future.[67] In general, however, while politically active Athenians may have availed themselves of *astrateia* suits against their rivals with some frequency (see Chapter 2), the special risks attending the prosecution of a *graphē lipotaxiou* or *graphē deilias* may have deterred them from using these very often as political instruments. If they hesitated to risk bringing formal charges against their opponents on these grounds, nothing stopped them, as we shall see, from publicly attacking their rivals for their allegedly unmanly behavior on campaign.

Hoplites returning to Athens appear on balance then to have faced little risk of prosecution for cowardice or related behavior on campaign. If prosecuted and convicted, the punishment of *atimia* was a fairly mild one compared to other available punishments, including exile and death. As observed in connection with convictions for *astrateia*, moreover, the penalty of *atimia* was not always strictly enforced in Athens (see Chapter 2).

[67] For the use of this general tactic in political rivalry, see Dem. 25, 26, and 58. If an individual failed to prosecute his political rival through a *graphē* before a court of hoplites immediately after a campaign, he could prosecute him later through the *dokimasia rhētorōn* on the grounds that his discarding of arms on the battlefield disqualified him from addressing the public. Among the various grounds specified for bringing a *dokimasia rhētorōn* were draft evasion and shield-tossing (ῥιψασπία) (Aeschin. 1.28–9; cf. MacDowell 2005). The case alluded to in Lys. 10.1, in which ῥιψασπία figured, was presumably pursued before a regular jury under this rubric; the defendant was apparently not convicted (Lys. 10.3, with Todd 2000: 101 n.1). Individuals undergoing *dokimasiai* before entering public offices might also find their military credentials challenged by opponents, as in Lys. 16 and 31: see Roisman 2005: 117, with n. 42.

Just as Athens' moderate approach to the problem of *astrateia* stands in sharp contrast to Sparta's apparently harsh response to this (see Chapter 2), so too Athens appears to have acted more mildly than Sparta in its measures concerning cowardice and related offenses on campaign. Spartans who fell short of military standards on campaign were liable not only to loss of civic privileges upon returning home (Plu. *Ages.* 30.2; Th. 5.34.2) but also public degradation and humiliation as members of a class formally designated as "Tremblers" (*Tresantes*) (Plu. *Ages.* 30.2–3; Hdt. 7.31; cf. X. *Lac.* 9.4–6).[68] Such men, according to Plutarch, were readily recognizable: "they wear cloaks with colored patches, and they shave one part of their beards and grow the other part" (*Ages.* 30.3–4). Although D. M. MacDowell (1986a: 45) suggests that "[t]he adoption of a ridiculous style of dress and shaving is the kind of thing which the coward's fellows would impose on him informally, by exercising their right to hit him if he did not fall in with it," it is quite plausible that humiliation along these lines was more formally institutionalized, as were other forms of social mockery in Sparta (cf. David 1989: 14–15).[69]

That Athenians did not have recourse to this harsher approach to cowardice and related offenses reflects the democratic moderation on which Athenians prided themselves (cf. Dem. 22.51) and, more particularly, Athenian sensitivity to the reciprocal relationship between city and citizen. From an Athenian perspective, the natural way to punish a flagrant breach of citizenship obligations by a citizen-soldier, which entailed a violation of his reciprocal relationship with the city, was to revoke his civic privileges through *atimia*. Thus Demosthenes (15.32) asserts before the Assembly: "You consider that the man who deserts the post that his general has assigned him deserves to be *atimos* and deprived of his share in our common privileges." To go farther than this, as Spartans did, by exposing the offender to persistent public humiliation, would risk putting the city in a despotic role vis à vis its

[68] On the *Tresantes*, see MacDowell 1986a: 44–6; Loraux 1995: 68–9; Velho 2002: 251–6.

[69] For public humiliation of cowards, see also D.S. 12.16.1–2, claiming that in Thurii, "Charondas ordered that they [i.e. draft-dodgers and deserters of the ranks] should sit in the agora for three days dressed in women's clothing"; cf. Pl. *Lg.* 944e-945a; Plu. *Art.* 14.

citizens.[70] As a practical matter too, Athenians may not have wished to call attention to tensions between the city and its citizens over civic obligations by creating an identifiable and conspicuous class of individuals like the Spartan *Tresantes*. Instead, Athens submerged those found guilty of cowardice and related offenses in the larger and more diffuse class of *atimoi*, which included state-debtors and others (And. 1.73–6). *Atimoi* bore no visible stigma of their demotion in civic status; only if they attempted to exercise civic privileges and were prosecuted for this would the public be reminded of the specific source of their *atimia*.

Critics of Athenian democracy often found its enforcement of citizen obligations too lenient (cf. Pl. *R.* 557e) and compared this unfavorably with that found in Sparta, where citizens were said to do their duty largely out of fear of the law. Xenophon, an Athenian exile who was on intimate terms with the Spartans, contrasts the shame heaped upon cowards in Sparta with their treatment elsewhere, including presumably in his native Athens:

> Clearly, what Lycurgus did [sc. through his laws] was to ensure that the brave should have happiness, and cowards misery. For in other states when a man proves a coward, the only consequence is that he is called a coward. He goes to the same market as the brave man, sits beside him, and frequents the same gymnasium, if he chooses. (*Lac.* 9.3–4)

In fact, Athenians were not quite as lenient as Xenophon may imply here. There was at least some risk of prosecution for cowardice under the city's laws, as we have seen, and fear of the city's laws could plausibly be invoked, therefore, as a motive for acting honorably on the battlefield. Thus one of the younger Alcibiades' prosecutors could assert before a jury of hoplites, "you did not venture to desert your ranks or choose what was most agreeable to yourselves, but were far more afraid of the city's laws than of the danger of meeting the enemy" (Lys. 14.15). Similarly, Aeschines, in rebuking Demosthenes for his alleged cowardice at Chaeronea, asserts that indictments for cowardice exist, "in order that each one of us, fearing the punishment of the laws

70 Athenians used public humiliation sparingly as a form of punishment for citizens (see Hunter 1994: 154–84; Allen 2000a: 213–15) and not for breaches of the basic duties of citizenship.

more than he fears the enemy, may become a better champion of the fatherland" (3.175). While both of these speakers have a vested interest in amplifying the importance of "fear of the laws" in the military sphere (cf. Lyc. 1.130), Athenian hoplites did indeed have to take into account the possible legal as well as social consequences for shortfalls in courage.[71]

If fear of the city's laws had its place in discouraging Athenian hoplites from engaging in behavior that might be deemed cowardly, however, Athenians clearly did not rely upon this threat as heavily as Spartans did (Lyc. 1.129–30).[72] It was a point of pride among Athenians, in fact, that living as free men, without the harsh restrictions and regulations of the Spartan way of life, they willingly went to battle and fought bravely (Th. 2.39).[73] While the freedoms that Athenians enjoyed may well have encouraged them to fight bravely for their city (see Chapter 1), so too did public discourse, a hallmark of their free society.

Courage and Cowardice in Democratic Discourse

Athenian public discourse provided citizens with many opportunities to reflect upon the place of hoplite courage and cowardice in the democratic city. Whether this discourse focuses on praising hoplite courage or condemning its opposite, it provides valuable evidence of how Athenians addressed concerns over hoplite performance.[74] One

[71] Cf. Arist. *EN* 1116a17–22: "First, as most closely resembling true Courage, comes the citizen's courage. Citizen troops appear to endure dangers because of the legal penalties and the reproaches [sc. attaching to cowardice] and the honors [sc. awarded to bravery]; hence those peoples appear to be the bravest among whom cowards are degraded and brave men held in honor." On "fear of the laws" under the democracy, see also A. *Eu.* 696–9; Th. 2.37.3; Balot 2004b: 420–2 (with my comments in note 79 below); Roisman 2005: 186–8.

[72] Cf. Sophocles' representation of the Spartan Menelaus on the subject of fear and military authority: "The laws of a city can never function well where no one is afraid, nor can an army be sensibly controlled when it has not the protection of fear and respect" (*Aj.* 1073–6).

[73] Cf. Arist. *EN* 1116b2: "A man ought to be brave not because he is compelled to be, but because courage is noble."

[74] On the complementary relation of praise and blame in this context, see Lyc. 1.74 ("As you praise and honor brave men, so too you must hate and punish cowards"); Arist. *EN* 1116a17–21.

rich source of evidence for the place of martial courage and cowardice within democratic citizenship is the Attic funeral orations (*epitaphioi*) for the state war dead. Although these orations most conspicuously celebrate and idealize the courage of Athenian hoplites, they also engage in intriguing ways with the problem of cowardice. After considering how the patriotic *epitaphioi* acknowledge and respond to the possibility of hoplite cowardice, we will turn to explore charges of cowardice against political figures as vehicles not only for character assassination but also for public reflection on citizen obligations.

Epitaphioi. It is not surprising, given their civic circumstances and rhetorical goals, that the extant Attic funeral orations highlight the manly excellence (*aretē*) and courage (*andreia*) of the city's hoplites. If, as observed earlier, the evaluation of hoplite courage and cowardice on the battlefield must often have been difficult, the *epitaphioi* at a great remove from the battlefield confidently assert that the war dead acted uniformly with courage;[75] their deaths were due to a turn of fortune (*tuchē*), not to any deficiency of character.[76] The vehemence with which the *epitaphioi* assert the uniform valor of Athenian hoplites in the face of battle leads us to suspect that here, as elsewhere, these ideology-laden speeches are working to suppress social tensions and anxieties (cf. Loraux 1986; Ober 1998: 86–9).[77] This suspicion is confirmed by the polemical stance that the *epitaphioi* adopt vis à vis citizen cowardice.

In praising the courage of Athens' dead soldiers, the *epitaphioi* assert that they consciously and deliberately chose to act courageously rather than cowardly. They chose to act nobly, "considering it better to keep fighting and die than to save themselves by giving in" (Th. 2.42.4; cf. 2.43.1); they "preferred to die rather than live as cowards" (Dem. 60.28; cf. Isoc. 4.77). Thus, if the war dead could speak, they might

[75] Loraux (1995: 87) observes, "The Athenians wish to hear of nothing but courage, and fear, this undesirable word, has disappeared from the official phraseology of war."

[76] See Lys. 2.58; Dem. 60.21; cf. Plu. *Nic.* 17.4 (Euripides' epitaph for the Athenians who fell in Sicily); Dem. 18.208; Lyc. 1.49. Athenians would have agreed with Democritus (68 fr. 269 D–K) that "Boldness is the beginning of action, but fortune (*tuchē*) is in control of the outcome." On the Athenian "rhetoric of military defeat," see Roisman 2005: 67–71.

[77] Cf. Lyc. 1.46: "The praise of brave men provides an unanswerable refutation of all whose conduct is opposed to theirs."

seek praise on the grounds that, "Although it was possible for us to live dishonorably, we have chosen rather to die nobly" (Pl. *Mx.* 246d2–3; cf. Isoc. 4.94–5). Consistent with this, the *epitaphioi* bestow praise on the war dead for *not* turning away from danger (Th. 2.40.4); *not* playing the coward (2.42.4); *not* being too fond of life (Lys. 2.25); and *not* being sparing even of their lives (Dem. 60.18; cf. Lys. 2.25). While the *epitaphioi* emphatically assert that the war dead did not succumb to cowardice, their repeated acknowledgement of this as a real and plausible alternative to courage suggests that, outside the ideal world of the *epitaphioi*, citizen-soldiers might well fall short in courage.[78]

Although the *epitaphioi* refuse to allow for any hesitation in the face of risk on the part of the war dead, they sometimes assume that the future hoplites in their audiences are fallible and therefore admonish them to emulate the courage of the dead (cf. Ziolkowski 1981: 156–60). Thus, for example, Thucydides' Pericles, in exhorting his audience to imitate the heroic war dead, urges them "Do not watch from the sidelines (μὴ περιορᾶσθε) the dangers of war" (2.43.4, with Rusten 1989: 171), and sets out precisely how they should weigh the alternatives of cowardice and courage: "The degradation arising from cowardice (μετὰ τοῦ μαλακισθῆναι) is more painful than an unperceived death in a moment of strength and common hope" (2.43.6). Similarly, in Plato's *Menexenus* the children of the war dead are exhorted "not to leave the ranks of their ancestors nor to yield to cowardice and beat a retreat" (246b4–5); their fathers would warn them, "if you neglect these precepts and play the coward, no one will receive you gladly" in Hades (247c2–3; cf. *Grg.* 522e). The fact that the *epitaphioi* actively work to persuade the living to choose courage over cowardice is consistent with their view that democratic citizenship involves free and deliberate choices on the part of free men (see Chapter 1).[79]

[78] Likewise, Tyrtaeus envisions cowardice as a very real possibility as he exhorts hoplites to valor (see e.g., frr. 10 and 11).

[79] Balot 2004b: 408–15 (cf. 2001b) makes a good case on the basis of passages including Th. 2.40.2–3, Dem. 60.17–18, and Hyp. fr. A.4 Burtt, that "rational courage," i.e. courage grounded in reason and growing out of intelligent deliberation, figured prominently in Athenian democratic ideology from the late-fifth century on. I am not persuaded, however, by Balot (2004b: 417, 420–2) that Athenian discourse de-emphasized

If the *epitaphioi* characterize the courageous self-sacrifice of the individual as a free choice under democracy, they also suggest that Athenian democracy is uniquely equipped to make this choice an attractive one for its citizens. The city promises the greatest rewards for *aretē* (Th. 2.46), not least of which is the commemoration of its citizens' noble sacrifices in perpetuity through funeral orations and annual ceremonies for the dead (cf. 2.43.2; Ziolkowski 1981: 109–10). At the same time, however, the *epitaphioi* make it clear that cowardice comes at a cost, because shame will accrue to those who betray the city's ideals. While the *epitaphioi* do not typically dwell on this negative theme, Demosthenes' funeral oration expounds upon this and places it within a democratic framework:

> It is impossible [in democracies] to deter freedom of speech (τὴν παρρησίαν), which depends upon speaking the truth, from exposing the truth. For it is not possible for those who commit a shameful act to appease all the citizens, so that even the lone individual, uttering the deserved reproach, makes the guilty wince; for even those who would never speak an accusing word themselves are pleased at hearing the same, provided another utters it. Through fear of such condemnation, all these men [i.e. the war dead], as was to be expected, for shame at the thought of subsequent reproaches, strongly faced the threat arising from our foes and chose a noble death over a disgraceful life. (60.26)

Democratic free speech, according to this assessment, ensures that cowards will suffer the shame that they deserve and thus encourages citizens to choose the noble course of courage (cf. Balot 2004a: 254–5; 2004b: 420).

Although the *epitaphioi* tend to treat cowardice obliquely and more as a potential than an actual problem for the city's hoplites, the spectre of cowardice looms over them and shapes how they address the future hoplites in their audiences who have not yet proven themselves the equals of their dead ancestors. Other forms of public discourse gave

shame and fear of the law as inducements to courage in the late-fifth century and only came to emphasize these in the fourth century (as in Aeschin. 3.175, Dem. 60.26, Lys. 14.15, Lyc. 1.129–30); these inducements are present in the fifth-century record (e.g., Th. 2.42.4, 2.43.1), as Balot (410, 417–18) acknowledges, and our fragmented historical record does not allow us to determine Athenian ideological preferences for one view of courage over another in the late-fifth century.

wider scope to the subject, and allowed for a more blunt treatment of it, at least in evaluating the martial behavior of prominent individuals.

Courage, Cowardice, and Political Leadership. While any Athenian might find his courage or cowardice on campaign a matter of public discussion, for example, when he appeared as a litigant in the popular courts, this was especially common for the elected generals (*stratēgoi*) and self-selected public speakers (*rhētores*) who provided political leadership for the *dēmos*.[80] Political prominence invited close scrutiny not only because it placed individuals in the public limelight but also because it was viewed as a privilege and distinction of which individuals should prove themselves worthy (cf. Ober 1989; Piepenbrink 2001: 148–50). Athenians, like citizens of modern democracies, expected good citizenship of those seeking to lead other citizens (e.g., Aeschin. 1.28–32), including honorable military service; Lysias' client Mantitheus thus alludes to the public's anger at "those who deem it right to manage the city's affairs and yet evade its dangers" (16.17; cf. Din. 1.71).[81] While the ongoing discussion of the citizenship of public figures, including their courage and cowardice, is linked most immediately to the question of political leadership within the city, it is ultimately inseparable from the larger Athenian dialogue concerning the basic obligations of all citizens.

To participate actively in public life in Athens was to expose oneself to abuse of all sorts (cf. Winkler 1990: 46, 55, 58–9; Sommerstein 1996a), including insinuations and allegations concerning bad citizenship in the military sphere. As we have seen, politically prominent individuals were magnets for charges of draft evasion, some of which may have been valid. No less did they draw attacks concerning cowardice and related offenses on campaign. While many of these claims may be outright fabrications, others may have some basis, however thin, in reality. If, for example, a prominent person fled the battlefield in a

[80] For surveys of the many passages in the orators that treat hoplite service, see Voegelin 1943: 33–44; Burckhardt 1996: 154–256; Roisman 2005: 105–29. Military service, like the performance of liturgies, could provide the basis for appeals to public gratitude (*charis*): see e.g., Lys. 16.15–17.

[81] On military service as an important qualification for public speakers, see Roisman 2005: 118–20.

rout along with his comrades, his enemies at home might single out his unheroic behavior for rebuke and ridicule. The attacks on the late-fifth century politician Cleonymus, whom Aristophanes casts repeatedly as an effeminate shield-tosser and coward, probably stem from his participation in the Athenian rout at Delium (424 B.C.).[82] Likewise, the repeated charges of cowardice against the politician Peisander may have arisen from his presence at an Athenian rout.[83] As we shall see, it was Demosthenes' participation in the rout at Chaeronea (338 B.C.) that gave his enemies a foothold for alleging that he was a coward (e.g., Aeschin. 3.152; Din. 1.12). The public may have been receptive to such claims as it sought scapegoats for collective failure; the temptation may have been especially strong, if the public figure – as in the case of Demosthenes – had been an outspoken advocate of the unsuccessful campaign.[84] That the grounds for the charges against these individuals were thin is suggested by the fact that no political rival, as far as we know, actually sought to prosecute any of them for cowardice.

While a public figure's behavior on the battlefield could lead to attacks on his courage and manliness, so too could his public stance concerning martial enterprises. Pericles' critics thus rebuked him as unmanly (Plu. *Per.* 33.6) for his failure as general to lead the Athenians out against the enemy when they were ravaging Attica at the outbreak of the Peloponnesian War. The comic poet Hermippus derides

[82] For these attacks, see Ar. *Nu.* 353–4, 672–80; *V.* 15–27, 592, 821–3; *Pax* 444–6, 674–8, 1295–1304; *Av.* 288–90, 1473–81; Eup. fr. 352 (undated); cf. Ael. *NA* 4.1. The Aristophanic attacks on Cleonymus' cowardice and shield-tossing begin only after Delium and likely stem from his alleged behavior in the rout there: see e.g., Sommerstein 1983: 153; Olson 1998: 167. In Aristophanes' *Knights* (424 B.C.), which antedates the rout at Delium, Cleonymus is mocked as a draft-evader (1369–72), not as a shield-tosser: see Sommerstein 1981: 218; cf. Olson 1998: 167; *pace* Storey 1989: 251.

[83] For these charges, see Ar. *Av.* 1556–8; Eup. fr. 35; Phryn. Com. fr. 21; X. *Smp.* 2.14 (including also the insinuation of draft evasion); cf. Ael. *NA* 4.1; Apostol. 14.14; *Suda* δ 319; Olson 1998: 153–4. Peisander may have participated in the Athenian rout at Spartolus in 429 B.C. (Th. 2.79), if the reference to Pactolus in Eup. fr. 35 is an error for Spartolus (cf. D.S. 12.47.3); see K-A *ad loc.*; Sommerstein 1987: 301; but cf. Storey 2003: 77–8.

[84] Peisander was likely an advocate of the Peloponnesian War (Ar. fr. 84; cf. *Pax* 395); Cleonymus may also have been a hawk, like other popular politicians (see Olson 1998: 167). Cf. how Thucydides (5.10.9) casts the hawkish Cleon as a coward at the rout at Amphipolis. Eup. fr. 394 may be a barb at the alleged cowardice of one of these prominent individuals (see K-A *ad loc.*).

Pericles' impotence, inquiring: "O king of the Satyrs, why ever are you unwilling to get your spear up but rather you provide dire words concerning the war while the soul of a Teles [i.e. a coward] is in you?" (fr. 47.1–4; cf. Th. 2.21.3; Isoc. 8.77; Balot 2004b: 411–12).[85] Similarly, Thucydides reports that Cleon taunted Nicias for failing to seize the military opportunity offered at Pylos (425 B.C.), asserting that "it would be easy if they had men for generals" to succeed (4.27.5; cf. Plu. *Nic.* 7.2).[86] So too, Phocion, who reportedly served some forty-five times as general in the fourth century (Plu. *Phoc.* 8.1), regularly came under fire for his reluctance to take the Athenians out in the field. Plutarch reports that on one such occasion, when the Athenians "called him cowardly and unmanly, he said, 'You cannot make me bold, nor can I make you cowards. However, we know one another'" (*Phoc.* 9.2).

Although the courage of public figures might come under scrutiny in public deliberations over military campaigns, the rhetoric of political debate could turn a proposed campaign into a test of collective manliness (cf. Roisman 2003: 133–6; 2005: 113–16; Balot 2004c: 87–90). Advocates of war in Athens do not hesitate to invoke the city's manly traditions as grounds for embracing a military venture (e.g., Th. 1.144.4; Dem. 3.30, 36; 9.36–40). Their opponents, by contrast, characterize a decision to go on campaign as rash rather than courageous. Thus when Thucydides' Nicias seeks to dissuade the Assembly from pursuing the expedition to Sicily (415 B.C.), he insists it is anything but cowardly for his audience to vote against this dangerous and reckless policy, which he attributes to Alcibiades and his youthful supporters:

It is of such youths, when I see them sitting here in answer to the appeal of this same man [i.e. Alcibiades] that I am afraid; and I make a counterappeal to the older men, if any of you sit by one of these, not to be ashamed that

[85] Contrast the traditions concerning Pericles' bravery on the battlefield found in Plu. *Per.* 7.1, 10.1.

[86] According to Plutarch (*Nic.* 8.1), Nicias' resignation of his command to Cleon, who succeeded at Pylos, "brought great discredit on Nicias. He was thought not merely to have cast away his shield, but to have done something far more disgraceful and base in voluntarily throwing up his command out of cowardice, and in abandoning to his enemy the opportunity for so great a success – actually voting himself out of office."

he may seem to be a coward (μαλακὸς) if he does not vote for war. (6.13.1; cf. Dem. 14.7–8; *Prooem.* 50.1)

Once a campaign was completed, political opponents might continue to contest its implications for manliness, individual and group, especially if the result was defeat; as we shall see, when Demosthenes sought after the battle of Chaeronea (338 B.C.) to justify his role in encouraging Athens to oppose the Macedonians, he argued that he had courageously urged this course of action and that the Athenians, in embarking upon it, had acted consistently with their manly traditions.

While the Athenian public appears to have looked closely at the courage and cowardice of political leaders throughout the classical period, the nature of this scrutiny was affected by an important development. In the fifth century B.C., for the most part the same group of individuals advised the people as public speakers (*rhētores*) and led them on campaign as generals; in the fourth century, however, these two roles diverged and became more specialized, and usually different individuals filled them (Hansen 1991: 268–70). This division may have heightened the public's expectations of generals as members of a professional cadre who should be held accountable for any deficiencies in judgment or courage on campaign (cf. Dem. 18.194). At the same time, this may have increased the likelihood that *rhētores* would be perceived as men of words rather than deeds, and their bold words in endorsing a military campaign as empty rhetoric divorced from experience of war (cf. Roisman 2005: 120–1).[87]

Consider, for example, an anecdote that Plutarch relates concerning the fourth-century general Phocion and the orator Polyeuctes:

When Phocion saw Polyeuctus the Sphettian on a hot day advising the Athenians to go to war with Philip, and then, from much panting and sweating, since he was really very fat, frequently gulping down water, Phocion said: "It is meet that you should be persuaded by this man to go to war; for what do you think he will do under breastplate and shield when the enemy are

[87] Throughout the classical period, Athenians, like other Greeks, were sensitive to the gap between courageous words and cowardly deeds. See e.g., Ant. Soph. 87 fr. 56 D–K: "He is cowardly who is bold in speech concerning absent and future dangers, and hurries on in resolve, but shrinks back when the fact is upon him"; cf. Ar. *Pax* 1172–90; S. *Ph.* 1305–6; fr. 724.

near, if, in making you a premeditated speech, he is in danger of choking to death."(*Phoc.* 9.5; cf. 10.2)[88]

When *rhētores* actually served as hoplites on the expeditions they had endorsed, the public may have been especially on the lookout for any hint of cowardice on their part and been quick to interpret this as evidence that their deeds did not match their words.

Case Study of Demosthenes. Because Demosthenes' career is better documented than that of other Athenian political leaders, it provides our best evidence of how issues of courage and cowardice could arise for public figures. Questions of courage and cowardice on and off the battlefield are prominent in the cross-fire between Demosthenes and his enemies at several points in his career.

Charges of cowardice crop up conspicuously within the ongoing bitter rivalry between Demosthenes and his arch-enemy Meidias, a wealthy man, who – like Demosthenes – was active as a public speaker (Dem. 21.202–3).[89] While the two had been personal enemies since 364/3 B.C. (21.78–80), hostilities between them flared up when Meidias struck Demosthenes in the face when he was serving as *chorēgos* at the City Dionysia in spring of 348; this eventually led to Demosthenes' prosecution of Meidias in 347/6.[90] In his speech from this prosecution, Demosthenes asserts that sometime after the assault (cf. 21.106) Meidias induced a certain Euktemon to initiate a prosecution for desertion of the ranks against him:

Now, I shall say nothing of the fact that he procured a prosecution for desertion (*lipotaxion*) against me, and hired the man to do this, that overly pliable scoundrel "dusty" Euktemon. That sykophant did not even proceed to the preliminary inquiry in the case, nor did Meidias hire him for any purpose except to get posted up in front of the eponymous heroes for all to see, "Euktemon of Lousia prosecuted Demosthenes of Paiania for desertion" – and

[88] On demagogues as physically unfit for war, see X. *Cyn.* 13.11 ("in body they are disgracefully unfit for war, because they are incapable of toil"); cf. S. fr. 963. On fat men as bad soldiers, see Pl. *R.* 556d; cf. X. *Mem.* 3.12.1–3.

[89] On the history of their enmity, see MacDowell 1990: 1–13; cf. D. Cohen 1995: 90–101. I rely on MacDowell's chronology in what follows.

[90] On the question of what legal action Demosthenes employed, see MacDowell 1990: 13–23.

I think he would gladly have had added, if it had somehow been possible, that Meidias hired him to prosecute! But I pass over that; for a prosecution for which the man has disfranchised himself by not proceeding, I need no further compensation, I have sufficient. (21.103; cf. Aeschin. 2.148)

The most plausible context for this allegation of desertion is that Demosthenes had left his fellow hoplites on the Euboean campaign of early 348 (21.133) to perform a *chorēgia* in connection with the Dionysia in spring of that year; this was, in fact, probably in keeping with Athenian rules concerning release from military service and Euktemon's charge therefore a false one (MacDowell 1990: 5–6, 9). If Demosthenes felt vindicated by Euktemon's disfranchisement for failing to pursue this trumped-up charge, however, this did not stop him from retaliating directly and in kind against Meidias for this attack on his manly reputation.

In his prosecution of Meidias for the assault at the Dionysia, Demosthenes turns the charge of desertion back against him. Soon after relating the Euktemon episode, Demosthenes states with indignation, "he [Meidias] got me prosecuted for desertion, though he has deserted his post three times himself" (21.110). Later in his speech, Demosthenes elaborates on this claim, casting Meidias as a "damned coward" (21.164), who in the course of the Euboean campaign deserted the cavalry twice and active service as trierarch once (21.160–6).[91] This clearly was tit-for-tat, because Meidias had arranged for a charge of *lipotaxion* to be brought against Demosthenes in connection with the same campaign. While neither charge nor countercharge appears to have any firm basis (MacDowell 1990: 6–7, 9), this exchange well illustrates how central such claims could be in public life and how sensitive public figures might be to them.

Just as Demosthenes was angered by Meidias' attack upon his military record, so too was Demosthenes' political rival Aeschines incensed when Demosthenes took a potshot at his record. In the course of his prosecution of Aeschines in 343 B.C. for his role as envoy to Macedon three years earlier, Demosthenes alleges that once, when Aeschines was shouted down in the Assembly for supporting a petition from Philip's

[91] On Demosthenes' claim that Meidias deserted thrice, see MacDowell 1990: 334.

envoys, as he descended from the speakers' platform, "he said that there were plenty of shouters, but few ready to go on campaign when it is necessary"; Demosthenes then immediately snipes, "He is a wondrous soldier himself I suppose, O Zeus!" (19.113; cf. 282; 18.129).[92] Demosthenes' sarcasm evokes a lengthy reply from Aeschines in his defense speech (2.167–9); taking Demosthenes' snipe as his starting point (2.167), Aeschines details his very full and distinguished military record – he even received a crown on the spot for his bravery in the battle of Tamynae and another on his return home (2.169).[93] In light of Aeschines' military record, which he corroborates by citing a decree and calling witnesses (2.170) – including a taxiarch from Demosthenes' own tribe, Pandionis (2.169; cf. Dem. 21.13), Demosthenes' barb appears to have been entirely gratuitous, and Aeschines' anger at it understandable.

Demosthenes' snipe at Aeschines' hoplite service in 343, which clearly struck a raw nerve at the time, may help explain the curious fact that Aeschines, in his prosecution of Ctesiphon (330 B.C.), repeatedly characterizes Demosthenes as a coward and deserter of the ranks at Chaeronea (338 B.C.). Scholars have puzzled over why Aeschines would place such weight on these charges, especially because the Athenian public would not have selected Demosthenes to deliver the *epitaphios* for the war dead from Chaeronea (Dem. 18.285–6; Aeschin. 3.152), if such a view were widely held (thus e.g., Yunis 2001: 245). One explanation, I would suggest, is that Aeschines viewed Demosthenes' participation in the Athenian rout at Chaeronea – in pursuit of Demosthenes' policy of confrontation with Macedon (3.244) – as a golden opportunity to retaliate in kind for Demosthenes' attack upon

[92] Cf. Demosthenes' similar claim that Meidias rebukes the Assembly, "You don't go out on campaigns, and you don't think you need to pay the war tax" (21.203). As MacDowell (1990: 408) observes, Demosthenes himself sometimes levels these very criticisms against Athenians in his harangues: see e.g., 8.21–3; cf. Plu. *Phoc.* 23.2 (attributing such criticisms to Phocion).

[93] While Aeschines claims he is presenting his military record not because of the slander against him but rather due to his vulnerability as a defendant in a public trial (2.167), he is likely doing so for both reasons. Note also that Aeschines attacks Demosthenes' military record, recalling his indictment for *lipotaxion* (2.148; cf. Dem. 21.103). On this exchange between Demosthenes and Aeschines concerning military service, see Burkhardt 1996: 237–9; Paulsen 1999: 406–8; Roisman 2005: 118–19.

his hoplite service. If Aeschines' prosecution of Ctesiphon for proposing that Demosthenes be honored with a crown in the Theater of Dionysus can be viewed as retaliation for Demosthenes' prosecution of Aeschines in 343 (D. Cohen 1995: 77–82), this also provided Aeschines a venue for retaliating against Demosthenes for specific claims made on that earlier occasion, including the snipe at his military service.[94] In any event, the exchange between Aeschines and Demosthenes at the trial of Ctesiphon, where Demosthenes spoke in support of Ctesiphon and in defense of his own record as statesman which was under attack, provides an intriguing glimpse into the politics and poetics of cowardice in Athenian public life.

At the opening of his prosecution, Aeschines portrays his opponents as perverse hoplites who are forming their "battle line" (τὴν παράταξιν) for the current trial to keep justice from taking its proper course (3.1). Consistent with this martial imagery, he seeks to enlist the jury for the upcoming battle: "But as each of you would be ashamed to desert the post (τὴν τάξιν λιπεῖν) to which he had been assigned in war, so now you should be ashamed to desert the post to which the laws have called you as guards of the democracy this day" (3.7). The full significance of this military imagery emerges when, about halfway through his speech (3.148), Aeschines begins his assault on Demosthenes as coward and deserter.

At the root of Aeschines' attack is his assertion that Demosthenes abandoned the ranks at Chaeronea and, upon returning home, "ran away" from the city (e.g., 3.159, 253). The first charge is most likely a distortion of the fact that Demosthenes fled the field at Chaeronea with the routed Athenian force (D.S. 16.86.4; cf. Din. 1.12).[95] The second charge is a hostile interpretation of the fact that Demosthenes left the city after Chaeronea to collect money from Athenian allies (cf. Din. 1.80–1); while Demosthenes, as a prime instigator of the

[94] Cf. Carey 2000: 162: "One interesting aspect of the duel is the complex dialogue between the speeches of 330 and those of 343."

[95] Later tradition embellishes the slander further: see Plu. *Dem.* 20.2; [Plu.] *Mor.* 845f. G. L. Cawkwell (*OCD*[3] 457 s.v. "Demosthenes"), however, makes too little of Demosthenes' participation in the rout: "Demosthenes was present at the battle, and returned so quickly to organize the city's defences that Aeschines could accuse him of running away."

campaign, may have feared for his safety after the Macedonian victory and have been happy to be away from the city for a time (Ellis 1976: 200, with 296 n. 88; cf. Worthington 1992: 247, 250), this was hardly flight, pure and simple (Dem. 18.248; [Plu.] *Mor.* 846a).[96]

Although the basis of these charges can be reconstructed from Aeschines' invocation of them (cf. Din. 1.80–2), Aeschines does not present them methodically or coherently, but rather peppers his speech with frequent references to Demosthenes' cowardice, *astrateia*, and *lipotaxion*.[97] There are two likely explanations for Aeschines' approach here. First, Aeschines is seeking to exploit charges that are already familiar to his audience (3.175); when Demosthenes came under public attack and prosecution soon after Chaeronea (Dem. 18.249–50), his enemies no doubt availed themselves of these and other allegations.[98] Second, the bases of these claims are sufficiently thin that Aeschines does not wish to expose this by dwelling in detail on them; he probably had no specific information concerning Demosthenes' flight from Chaeronea and no evidence to prove that he had left the city subsequently for anything but patriotic motives.[99]

While Aeschines' assault on Demosthenes is rooted in his alleged violations of the basic duties of a hoplite, he weaves these charges into his indictment of Demosthenes as a *rhētōr* who deserves public censure rather than honor. Aeschines repeatedly points to the paradox that the very public speaker who had ill-advisedly pressed the Athenian

[96] Cf. how ambassadors are sometimes attacked as draft-evaders (Ar. *Ach.* 598–609; *Nu.* 685–93, with MacDowell 1971: 139).

[97] See Aeschin. 3.148, 151, 152, 155, 159, 160, 161, 163, 167, 170, 175, 181, 187, 212, 214, 226, 231, 243, 244, 247, 253.

[98] As observed above (note 63), the general Lysicles, who survived Chaeronea, was condemned to death on his return (D.S. 16.88.1). Aeschines (3.252) alludes to two further prosecutions in the aftermath of Chaeronea: 1) the immediate prosecution, and condemnation to death, of an individual who had sought to flee from Athens to Samos after the battle; 2) the very recent prosecution of Leocrates, who had fled Athens for Rhodes after Chaeronea. Lycurgus 1: *Against Leocrates*, the prosecution speech in the latter case, survives. Sullivan (2002: 4; cf. Allen 2000b: 28–9) suggests that Aeschines may be mimicking elements of Lycurgus' prosecution – which she believes was successful – including its emphasis on cowardice and desertion.

[99] Note that Aeschines stops short of claiming that Demosthenes had abandoned his weapons on the battlefield; as mentioned above in the text, an unsubstantiated allegation of this could lead to a slander suit.

people to confront Philip fled in a cowardly manner from Chaeronea: "how outrageous then fellow citizens, if Demosthenes, who made the motion for that final campaign, and then betrayed the soldiers, is to receive honor from you" (244–5; cf. 152, 226).[100] Consistent with Demosthenes' unmanly behavior on the battlefield, Aeschines claims, is his cowardice as a *rhētōr* after Chaeronea, which has kept him from advocating action against Alexander when opportunities have presented themselves: "And yet the public opportunity does not wait for the cowardice of the orator (ῥητορικὴν δειλίαν)" (163). A proper, democratic *rhētōr*, Aeschines asserts, "ought to be a man of brave heart, that in danger and peril he may not desert the people" (170). Demosthenes in his reply, as we shall see, chooses to focus on this assault on his courage as *rhētōr* rather than on the question of his battlefield mettle.[101]

Demosthenes responds shrewdly to his opponent's indictment of him as a coward. His only direct reply to the charges of *lipotaxion* is to characterize these twice as mere taunts. On the first occasion, he inquires: "Are you not ashamed to taunt a man for cowardice (εἴς τε μαλακίαν), and then to require that same man to overcome the power of Philip single-handed, and to do it by mere words?" (18.245). On the second occasion, as Demosthenes mocks Aeschines for his earlier career as actor, he quips, "there was no truce or armistice in the warfare between you and your audiences, and since you received many wounds from them it is no wonder you taunt as cowards (ὡς δειλοὺς) those of us who have no experience of such engagements" (18.262). Demosthenes presumably calculated that he had nothing to gain by dwelling on Aeschines' particular allegations: he therefore passes over

[100] Cf. the assertion attributed to Demades (fr. 28 Burtt): "But the cowardly statesmen, leading out the flower of the city to Boeotia, led them to a graveyard." Demades himself, who was taken prisoner at Chaeronea (D.S. 16.87.1), came under fire later for "desertion" (Polyeuctus fr. 1 Baiter-Sauppe, cited by Yunis 2001: 245).

[101] On "courage" in advising the Athenian public as a frequently invoked trait of the ideal, democratic *rhētōr*, see Balot 2004a: 243, 246–53; Roisman 2004: 268–76; 2005: 142–5; cf. the kindred construction of the comic poet as a courageous adviser to the public (Rosen and Sluiter 2003b: 13–20; Rademaker 2003: 121). While in many instances Athenian *rhētores* were translating military ideals to the civic realm when they spoke of their own courage as speakers (Balot 2004a: 249), the question of actual military behavior pervades the exchanges between Aeschines and Demosthenes.

not only the charge of *lipotaxion* at Chaeronea but also the claim that he had abandoned the city when he went on his diplomatic mission after the battle (cf. 18.248).

It was not sufficient, however, for Demosthenes simply to dismiss Aeschines' allegations. These charges, which Aeschines had made central to his speech, were potentially damaging within the current trial and for Demosthenes' reputation after the trial.[102] Demosthenes, therefore, seeks to undercut these by transforming the issue of martial cowardice raised by Aeschines – which he did not wish to address directly – solely into a question of his courage and patriotism in advising the *dēmos* as *rhētōr* (cf. Dem. 8.68–70). While this does not constitute a direct rebuttal of Aeschines' charges of cowardice in battle and in fleeing the city, it allows Demosthenes to turn the charge of "desertion" back upon Aeschines in his deficient role as *rhētōr*.[103]

Central to Demosthenes' transformation of the contest between himself and Aeschines from the battlefield to the political arena is his application of military metaphors to public life. While Aeschines, at the opening of his speech, had applied these critically to Demosthenes' maneuvering in advance of trial, Demosthenes marshals these metaphors to advance an image of himself as a public figure who presents himself for "review at muster" (*exetasis*) and courageously remains in his post (*taxis*) in the battles of public life:

> Alone among your orators and statesmen I did not desert the post of patriotism (τὴν τῆς εὐνοίας τάξιν) in time of peril, but I was present at the muster (ἐξηταζόμην), advocating and proposing what should be done on your behalf in the midst of panic.(18.173; cf. 304)

Although Aeschines' attack on Demosthenes singles him out as a deserter of the ranks at Chaeronea (cf. Din. 1.12) and seeks to hold him solely responsible for the city's defeat by Philip (cf. Dem. 18.212, 245), Demosthenes asserts that he *alone* stood his place in the ranks as *rhētōr* in time of crisis. On the basis of his courage in doing so, Demosthenes asserts his superiority to Aeschines: "I am a better citizen than you,

102 They continued, in fact, to hound Demosthenes up until the end of his career: see e.g., Din. 1.12, 80–2 (323 B.C.).

103 Yunis (2001: 245) is not entirely right therefore to say, "Mostly D[emosthenes] ignores the charge of cowardice . . . "

insofar as I devoted myself to a course of action that seemed expedient to all, neither shirking nor even counting any personal danger" (18.197). Indeed, while Demosthenes bravely stood at his political post, Aeschines and other public speakers were ready to appear for muster (*exetasis*) and stand at their post (*taxis*) to serve the city's enemies after Chaeronea (18.320).[104]

Some scholars have been reluctant to accept that Demosthenes' invocation of these military metaphors was prompted by Aeschines' attack on him for *lipotaxion*; they point out that Demosthenes had used these in earlier orations (e.g., 3.36; 15.32–3; 19.9) and argue, therefore, that they need have no special significance here (Yunis 2001: 207; cf. Wankel 1976: 1.379, 2.866). While it is true that Demosthenes had employed these figures on earlier occasions, the frequency with which he uses them in this oration and the manner in which he does so are best explained by Aeschines' multiple attacks upon him in the current context as a deserter of his comrades at Chaeronea and of the city after the battle (cf. Dorjahn 1940: 340; Usher 1993: 232).

Although Demosthenes invokes military metaphors to glorify his performance as *rhētōr* and to undercut Aeschines' attacks on him as coward, he is careful to distinguish his responsibilities from those of the city's generals. In keeping with the split between the two offices that had emerged in the fourth century, Demosthenes insists that he should be held accountable for the policy of confrontation with Macedon that he had advocated, not for the execution of this policy on the battlefield because this was in the hands of the city's generals (18.194, 212, 245, 303–4). Demosthenes for his part had fulfilled his duty as *rhētōr* (18.173, quoted above) by advocating a courageous policy that was worthy of the Athenian people and their traditions (18.68, 193) and by encouraging others to "an eager desire to do their duties (τὰ δέοντα)" as citizens (18.246). To hold him personally responsible for the city's military failure at Chaeronea is to misunderstand his obligations as *rhētōr* and to fail to appreciate his courage in fulfilling his self-appointed political post (18.221).

[104] For the the *exetasis* metaphor, see 18.173, 197, 217, 277, 310, 320; for the *taxis* metaphor, see Dem. 18.62, 138, 173, 192, 221, 304, 320.

While individual political reputations are at stake in the exchange between Aeschines and Demosthenes over courage and cowardice, both orators suggest that broader questions of citizen valor are involved. Thus Aeschines warns the jurors:

> Cast your vote, then, not only as men giving a verdict, but also as men in the public eye, to be called to account by the citizens who, though they are not now present, will nevertheless ask you what your verdict was. For be assured, men of Athens, the city will be held to be of like character with the man who is proclaimed [i.e. when crowned in the Theater]. And it is a reproach for you to be likened, not to your ancestors, but to the cowardice (τῇ ἀνανδρίᾳ) of Demosthenes. (3.247)

Demosthenes, by contrast, invites his audience to identify his courage with their own. His personal courage in public life and the courageous policy he had advocated are consistent with Athenian shared values and citizen ideals (18.193; cf. 68). If Demosthenes' policy of confrontation led Athenians to face Philip at Chaeronea and the Macedonians prevailed, this brings no shame to the *rhētōr* who courageously pursued this policy or to the Athenians who fought bravely at Chaeronea; neither can be held accountable for turns of fortune (*tuchē*) (18.192–4; cf. Yunis 2001: 17). The Athenian jurors who voted overwhelmingly against Aeschines in this trial (Plu. *Dem.* 24.2–5; [Plu.] *Mor.* 840c) chose not to hold Demosthenes accountable for Chaeronea and simultaneously exculpated themselves and their fellow Athenians from any shame that might attach to their collective rout and defeat.

The conspicuous place of charges and countercharges of cowardice in Demosthenes' political career confirms their importance in the competition among Athens' political elite before the public. The public's interest in these exchanges can be explained in part by their expectation that those providing political leadership to other citizens should themselves embrace a high standard of citizenship. At the same time, however, this interest likely reflects broader Athenian concerns about hoplite performance and the obligation of citizens to serve honorably on campaign. The fact that politically active individuals were perhaps most likely to come under fire for cowardice when they had participated in Athenian routs, as Demosthenes had at Chaeronea, suggests the close link between this individual scrutiny and group experience. While politically prominent Athenians, as magnets for charges of cowardice in such circumstances, were vulnerable to isolation from the group and scapegoating, Demosthenes' successful rebuttal of Aeschines' attacks upon him suggests that the Athenian public was not always eager to blame its political leaders for collective military failures; indeed, it might – on occasion at least – identify with, rather than scapegoat, members of the political elite who shared in their military defeats.

The subject of citizen cowardice was a highly sensitive one for the Athenian democracy. Notwithstanding civic and cultural ideals of martial valor, Athenian hoplites – like other Greek hoplites – sometimes fell short on the battlefield, and engaged in behavior individually and collectively that could be construed as shameful. Naturally, those involved put the best face on their behavior in the immediate aftermath of battle, denying any charges of shameless behavior and shifting blame to others in keeping with the dynamics of honor competition that operated throughout a campaign. Because hoplites had only limited knowledge of the behavior of their fellows during a battle and, in particular, in the course of a rout – where dishonorable behavior was most likely to occur – there was considerable latitude for finger-pointing and face-saving after a battle.

The city responded selectively to the performance of hoplites when its forces returned home from a campaign. In the case of group performance, the city was prepared to bestow praise and honor on victorious forces, as long as the city itself was allowed to share in the glory of their achievements. By contrast, it largely overlooked any deficiencies in group performance, allowing routed forces to disband upon their return without any institutional scrutiny or public humiliation. Not surprisingly, Athenians chose not to dwell on moments of collective embarrassment that might damage the city's reputation and call into question the claim of civic ideology that democratic citizens consistently act with courage. This did not, however, stop Athenians from scapegoating the generals of defeated forces and holding them accountable for what had transpired on campaign.

In the case of the performance of average hoplites, the city sometimes singled out individuals not only on the basis of outstanding performance in battle but also for deficient behavior. The city's laws allowed for the prosecution of cowardice and related offenses on the part of individuals. Such prosecutions, however, appear to have been uncommon because of practical and social obstacles to bringing them, and the penalty of *atimia* imposed on those convicted was in any case a moderate one in keeping with democratic values. By contrast, there was considerable scope to the public discussion of politically prominent persons who were alleged to have shown cowardice in battle. This discussion had a twofold significance for Athenians: through it the public could reflect on what qualified exceptional individuals to provide political leadership and on the citizen ideals that average Athenians were to embrace while serving as hoplites.

4

THE ARTFUL TAX DODGER

> What is the duty of a respectable citizen?... Is it not his duty, when the city needs money, to be among the first to pay the war tax and not to conceal any part of his wealth? (Is. 7.40)

A fundamental obligation of Athenian citizenship, as we have seen, was to serve the city in time of war and to perform this service honorably, even up to the point of death on the battlefield. The Attic funeral orations envision the sacrifice made by Athens' hoplites as a worthy and necessary "expenditure" on behalf of the city that all citizens should be willing to make.[1] If good citizenship could entail this ultimate, metaphorical expenditure, it comes as no surprise that it could also require a man to put his financial resources at the city's disposal. This obligation, however, fell primarily on the city's wealthiest citizens, who were called upon to pay the irregularly imposed war tax (*eisphora*) and, more routinely, to perform expensive public services (liturgies), including the maintenance and supervision of a trireme (the trierarchy) or the financing and training of a chorus for one of the city's festivals (the *chorēgia*). Taxation in most societies is unpopular and a source of complaint and resentment; this was conspicuously the case in democratic Athens, where it fell exclusively on a small but powerful group of individuals. This chapter explores the often tense

[1] For this trope in the *epitaphioi*, see Ziolkowski 1981: 111; cf. Dem. 18.66; Ar. *Lys.* 651–5, with 589–90. For challenges to the equation of lives with money, see E. *Supp.* 775–7; A. *A.* 437–44.

relationship between the city and its wealthiest citizens over financial obligations.

In examining this subject, I seek to build upon my earlier treatment of it (Christ 1990) and, in particular, to locate the attitudes and actions of elite citizens in the broader context of citizen psychology and behavior in Athens. Viewed in isolation, devious behavior among the elite may appear to be *sui generis*, a product of the unique circumstances and anxieties of a class responding to the demands placed upon it by the democracy. Viewed together with other forms of unpatriotic behavior, however, bad citizenship among the elite looks more like a variation on a common Athenian pattern of behavior. As we shall see, while evasive practices on the part of the wealthy could arise from oligarchic opposition to the democracy, these – like other manifestations of bad citizenship in Athens – were often inspired by more mundane and selfish motivations. Indeed, rich Athenians may have been no different fundamentally from their fellow citizens in responding to civic obligations; they just had more money.[2]

Further impetus for a fresh look at tax evasion in Athens comes from the appearance of new scholarship relevant to it. Of particular interest are in-depth studies of the trierarchy (Gabrielsen 1994) and *chorēgia* in Athens (Wilson 2000), which illuminate the institutions governing liturgies and thus pave the way for a better understanding of how evasion might be effected. Although I will draw repeatedly on the institutional insights of each study, in my view both tend to overestimate how much wealthy men were driven by "love of honor" (*philotimia*) to perform liturgies and underestimate the scope of liturgy avoidance and the challenges this posed for the city.[3] While public discourse lauded *philotimia* in the liturgical sphere, not all men were equally drawn to

[2] Cf. Ernest Hemingway's famous quip on the rich (Bartlett 1980: 845: 7).

[3] Wilson underestimates opposition to the liturgical system, restricting it largely to oligarchic individuals (2000: 184–7). Although Gabrielsen uncovers serious and ongoing resistance to the trierarchy (1994: 84, 180; 224–5), he still maintains that *philotimia* persisted in this sphere and that the system ultimately worked (48–9; 59–60; 90; 101; 219–20; 225–6). Each study's focus on a single type of liturgy also discourages a broader view of strategies that the wealthy may have adopted vis à vis their diverse obligations: see below in the text.

this civic virtue and even those who were enticed by it prudently balanced the pursuit of honor with the preservation of wealth.

In calling for a reassessment of the role of *philotimia* in the behavior of the wealthy, I build on the observations of E. E. Cohen (1992). In his study of Athenian banking, Cohen argues that wealthy Athenians frequently concealed money in banks to dodge their financial obligations to the city; he therefore rejects "the romantic notion that Athenian taxpayers gloried in paying governmental charges and contended in *agonistic* fervor to advance ever-greater sums" (199). While Cohen goes too far in questioning the contemporary significance of *philotimia* (cf. Millett 1998: 246 n. 28), in my view he is right to emphasize that Athenians tended to behave rationally and cautiously concerning their fortunes. In fact, as we shall see, a wealthy man might seek to have his cake and eat it too, by balancing the pursuit of prestige, which carried both symbolic and concrete advantages, with his obvious interest in preserving his fortune.[4]

I will begin with an overview of the rather complex rules and institutions governing the liturgical system and collection of the *eisphora*, and then consider how friction between the wealthy and the city may have shaped these arrangements as they took form over time. I will then examine closely why wealthy men regarded their financial obligations with ambivalence, concern, and sometimes outright resentment, notwithstanding the appeal of *philotimia*, and explore the options available to them to evade their obligations or to reduce their liability to these.

[4] In characterizing wealthy Athenians as "rational," I do not mean to suggest they pursued only material well-being in the manner of the "rational actors" of modern economic theory; it was rational in this social context for wealthy Athenians to pursue status as well as material prosperity (cf. Amemiya 2005: 158–9). For an attempt (unsuccessful in my view) to apply a rational-actor perspective to the emergence of liturgies in Athens, see Lyttkens 1997.

On the Athenian pursuit of economic and financial interests within social parameters, see Christesen 2003: 31–4; cf. Osborne 1991: 129–32, 135–6; Burke 1992; Shipton 1997: 411–12; 2001; Cartledge 2002a: 160–2. In my view, Meier (1990: 146) is mistaken in positing (in Weberian terms), "we may say that the Athenians, as *homines politici*, were less concerned with their economic needs and hardships than we *homines oeconomici*." For surveys of the ongoing debate over the Athenian economy, see Morris 1994; Cartledge 2002b; cf. Morris and Manning 2005.

FINANCIAL OBLIGATIONS: RULES AND INSTITUTIONS

Wealthy Athenians were called upon to support their city in two distinct ways, through the regular performance of liturgies and the payment of the *eisphora*, a tax which was imposed as needed in time of war. While liturgies typically required not only the expenditure of large sums of money but also personal service, the *eisphora* was a tax that entailed simply the payment of money. Although the performance of liturgies was ultimately compulsory, voluntarism was encouraged and lauded by the city, and the wealthy often had some choice concerning which liturgy to perform, when to do so, and how extravagantly to carry it out. By contrast, there was no veneer of voluntarism with the *eisphora*; its payment was mandatory, and the city determined how much was due and when.

Liturgies can be divided into two groups, festival and military (Davies 1967: 33).[5] Festivals were an integral feature of civic life, and their success depended largely on the efforts of liturgists. Each year, the city needed at least 97 wealthy men to perform festival liturgies; in years of the quadrennial Great Panathenaia, the number rose to over 118 (*ibid.* 40). While these liturgies took many different forms, the most important and best attested is the *chorēgia*, which entailed training and financing a chorus for a tragic, comic, or dithyrambic performance.[6] A festival liturgy could cost anywhere from a few hundred drachmas to several thousand, depending on the type of service and the extravagance with which it was carried out; a successful *chorēgia* might well involve costs at the upper end of this range (Lys. 21.1–5; Davies 1971: xxi).[7]

In the military sphere, the city relied on wealthy men to perform the trierarchy, that is, to maintain a trireme in the city's navy and supervise its crew for a year. While the city provided the ship and some initial funds for the crew, effective operation of a trireme could require a trierarch to spend heavily on the ship, its officers, and its crew.

5 Wilson (2000: 46–7) points out, however, that the festivals supported by liturgies sometimes cultivated military practices and values.

6 In discussing festival liturgies in this chapter, I will therefore focus on the *chorēgia*.

7 These were very large sums by the standards of average Athenians: In the late-fifth century, a skilled worker might receive a drachma for a day's labor; by the late fourth century, the daily wage for such a worker was twice this (see Markle 1985: 265, with n. 1; cf. Loomis 1998: 232–50).

Typical costs may have ranged between 4,000 and 6,000 drachmas (Davies 1971: xxi–xxii; Gabrielsen 1994: 49–50). The city needed several hundred trierarchs each year to support its fleet in the late-fifth century B.C. ([X.] *Ath. Pol.* 3.4; Gabrielsen 1994: 176–9). When difficulties surrounding the recruitment of trierarchs led to the sharing of trierarchic duties between two men (the syntrierarchy) in the last decade of the fifth century, this increased the number of trierarchs needed. Further problems led to the establishment in 357 B.C. of naval tax groups (*symmoriai*), 20 groups of 60 men each; the members of each *symmoria* shared trierarchic costs and obligations. This arrangement was, in turn, refined further in 340 to improve the distribution of costs within groups. I will return to these developments and their circumstances below.

The *eisphora* is best documented in the period after its reform in *ca.* 378/7 B.C. (Hansen 1991: 112–15). From this time, eligible individuals were divided into 100 tax groups (*symmoriai*) of up to 15 members each; within each group, the three wealthiest members were responsible for the advance payment (*proeisphora*) of the group's tax liability, and it was up to them to collect from each member his share.[8] The *proeisphora*, with the risk of financial loss that went with it, was treated as a liturgy and was subject to the same rules as other liturgies. How exactly the *eisphora* was administered through the *symmoriai* is controversial. In my view, whenever the Assembly voted to collect the *eisphora*, it divided the total sum sought equally among the 100 *symmoriai*; within each *symmoria* each individual paid a share of the group's collective liability in proportion to his own assessment (*timēma*) of his total wealth, which was subject to review by the members of his group (Harp. s.v. διάγραμμα; cf. Isoc. 17.41).[9] From 347/6 a regular *eisphora* was levied

[8] Scholars continue to debate whether these *symmoriai* and those established in 358/7 B.C. for naval purposes were identical: see e.g., Hansen 1991: 112–15, arguing for identity; and Gabrielsen 1994: 183–90, arguing against this. The *proeisphora* may have been established only some years after 378/7: see Wallace 1989: 483–5, 487; Christ (forthcoming).

[9] For this reconstruction of how the *symmoriai* worked, see Christ (forthcoming); cf. Andreades 1933: 1.337–8. I am not persuaded by Ste. Croix (1953: 34, 58) that the Assembly simply levied the *eisphora* as a percentage tax of between one and two percent on each individual's *timēma*. While the total amount the city sought to raise on a particular occasion could be expressed as a percentage of the most recent figure available for the aggregate *timēma* of the *symmoriai* (Dem. 14.27, 19), this does not necessarily

each year to raise ten talents (*IG* II^2 244.12–13; 505.14–17); irregular levies, however, were still sometimes imposed by the Assembly (Din. 1.69).

The arrangements governing the *eisphora* before 378 are not at all clear.[10] From 428, when the *eisphora* first appears in our record (Th. 3.19.1; see below), to 378 wealthy men were probably directly liable for their individual payments. Wealthy citizens during this period may have paid a fixed amount, rather than an amount in proportion to their declared wealth (*timēma*) as was the case later.[11] There is no secure evidence, in fact, that citizens produced a *timēma* of their wealth before the reforms of 378/7;[12] while the *timēma* is attested in connection with a metic *eisphora* of *ca.* 394/3 (Isoc. 17.49, with 41), special rules apparently governed metics and we cannot assume that the citizen *eisphora* was handled in the same manner at this time.[13] Although fixed *eisphora* payments for citizens would not take into account their different levels of wealth, this would be consistent with the fact that the city's liturgical system apparently did not do so in this period (see below).

Selection

How were wealthy men identified and selected to pay the *eisphora* and to carry out liturgies? The procedures surrounding selection of those

mean that individuals within the *symmoriai* paid this same percentage. It was efficient for the city to divide the total *eisphora* equally among the one hundred *symmoriai*, as this facilitated speedy payment of the *proeisphora* by the three wealthiest members of each *symmoria*; the tax shares of individuals within the *symmoriai* could then be worked out later at leisure on the basis of their current *timēmata*, which took into account changes in their wealth.

[10] The views set forth in this paragraph are developed in detail in Christ (forthcoming).

[11] In this earlier period, there is no suggestion that citizens who are liable to the *eisphora* pay different amounts: individuals simply assert that they have paid large sums in *eisphorai* (Lys. 21.3; 19.43; cf. Ant. 2.2.12), not that their payments exceeded those of their wealthy peers.

[12] Scholars have too often assumed that the *eisphora* was based on an individual's *timēma* through its life: see e.g., Thomsen 1964: 183; Davies 1971: 593; 1981: 146; Brun 1983: 9; cf. Ste. Croix 1953: 34 n. 20. Although a fragmentary decree passed in 415 B.C. in connection with the launching of the Sicilian expedition (*ML* 78 fr. c) contains the words ἀπὸ τô τιμέματος (l. 2) and ἐσφέρεν (l. 5), the sense of τίμημα is obscure here (Rhodes 1981: 136–7) and its connection to ἐσφέρεν, which may not even refer to taxation in this context, is not clear.

[13] On the metic *eisphora*, see Ste. Croix 1953: 32 n. 5; Whitehead 1977: 78–80.

liable to the *eisphora* are not clear. The generals were probably responsible throughout the life of the *eisphora* for its administration: we know that after 378 B.C. the generals designated the *proeispherontes* (Dem. 42.5, 14), and they likely also formed the *symmoriai* within which these individuals served (Dem. 39.8) (Wallace 1989: 481, with n. 25); they are the logical candidates for administration of the war tax before 378 as well, because they were responsible for military expeditions. Before the reforms of 378, whenever the Assembly voted to impose an *eisphora*, the generals may have called upon the demarchs to report to them concerning wealthy individuals in their demes, and used this information to compile a list of men liable to the *eisphora* (cf. Ar. *Eq.* 923–6); the generals may then have relied upon the demarchs to collect the tax from these individuals (Davies 1981: 143–50; Rhodes 1982: 13–14; Whitehead 1986: 132–3). After 378, this awkward arrangement of identifying payers of the *eisphora* whenever it was levied was probably abandoned: once wealthy men were assigned to symmories, they appear to have remained in these, with some adjustments in membership made periodically to keep the wealth of each *symmoria* in rough parity with all others (*Suda* α 2092, s.v. ἀνασύνταξις). The generals designated within each symmory the three wealthiest individuals as payers of the *proeisphora*; these persons, as noted above, paid their group's total tax straightaway and then collected payments from their fellow members.[14] Throughout the history of the *eisphora*, those assigned to pay it had no way – within the bounds of the law at least – to win release from this obligation: no regular exemptions were recognized (Dem. 20.18) and no legal procedures available for seeking release.[15]

The process by which liturgies were assigned is somewhat better attested. Civic officials were responsible for matching up wealthy men with the festival and military liturgies that fell under their supervision. For example, the eponymous archon directly sought out candidates to serve as *chorēgoi* for the tragedies at the City Dionysia, but relied

[14] Wallace (1989: 481–2) argues on the basis of [Dem.] 50.8 that the three hundred *proeispherontes* were identified anew through the demes each time the *eisphora* was levied.

[15] While a man could win release from the liturgy of the *proeisphora* through *antidosis* (Dem. 42.3–4, 25), he presumably remained liable for his individual share of the *eisphora*.

upon the tribes to submit to him names of *chorēgoi* for the men's and boys' dithyrambic choruses at this festival and the Thargelia; he also selected *chorēgoi* for the comedies at the City Dionysia until sometime in the mid-fourth century when the tribes began providing him with candidates ([Arist.] *Ath. Pol.* 56.3, with Rhodes 1981: 623–4). The *archōn basileus* was personally responsible for finding *chorēgoi* for comedies and tragedies at the Lenaia, while the tribes provided him with candidates to serve as gymnasiarchs (57.1, with Rhodes 1981: 624, 638–9). In Aristotle's time, one of the generals, the στρατηγὸς ἐπὶ τὰς συμμορίας, was responsible for selecting trierarchs (61.1) and placing them in the trierarchic *symmoriai*; in earlier times the generals probably shared responsibility for naming trierarchs (Hamel 1998a: 28–31).[16]

How exactly the city's officials went about filling liturgical posts when these were not filled by tribal nominees is unclear. After soliciting volunteers, they had to identify and select individuals to complete their lists. Because the number of wealthy Athenians was too large for any individual to be intimately familiar with all potential candidates (see below), an official often had to rely on other sources of information. In some cases, individuals hostile to a wealthy man or eager to avoid the liturgy themselves might come forward and provide a name (And. 1.132). Officials could also consult any records passed on by their predecessors. The generals, for example, would have had ready access to the previous year's list of trierarchs (Rhodes 1982: 3) and, after 378 B.C., probably to the declarations of wealth (*timēmata*) of individuals from the most recent levying of the *eisphora*; generals who had served in the previous year and had been reelected, as was common, could help ensure that information from one year would be available the next.[17] While the generals and the magistrates organizing

[16] Gabrielsen (1994: 74–5, 78) is skeptical that the generals played an active role in selecting trierarchs; he believes that deme members and officials (57–8) provided information to the city concerning liturgical liability (cf. [Dem.] 50.8).

[17] Gabrielsen (1994: 68–73) may be right that there were no standing lists (*katalogoi*) of all men eligible for the trierarchy; cf. the *ad hoc* hoplite *katalogoi* that were generated up until the mid-fourth century whenever a campaign was launched (Hansen 1985: 83, 89; Christ 2001: 400–3). Stanley (1993: 29–31) posits that there must have been a list of individuals eligible for liturgies, but offers no evidence that this existed.

festivals could share information with one another concerning potential liturgists, cooperation may not have been common because they were competing to fill their rosters from the same group of candidates (see further below).

Exemptions

Individuals who were selected to perform liturgies could seek release from service on the grounds that they were exempt. Certain categories of persons were exempt from the performance of some or all liturgies.[18] While metics were eligible for some festival liturgies (Dem. 20.18; Lys. 12.20), they did not normally serve as trierarchs (Dem. 20.20).[19] Minors were exempt from all liturgies (Dem. 21.154; Arist. *Rh.* 1399a; cf. Lys. 32.24; Dem. 14.16), but liable to the *eisphora* if they inherited a large estate (Dem. 27.37). Disability or sickness may sometimes have been deemed grounds for exemption (Dem. 14.16).[20] The nine archons were exempt from the trierarchy (Dem. 20.28) and presumably also festival liturgies, which some of them administered; other major officeholders, including the ten generals, were likely exempt from all liturgies as well.[21] Some individuals were honored by the *dēmos* with grants of *ateleia*, which made them permanently exempt from festival

[18] On exemptions, see Harrison 1971: 2.234–5; MacDowell 1978: 162; Gabrielsen 1987a: 8 n. 4; 1994: 85–90; Wallace 1989: 486; Christ 1990: 149–50 n. 9; Hansen 1991: 111.

[19] Thus Whitehead 1977: 80–2; Gabrielsen 1994: 61, with 240–1 n. 25; but cf. Jordan 2001.

[20] When Dem. 14.16 speaks of exemption from the trierarchy "if someone is ἀδύνατος," this likely refers to an individual who is physical disabled (cf. Rhodes 1982: 9–10; MacDowell 1986b: 441) rather than to one who is carrying out another liturgy as Gabrielsen (1994: 188–9) argues. The generals, however, may have been reluctant to grant exemptions on this basis: see below in the text.

[21] Although some scholars believe that members of the cavalry were automatically exempt from the trierarchy (e.g., Rhodes 1982: 4, 15 n. 13; cf. Gabrielsen 1994: 90, 179), this would have provided an enormous loophole for wealthy men seeking to dodge the costly trierarchy and would probably appear somewhere in our relatively rich record concerning the trierarchy. In fact, it is more likely that selection for trierarchic service, which relatively few men could afford, trumped that for cavalry service, which was less costly and which a larger pool of men could carry out (cf. Bugh 1988: 39–78). Although Demosthenes (21.160–7) attacks Meidias as a deserter and evader because he volunteered to serve as trierarch to get out of cavalry service, Meidias was likely availing himself of a legitimate option.

liturgies (Dem. 20.28; 20.18).[22] Property in cleruchies – that is, Athenian settlements in conquered lands – and that of corporations (τὰ κοινωνικά) were also exempt from trierarchies (Dem. 14.16, with Gabrielsen 1994: 87–90) and possibly festival liturgies as well. Cleruchs themselves probably enjoyed a *de facto* exemption from liturgies, even if they owned considerable property in Attica (*pace* Gabrielsen 1994: 88); their residence abroad would make it very awkward to designate them as liturgists. While there was no exemption for persons who claimed they were too poor to perform service, an individual could seek to transfer his burden to a wealthier man on this basis through the *antidosis* procedure (see below).[23]

In addition, current and past performers of public service received special consideration:

1) An individual could not be required to perform more than one liturgy in a given year ([Dem.] 50.9; cf. Dem. 20.19; 21.155) or the same festival liturgy more than once in his life ([Arist.] *Ath. Pol.* 56.3) (Rhodes 1982: 15 n. 2).
2) A performer of a festival liturgy was entitled to a one-year respite from all public service upon completion of his office (Dem. 20.8).
3) A trierarch, due to the financial and personal demands of his liturgy, could claim a two-year reprieve from (apparently) all liturgies (Is. 7.38; cf. Lys. 21.2, 5).[24]

It was inevitable that some of those selected to perform liturgies could legitimately claim exemption. In the absence of a central liturgy authority in Athens with consolidated record-keeping, officials may often have inadvertently assigned liturgies to individuals who could claim an exemption. In some cases, however, officials may have

[22] Leptines' law of 356/5 B.C. sought to abolish this exemption. Rhodes (1982: 13) believes that the law probably survived the attack on it to which Demosthenes 20: *Against Leptines* belongs; Gabrielsen (1987a: 15) views it as not clear whether this was so.

[23] Rhodes (1982: 4) cites Dem. 20.19 as evidence that perhaps "men who fell short of some stated requirement for liability were legally exempt from liturgies," but the passage makes no explicit claim that this was so.

[24] It is controversial how this rule operated in connection with the trierarchic *symmoriai* established in 358/7 B.C.: see Gabrielsen 1994: 87, with 245 nn. 3 and 6.

knowingly ignored a candidate's exemption – especially when this derived from recent performance of a liturgy – in the hope that he would choose not to exercise it (cf. Wallace 1989: 486). In either case, it was incumbent on an individual who believed that he was exempt and wished to be released from service to bring his exemption to the attention of the official who had selected him; it was the official's obligation to bring the claim as a suit (*skēpsis*) before a panel of jurors for adjudication ([Arist.] *Ath. Pol.* 56.3).[25]

A different legal procedure, *antidosis*, was available to anyone who, though eligible for service, believed that he could identify a wealthier candidate for it (Gabrielsen 1987a; Christ 1990: 160–9). The individual initially assigned to a liturgy could formally challenge another man either to perform it in his place or to exchange property, both real and personal, with him, in which case the challenger would carry out the liturgy from his new estate.[26] If the challengee rejected both options or if difficulties arose during an exchange to which the parties had agreed, the case could be brought before a popular jury as a *diadikasia* (Dem. 28.17); it was up to the jury then to assign the disputed liturgy to the man it deemed wealthier.[27]

[25] On *skēpsis*, see Harrison 1971: 2.232–6; Rhodes 1981: 625, 681. On the officials supervising this and *antidosis*, see Gabrielsen 1987a: 13 n. 13. MacDowell (1978: 162) envisions magistrates granting some exemptions on their own authority, but [Arist.] *Ath. Pol.* 56.3 appears to rule this out even for exemptions claimed on the basis of recent service (see Gabrielsen 1994: 85).

Gabrielsen (1994: 92) argues on the basis of [Arist.] *Ath. Pol.* 56.3 and 61.1 that *skēpsis* and *diadikasia* were "used synonymously for suits arising in connection with claims to exemption." While these two passages use these terms interchangeably, *diadikasia*, the term used in 61.1, is a broader rubric in Athenian law (see Todd 1993: 119–21) and encompasses suits initiated through *skēpsis* (as in 61.1) or *antidosis* (Dem. 28.17); when [X.] *Ath. Pol.* 3.4 uses διαδικάσαι in a liturgical context, it may well be referring to both types of suits.

[26] Although most individuals were probably reluctant to go so far as to exchange property, this was a real possibility: see Lys. 4.1; 24.9; Dem. 20.40; 21.79; 28.17; 42.19, 27; MacDowell 1978: 162–4; Gabrielsen 1987a: 14–17; Christ 1990: 161 n. 68.

[27] Gabrielsen (1987a: 23–4; cf. 1994: 91–5) argues that the case only came to court if difficulties arose during the exchange, but the ancient sources do not speak of any such restriction (see Christ 1990: 161 n. 68, and 166 n. 82; cf. Hansen 1991: 112, with n. 312). I am also not persuaded by Gabrielsen (1994: 91) that there were two rounds (rather than one round) of *antidosis* challenges per year in connection with trierarchic assignments.

The Liturgical Class

The number of Athenians who were liable to carry out liturgies and pay the *eisphora* is controversial.[28] The fact that the trierarchic *symmoriai* that were established in 358/7 B.C. had 1200 members before exemptions were granted (Dem 14.16) may indicate that this was the approximate size of the liturgical class at this time. In the late-fifth and early-fourth centuries as well, a group of about this size would probably have sufficed to yield the trierarchs and festival liturgists needed after exemptions were claimed. The same group of 1200 may also have been responsible for payment of the *eisphora* from 378 on (Isoc. 15.145; but cf. Dem. 20.28). Before 378 as well the liturgical class may have been more or less coextensive with the group paying the *eisphora*.[29]

While those in the liturgical class of 1200 were not all equally wealthy, for much of the classical period the democracy made no formal distinction between the very rich and merely rich to ensure that the most expensive liturgies, including the trierarchy, would consistently fall upon the very wealthiest men; as suggested above, the *eisphora* may also have fallen equally on rich men for much of its history.[30] In the fourth century, however, recognition of wealth disparities among the rich eventually led to the identification of the wealthiest 300 individuals, who became responsible for the *proeisphora* from *ca.* 378 and who assumed primary responsibility within the trierarchic *symmoriai* from 340 (Hansen 1991: 113–14).[31]

[28] Recent treatments of the problem (with earlier scholarship) can be found in Hansen 1991: 112–15 and Gabrielsen 1994: 178–80.

[29] Wealthy Athenians in this period thus invoke their liturgical services and *eisphora* payments together as the basis for special treatment from the *dēmos* (Lys. 21.1–5, with 11–12, 25; 25.12–13; cf. Is. 5.35–7).

[30] Athenians may have had no means of distinguishing between the rich and very rich before 378 B.C., when, as suggested above in the text, the *timēma* was first introduced in connection with the *eisphora*. The fact that magistrates competed freely with one another to fill their liturgical slots at the start of the official year also worked against matching up the wealthiest men with the most expensive liturgies (see below in the text and note 92).

[31] If Davies (1981: 37) is correct that the distribution of wealth in Athens did not change markedly during the classical period, these reforms cannot be explained as a response to the fact that wealth had become more concentrated in the hands of a few. On the social and political bases of these reforms, see below in the text.

The city did not, as far as we know, set a minimum level of wealth that placed a man in the liturgical class (Gabrielsen 1994: 45–53). The size of this class was determined, first and foremost, by the number of trierarchs and festival liturgists that the city required in a given year. Membership in this class over time was determined largely through the *antidosis* procedure.[32] While we do not have enough information about the wealth of those known to have performed liturgies to calculate a minimum or average level of wealth within the liturgical class, in practice a man probably needed to possess a fortune of at least several talents to carry out liturgies with any regularity (Davies 1971: xxiii–xxiv; 1981: 28–37). Although liturgists were very wealthy relative to average citizens,[33] their ability to sustain liturgies and *eisphorai* over time must have varied considerably with their levels of wealth and personal circumstances.

How well did this system work? In the estimation of Davies, it was "a (for Greece) unusually effective taxation system" (1971: xvii). In my view, this system was considerably less effective and more troubled than Davies and others have allowed. The modifications to this system over time provide strong indications of ongoing problems and tensions.

A SYSTEM UNDER PRESSURE

When we view Athenian arrangements concerning taxation as a system of rules and administrative structures, it is easy to miss the dynamic social and political forces that led to their formation and modification over time. The history of taxation in Athens is one of ongoing conflict between the wealthy and the city, and of increasing assertion of state authority over the wealthy and their fortunes. It is convenient to consider our sources within three periods: 508/7–432 B.C.; 431–404 B.C.; 403–321 B.C.

[32] On the continuing liability of a family over time, see Gabrielsen 1994: 60–7.

[33] Hansen (1991: 115) reckons that "the property of any one of the roughly 1200 liturgists would represent a lifetime's ordinary earnings" of an average Athenian.

508/7–432 B.C.

The tensions between the wealthy and the city that are richly attested, as we shall see, between 431–321 likely first appeared in the period 508/7–432. Although the dearth of sources makes it impossible to track the relations between the wealthy and the city over these years, key features of the liturgical system took shape during this period and, to judge from the form that they took, they did so amid tensions and controversy concerning the civic responsibilities of wealthy citizens.

Democratic Athens' liturgical system came into being gradually in the decades following the Cleisthenic reforms of 508/7, which laid the foundations of democracy. While the democracy's liturgical arrangements may have built on earlier ones, we are almost completely in the dark concerning these (Gabrielsen 1994: 19–26; Wilson 2000: 14–17); the liturgical system, as we meet it in classical sources, is administered by and for the democracy and is inseparable from its institutions. The *chorēgia* is attested at the City Dionysia from 502/1 for dithyramb (20 *chorēgoi* per year) and tragedy (three *chorēgoi* per year); and from 487/6 for comedy (five *chorēgoi* per year); the Lenaia required five *chorēgoi* for comedy annually starting around 440, and two for tragedy starting somewhat later (Davies 1967: 33–4). Many other festival liturgies, which are attested later, may also have been established in this period (*ibid.* 34–40). While our sources are sketchy, the trierarchy may have been established in the 480s in conjunction with Athens' rapid expansion of its fleet in the face of Persian imperialism; by 480, when the Athenians and their allies were victorious over the Persian fleet off Salamis, the city would have required a trierarch for each of its 200 ships (Gabrielsen 1994: 26–39). As the city established and maintained its naval empire in the next several decades, its need for trierarchs must have remained strong.

When democratic Athens developed these arrangements, it exploited not only the wealth but the aristocratic ethos of its richest citizens. Aristocrats in the Greek world had long been under pressure to validate their claims to prestige in the eyes of the community by competing with one another in a variety of public venues, including athletics and war; an integral part of this status competition was lavish expenditure. Democratic Athens, through its liturgical system, redirected this interpersonal aristocratic competition to serve the needs of the community.[34] Those who served the state through liturgies achieved prominence and put the city under a debt of gratitude (*charis*) to them; as we shall see, however, the precise nature of this debt and the terms of its repayment were subject to contestation and negotiation.

Athenian aristocrats may have embraced their emerging role as benefactors of the city in the first several decades of democratic rule. Indeed, these arrangements probably took shape largely with their consent, as they still enjoyed considerable political power in this period (Ober 1989: 75–82; Hansen 1991: 34–8) and the *dēmos* was not yet in a position, as far as we can tell, to impose such a system upon them. The earliest liturgies attested, festival ones, provided excellent opportunities for status display and fit well with aristocratic values (cf. Wilson 2000: 107–43), despite accommodations to the political climate of the new democracy. Even as the number of festival liturgies grew, therefore, wealthy men may have been drawn to them, as they were in later times, and often may have volunteered to perform them.[35]

Tensions concerning liturgical service most likely first arose in connection with the trierarchy in the decades after the defeat of the Persian fleet off Salamis (480 B.C.). It was one thing for wealthy men to help sustain the fleet that defended Athens against Persia; it was quite another for them to be on call, personally and financially, for the city's many naval enterprises in the decades following Salamis. As Athens asserted control over the members of the Delian League and acquired a naval empire from the 470s to 450s (Meiggs 1972: 42–128), it must frequently have called upon wealthy men to serve as trierarchs. While many members of the city's elite were complicit in the conversion of the Delian League into a naval empire and had a vested interest in maintaining it (Th. 8.48.5–6; Finley 1981: 44, 52–3, 58–9; Raaflaub 1994: 133), trierarchic service cannot have appealed to all equally. As we shall see, the trierarchy involved personal risk (cf. Th. 1.104, 109–10), large and unpredictable costs on top of outlays for festival liturgies,

[34] On this facet of the liturgical system, see Davies 1981: 98–9; Sinclair 1988: 188–90; Christ 1990: 150; Kurke 1992: 103–6; Gabrielsen 1994: 48–9.

[35] Cf. Arist. *Pol.* 1309a18–21, which argues that democracies should prevent wealthy men from undertaking "useless" liturgies like the *chorēgia* and torch-race, "even if they wish" (καὶ βουλομένους) to perform these.

and extensive periods of time away from family and personal affairs; trierarchic service, moreover, did not satisfy aristocratic desire for public acclaim as directly or efficiently as performance of a festival liturgy did. Thus, while the city may not have had much trouble inducing wealthy men to undertake festival liturgies in the decades after the Persian Wars, it likely had to apply coercion more regularly in this period to ensure that wealthy men in sufficient numbers would fulfill the significant demands of the trierarchy.[36]

It is probably against this backdrop of increasing liturgical demands on the wealthy and resistance by some to these that, perhaps as early as the 470s, rules concerning frequency of service were established. As the wealthy became liable not only for the *chorēgia* but also for the trierarchy, it was inevitable that some wealthy men would press for relief and that questions would arise concerning how often an individual should be required to perform liturgies. Perhaps the first rule of this sort formulated was that a man should not be required to carry out more than one liturgy per year. This would address a basic concern of the wealthy as the liturgy system grew and the likelihood that an individual might be called on to carry out two or more services in the same year increased. Temporary exemption from service upon completion of a liturgy may have been introduced at the same time or later as a separate measure: for less wealthy liturgists, service in consecutive years might be burdensome and some respite be necessary. Initially, all liturgies may have been treated equally in this regard, with a one-year exemption following performance of a festival liturgy or the trierarchy; the two-year exemption for the trierarchy, which recognizes its especially heavy costs and demands, may have been a later development in this period or during the Peloponnesian War when pressures on the wealthy mounted (Rhodes 1982: 3; Gabrielsen 1994: 86).[37] While these measures take for granted that a wealthy man is liable for service to the city unless exempt on designated grounds,

[36] Gabrielsen (1994: 36; cf. Kallet 1998: 57) underestimates the potential for conflict between wealthy men and the state over the trierarchy in this period.

[37] Lysias (21.2, 5) suggests that by *ca.* 411 B.C. a wealthy man was not legally required to serve continuously as trierarch from year to year, i.e. that service brought a period of exemption; Is. 7.38 may indicate that the two-year exemption for the trierarchy was operating by *ca.* 415 B.C.

they represent a significant concession to wealthy Athenians in setting a limit on the frequency of service required of them. The *dēmos* may have acceded to these measures not only in practical recognition of the finite resources of the wealthy but also in deference to the political power of the wealthy under the early democracy.

If the wealthy, according to this reconstruction, prevailed in setting limits on the frequency of obligatory service, the *dēmos* – perhaps in the 450s (see below) – asserted its authority over them and their fortunes in strictly limiting how a wealthy man could gain release from service. By regulating this through *skēpsis* and *antidosis* – legal procedures over which the popular courts had jurisdiction – the *dēmos* limited the ability of the wealthy to shirk their liturgical obligations.

While it may initially have been up to the officials assigning liturgies whether to allow or reject exemption claims, including those based on frequency of service, once *skēpsis* was introduced they apparently had to bring all claims before a popular lawcourt for adjudication.[38] This popular check on magisterial discretion may have arisen from the suspicion that these officials, who were themselves often members of the liturgical class, were allowing illegitimate exemptions to friends and cronies.[39]

Antidosis was probably also established as a popular measure to curtail abuse on the part of the wealthy. In the early years of the democratic liturgical system, wealthy men may have been able to win release from service by claiming financial hardship; such claims could be difficult to disprove and put a considerable burden on officials to find replacements. Once *antidosis* was introduced, if a wealthy man was unhappy with his assignment to a liturgy, the responsibility was his to provide a substitute; if he could not, the liturgy remained his obligation. These were rather strict conditions to set for those who believed they were being treated unfairly; the provision of property exchange, which

[38] [Arist.] *Ath. Pol.* 56.3 attests to this for the late fourth century B.C. The Old Oligarch, who may be writing in the 420s (Ostwald 1986: 182 n. 23; *pace* Hornblower 2000), suggests that the courts were busy with *diadikasiai* in connection with liturgies, i.e., with suits involving *skēpsis* and *antidosis* ([X.] *Ath. Pol.* 3.4, with note 25 above); this would be consistent with mandatory court review of exemption claims.

[39] On the ability of officials to favor their friends even after this reform, see below in the text.

cannot have been very attractive, as one recourse within the procedure also seems distinctly unsympathetic to wealthy citizens.[40] Viewed in this light, the *antidosis* procedure appears not so much as a measure intended to ensure equity among the rich in the bearing of liturgical burdens as a no-nonsense measure passed by the *dēmos* to ensure that wealthy men as a group would not shirk their obligations (cf. Christ 1990: 161–3; Gabrielsen 1987a: 37; 1994: 93–4).

The legal procedures of *skēpsis* and *antidosis* were likely introduced sometime between the 450s and the 430s. While these procedures are already in existence by the 420s when the literary record begins to blossom, they probably do not antedate the 450s, at least in the form we later meet them: they rely upon the existence of a system of popular lawcourts, which were not fully empowered before this time ([Arist.] *Ath. Pol.* 25.2, 27.4).[41] As it is hard to imagine the democracy's liturgical system, which must have been well developed by the mid-fifth century, operating very well without one or both of these mechanisms, it is tempting to place them in the 450s and to regard them as measures imposed on the wealthy by a newly assertive *dēmos*.[42]

40 Davies (1981: 75–6) cites the *antidosis* procedure as evidence of "the curious lack of emotional involvement among Athenians towards real property which they owned." The dearth of evidence for exchanges carried through to completion, however, argues against such detachment. The exchange alluded to in Lys. 4.1, which Davies (76 n. 5) cites as an instance of actual exchange, was not ultimately carried through (see Gabrielsen 1987a: 21–2).

41 The Old Oligarch (420s B.C.?) refers to *diadikasiai* in a liturgical context, i.e., to suits involving *antidosis* and *skēpsis* ([X.] *Ath. Pol.* 3.4, with note 25 above). *Skēpsis* is used in a legal context in 425 B.C. in Ar. *Ach.* 392 (see Olson 2002: 175–6), but it is not clear in this passage whether it refers to a claim of exemption in the liturgical sphere or outside it as in Ar. *Ec.* 1027 and *Pl.* 904. *Antidosis* appears in Cratin. fr. 290 (after *ca.* 425 B.C.: see K-A *ad* fr. 283); X. *Oec.* 7.3 (with a dramatic date of *ca.* 420–10 B.C.: see Pomeroy 1994: 18–19); *IG* I[3] 254, referring to *antidosis* on the deme level in Ikaria *ca.* 440–415 B.C. (see Whitehead 1986: 215–17; Gabrielsen 1987a: 29–30); Arist. *Rh.* 1416a28–35, attesting that Euripides, who died *ca.* 406 B.C., had been involved in an *antidosis* dispute with a certain Hygiainon. Most scholars do not take seriously the claim in Dem. 42.1 that Solon established *antidosis*. Davies (1971: xxii n. 8, followed by Christ 1990: 161 n. 68) argues that *antidosis* may date back to 502/1 B.C. when *chorēgiai* first appear in our record.

42 These measures suggest that the *dēmos* regarded liturgical expenditures as necessary for the well-being of the state, notwithstanding the rich revenues of empire. While it is true that the city could easily have taken over the financing of festival liturgies at the height of the empire (Kallet 1998: 55), it would have been costly for it to assume financial responsibility for trierarchies, given the huge expenses involved.

While the surveyed developments bear vestiges of the political circumstances that engendered them, they also point to a practical constraint that the city faced in the liturgical sphere in this period: it apparently had no way to distinguish degrees of wealth within the liturgical class. This is directly suggested by the nature of the *antidosis* procedure, which relies upon a private citizen to identify an individual (allegedly) wealthier than himself and, in the case of adjudication, to provide information concerning his opponent's wealth. Consistent with this also is the fact that the rules governing exemption during and after liturgical service do not distinguish between the very rich and the not so rich: apparently, any wealthy man could insist on performing only one liturgy at a time and on a respite after completing a liturgy. As noted above, it was much later, in 378 B.C., that the city, in reforming the administration of the *eisphora*, first sought information about the absolute wealth of citizens through self-assessment (*timēma*).

While the history of Athens in the period 508/7–432 is murky, the transformation of liturgies in this period from largely voluntary services into legal obligations that were increasingly difficult to avoid must be intimately linked with the emergence of popular rule. How much turmoil surrounded the development of liturgical arrangements is not clear, but just as the transition to democratic rule was not entirely smooth (cf. Th. 1.107; [Arist.] *Ath. Pol.* 25), so too the democratic liturgical system likely emerged in the face of controversy and sometimes resistance. The Old Oligarch looking at the results of this process in the 420s (?) cynically asserts that the liturgical system makes members of the *dēmos* "wealthy and the wealthy poorer" ([X.] *Ath. Pol.* 1.13); a wealthy Athenian incurring substantial and repeated liturgical costs did not have to be an oligarch for this point of view to resonate with him.

431–404 B.C.

The Peloponnesian War (431–404) placed considerable stress on the relationship between the city and its wealthy citizens. Already in 428 the costs of war strained the city's finances and prompted it to impose an *eisphora* of 200 talents (Th. 3.19.1). Although we do not know the precise number of occasions on which the city imposed the *eisphora* during the war or the amount levied each time, it is clear that the city had recourse to this tax repeatedly and that this heightened pressures on the wealthy.[43] These levies came at a time when they were serving as trierarchs with increased frequency and when their personal resources were diminished due to the ravages of war.

When the city levied the *eisphora* in 428, this may have been an innovation inspired by exigent circumstances. Thucydides speaks of the Athenians "even themselves for the first time paying an *eisphora* amounting to two hundred talents" (καὶ αὐτοὶ ἐσενεγκόντες τότε πρῶτον ἐσφορὰν διακόσια τάλαντα) (3.19.1). Scholars disagree on what this refers to: the debut of the *eisphora* (Sealey 1984: 77–80); its first imposition in the Peloponnesian War (Gomme 1956: 2.278); or the first time an amount so large was levied (Griffith 1977; cf. Hornblower 1991: 403–4). It is quite possible, given Thucydides' wording (Sealey 1984: 79–80) and the absence of compelling evidence to the contrary, that this was indeed the debut of the *eisphora*.[44]

Although Athens' imposition of a direct tax on the rich to meet war expenses may seem natural from a modern perspective, direct taxation was a striking development in the relationship between the city and the wealthy as this deviated sharply from the paradigm of the liturgical system. There was no pretense of voluntarism with the *eisphora*, which was a mandatory tax, and it provided no direct and immediate opportunities for status display before the public. The financial outlay required by the *eisphora*, its unpredictability as an irregularly imposed tax, and its operation outside the terms of the liturgical

[43] Three *eisphorai* are securely attested: one in 428 B.C. (Th. 3.19.1), and two between 410–404 (Lys. 21.3; cf. D. S. 13.47.7, 52.5, 64.4). The familiarity of the *eisphora* in Ar. *Eq.* 923–6 (424 B.C.) and Eup. fr. 300 (*ca.* 424 B.C.? see K-A V.471), however, suggests that it was imposed more than once in the period 428–424 (cf. Thomsen 1964: 172). Ar. *Lys.* 654–5 (411 B.C.) points to a recent *eisphora* (Sommerstein 1990: 190; cf. Thomsen 1964: 175); this would provide a fresh financial grievance for those who supported the oligarchy of 411 (Th. 8.48.1, 63.1). If ἐσφέρεν in *ML* 78 fr. c. line 5 (415 B.C.) refers to taxation (see above, note 12), the immediate qualification "whenever it is necessary" leaves doubt as to whether an actual *eisphora* resulted. Ant. 2.2.12, which speaks of payment of "many great *eisphorai*," may well date to the Peloponnesian War; on the problem of dating the *Tetralogies*, see Sealey 1984.

[44] While the Kallias decrees (*ML* 58 = *IG* I³ 52) are often taken as evidence of a prior imposition of this tax, it is not clear that decree B, which alludes to it (lines 17 and 19, with restorations) antedates 428 (see Kallet-Marx 1989: 112–13 n. 84).

system, made it a frequent source of complaint for wealthy Athenians through its history.[45] The *dēmos* recognized the unpopularity of such a tax, to judge by its provision that the Assembly had to vote to grant immunity (*adeia*) from prosecution before it allowed anyone to propose an *eisphora* (*ML* 58 B 15–19 = *IG* I³ 52; Thomsen 1964: 187).

While the ongoing war made Athens rely heavily upon the wealthy for the *eisphora* and trierarchy, the city provided some relief to them in the area of festival liturgies. It reduced from five to three the number of comedies performed at the Dionysia and Lenaia through much of the war, and thus also the number of *chorēgiai* required (Davies 1967: 33–4); it is possible that there was also some paring back of other festival liturgies. The attested concessions, however, seem rather modest in light of the elevated demands on the wealthy at this time, and tensions ran high.

Aristophanic comedy attests to tensions in a variety of ways. *Knights* (424 B.C.), for example, treats the financial obligations of the rich as a burden a man might wish upon his enemies: Cleon's comic stand-in, Paphlagon, threatens to take vengeance on his rival, the Sausage-seller, by enrolling him as a trierarch (912–18) and by registering him among the wealthy so that he will be "weighed down by *eisphorai*" (923–6).[46] Elsewhere, Aristophanes alludes to evasion of these responsibilities. The Chorus of Old Women in *Lysistrata* (411 B.C.) rebukes their male counterparts for not paying their *eisphorai*: "indeed, we're positively in danger of ruin thanks to you" (654–5). In *Frogs* (405 B.C.), Aeschylus protests that Euripides' dramatic exploitation of kings in rags has inspired wealthy men to imitate this to avoid the trierarchy: "That's why no rich man is willing to serve as trierarch, but instead wraps himself in rags and whines, claiming to be poor" (1065–6). That real tensions lie beneath these comic jibes is confirmed by forensic oratory, which speaks both of the burden of financial obligations (Lys.

[45] For evidence of this in the fourth century, see note 50. Wealthy Athenians were not alone among Greeks in their antipathy for the *eisphora*: see e.g., Arist. *Pol.* 1271b13 ("the Spartiates pay *eisphorai* badly").

[46] For the debate over whether Cleon might have introduced the *eisphora* in 428 B.C., see Thomsen 1964: 168–70; Bugh 1988: 108–9.

fr. 35 Thalheim; Isoc. 18.60) and evasive tactics (Lys. 20.23; 21.12; Isoc. 18.60).

The city's financial demands on the liturgical class during the Peloponnesian War, in fact, appear to have figured prominently in the oligarchic coup of 411. According to Thucydides, those eager to replace democracy with oligarchy were "powerful citizens . . . who are the very ones especially burdened (ταλαιπωροῦνται)" in war (8.48.1). Later, in elaborating on the motives of the oligarchs, Thucydides makes explicit the financial nature of the burdens in question:

> They had resolved [under the oligarchy] to contribute zealously from their own private resources either money or whatever else should be necessary [for the pursuit of the war], believing that from now on the burdens they would bear (ταλαιπωροῦντας) would be for no others than themselves. (8.63.4; cf. [Arist.] *Ath. Pol.* 29.5)

While political and financial motivations are intertwined here, the burden of financial obligations may well have spurred the oligarchs to pursue their political program and usurp power at this time (Gabrielsen 1994: 173; cf. Balot 2001a: 213).

When the *dēmos* regained power soon after this oligarchic episode, it provided some relief to the liturgical class, presumably in part to alleviate the pressures that had prompted some to join with the oligarchs. Although Athens' grave circumstances made it necessary to exact payment of the *eisphora* twice in the period 410–404 (Lys. 21.3), the city allowed wealthy men for the first time, as far as we know, to pair up and share costs and responsibilities for a trierarchy or *chorēgia*; the syntrierarchy and *synchorēgia* were both in use by 406/5.[47] While cost-sharing among liturgists was introduced as a temporary measure in troubled times, it endured in the case of the trierarchy. Although the *synchorēgia* passed out of use by *ca.* 398, the syntrierarchy became common in the first half of the fourth century (Gabrielsen 1994: 173–4, 178–9). This new arrangement, however, proved problematic for the city, as we shall see.

[47] On the dating of these innovations, see Davies 1967: 33–4 and Gabrielsen 1994: 174.

403–321 B.C.

Tensions concerning the financial obligations of the liturgical class persisted after the Peloponnesian War and up through the end of democratic rule in 322/1. The reforms introduced in this period attest to these tensions and provide interesting evidence of how Athens sought to balance its needs with the concerns of the wealthy, which it could not afford to ignore altogether. While the city in the face of pressures most dramatically altered the institutions governing the *eisphora* and *trierarchy*, it also modified somewhat those regulating the *chorēgia*.

Athens continued to rely upon the *eisphora* to support its military endeavors in the fourth century, levying it repeatedly from 395–338 (Brun 1983: 55; but cf. Wallace 1989: 484 n. 34). While individual levies would not normally have ruined wealthy men (Ste. Croix 1953: 69), cumulatively and in combination with liturgical obligations *eisphorai* heightened the financial pressures on the rich, in particular those with lesser fortunes (Davies 1981: 82–3; Millett 1991: 68–9, 270 n. 25). This was probably especially true in the first decades of the fourth century. The city's financial dependence on the liturgical class likely increased in this period, as it faced economic hardship after the Peloponnesian War (Strauss 1986: 42–69; E. E. Cohen 1992: 194–5). At the same time, many members of the liturgical class must have found their wealth diminished due to the devastation of war and the cumulative effect of their civic expenditures during the last intense phase of the war. When the *eisphora* was levied during the Corinthian War (395–386 B.C.) (Thomsen 1964: 180–1; Brun 1983: 26–8, 55), many wealthy Athenians may have found this burdensome (Lys. 28.3–4; 29.9; cf. Ar. *Ec.* 197–8, with Sommerstein 1998: 155; Is. 5.37).

It is against this backdrop of challenging times for the city and its wealthy citizens that we should place the reform of the *eisphora* in 378. First and foremost, this reform probably sought to reduce difficulties in collecting the *eisphora*: the establishment of standing *symmoriai* facilitated tax collection, as did the (perhaps) somewhat later introduction of *proeispherontes* who were responsible in advance for the payment of the *eisphora* of their tax groups.[48] The reform likely also

[48] The *diadikasia*-documents of the late 380s to the early 370s B.C. may attest to difficulties in the administration of the *eisphora* and/or liturgies: see Davies 1981: 133–50 (linking

addressed complaints among the wealthy concerning inequities: less wealthy members of the liturgical class, who would especially feel the effect of financial hard times, may have complained that no account was being taken of relative wealth among payers of the *eisphora*. If self-assessment (*timēma*) for citizens was introduced at this time, as suggested above, this made it possible for the city for the first time to levy the *eisphora* in proportion to total declared wealth rather than as a flat tax.

This reform appears to have been quite successful from the city's perspective. While *eisphorai* totaling about three hundred talents were levied in the period 378/7 to *ca.* 356/5, only 14 talents was unpaid when the city took action to collect arrears at the end of this period (Dem. 22.44).[49] One may infer that the *proeispherontes* were highly effective tax collectors for the city, and not surprisingly: they had a strong incentive to seek *eisphora* payments from those in their tax groups because they paid their group's liability in advance. Any pleasure that wealthy men may have taken in the improved equity of the new system may have been offset by their chagrin at the efficiency with which the *eisphora* was now collected. Payment of this direct tax, to all appearances, continued to be unpopular, and attempts to minimize liability to it were probably widespread.[50] While the reforms of 378/7 made it difficult for a man to avoid paying his share based on his declaration of wealth, he had great latitude in what he reported in the first place if he was able to conceal much of his wealth from public view (see below).

The trierarchy had a rocky history in the fourth century. In the troubled economic times of the first several decades of the century, the city apparently had difficulties recruiting trierarchs. The large number of

these documents to the *eisphora*); Rhodes 1982: 11–13 (linking them to the trierarchy or all liturgies); Gabrielsen 1987b and 1994: 70–1 (linking them with disputes over payment of public debts, including arrears for the *eisphora* and naval debts).

49 The city may have been collecting these arrears from individuals who had failed to make their payments to the *proeispherontes*: see Wallace 1989: 485. If the *proeisphora* worked as it was supposed to, the city had already received the total amount levied in this period from the *proeispherontes*; the arrears it collected at this time could therefore be applied to the city's current needs.

50 On the continuing unpopularity of the *eisphora*, see Dem. 2.24; 8.21–3; *Prooem.* 41.2; cf. 1.6; 2.27, 31; 4.7; X. *HG* 6.2.1; *Hier.* 9.7; Ste. Croix 1953: 69, with n. 152.

unallotted ships listed in naval records from the 370s – half the fleet in 378/7 and one-quarter of it in 373/2 – is likely due to a shortage of trierarchs (Gabrielsen 1994: 180–1; cf. X. *HG* 4.2.14); the situation was probably no better in the equally difficult times of the 390s and 380s. These problems are all the more striking in light of the fact that the city maintained a reduced fleet of perhaps 100 ships from the 390s to the 370s (*ibid.* 178–9). These difficulties help explain the state's lenience in the period before 357/6 toward the collection of outstanding debts for equipment from former trierarchs: more stringent debt collection might have exacerbated recruiting problems (*ibid.* 83–4; cf. 158). Likewise, the state appears to have allowed many men to share costs as syntrierarchs to make service less unattractive (*ibid.* 178–9). Even split costs, however, might seem too high to potential trierarchs in these hard times, especially because the costs of the trierarchy were rising as the city came to rely more heavily on private financing of the navy (*ibid.* 116–17). The syntrierarchy, moreover, may have contributed to recruiting problems for the city, as both men collaborating in a syntrierarchy were probably entitled to a two-year liturgical respite upon completion of service (*ibid.* 176, 224).

It is against this backdrop of persistent problems surrounding the trierarchy that Athenians passed Periandros' reform (358/7 B.C.), which addressed difficulties in both recruiting and debt collection (Gabrielsen 1994: 84; 157–60, 198–9). It assigned members of the liturgical class to 20 groups (*symmoriai*) of 60 each, and made these groups responsible not only for sharing costs of trierarchies and furnishing trierarchs but also for debt collection. This reform may have been more successful in the former area than in the latter one: while the number of unallotted hulls plummeted in 358/7 (*ibid.* 193), collection of debts continued to pose a problem (*ibid.* 162).

Periandros' reform represents a firm assertion of state authority over wealthy citizens in the sphere of the trierarchy. In assigning wealthy men to groups whose members shared responsibility for the trierarchy, it removed any remaining pretense that this service was voluntary. In effect, trierarchic expenditure had become a mandatory tax like the *eisphora*; the success of the *symmoriai* formed for collection of the *eisphora* presumably inspired the extension of this model to the trierarchy.[51] Like the earlier reform of the *eisphora* in 378, Periandros' reform looks as though it was implemented first and foremost to ensure that members of the liturgical class fulfill their civic obligations. Unlike the reform of the *eisphora*, however, it did not address concerns among the wealthy over the relative sizes of their contributions: within the trierarchic *symmoriai* no distinction was made between the amounts required of less and more wealthy members (Dem. 18.102–8; cf. 14.17; Isoc. 8.128; Gabrielsen 1994: 196–7).[52] Discontent over this led to the passage of Demosthenes' naval reform of 340, which established that a man's contribution was to be in proportion to his property and compelled the richest three hundred members of the naval *symmoriai* to bear a larger share of the costs within their groups (Dem. 18.102–8; Gabrielsen 1994: 207–13). While the reform of 340 angered the wealthiest three hundred individuals (Dem. 18.103), it likely helped reduce tensions between the city and the less wealthy members of the trierarchic *symmoriai* (Gabrielsen 1994: 212).[53]

An interesting development in the period after Periandros' reform was the introduction of voluntary naval contributions (*epidoseis*). An *epidosis* was a donation solicited by the Assembly or Boule to meet some public need; lists were publicly posted of those who kept their promises and of those who did not (Is. 5.37–8; Gabrielsen 1994: 200). While *epidoseis* were used in Athens for diverse public needs from at least the late-fifth century, the city apparently began to use them in the naval sphere starting in 357 (Dem. 21.161) and did so on several occasions after this (Migeotte 1992: 15–18; Gabrielsen 1994: 199–206). Gabrielsen (1994: 205) argues persuasively that these were

[51] Gabrielsen (1994: 198) does not go far enough when he observes of the reform: "The process of transforming the trierarchic obligation into a tax proper was well under way." The financial component of the trierarchy had now become in fact a "tax proper" that was indistinguishable from the *eisphora* (cf. Sinclair 1988: 190). In light of the unmistakably mandatory nature of this tax and the manner of its collection, it seems odd to speak, as Gabrielsen does (182) in introducing Periandros' reform, of "[m]aintenance of an appropriate balance between the elements of option and compulsion."

[52] A further inequity could arise if a very wealthy man collected the costs of a trierarchy from the members of his *symmoria* without contributing much himself (Dem. 21.155; 18.104). In my view, Cawkwell (1984: 342) is mistaken to see Periandros' reform as concerned primarily or exclusively with equitable sharing of trierarchic costs.

[53] Demosthenes (18.102–8) tendentiously labels the less wealthy members "poor men."

solicited to induce individuals to undertake voluntary service as trierarchs, rather than to donate ships as has been commonly believed. Although Gabrielsen (206) posits that naval *epidoseis* "should not be seen as a sign that the established trierarchic system had not stood the test of time," it is hard to see why these would be needed if the naval *symmoriai* were functioning efficiently (cf. Migeotte 1992: 16, 18).[54] The fact that *epidoseis* were solicited only periodically – and not every time trierarchs were needed – may suggest that these were intended to remedy shortfalls.

The *chorēgia*, unlike the trierarchy, appears to have operated fairly smoothly during the fourth century. As noted above, the *synchorēgia*, which appeared along with the syntrierarchy near the end of the Peloponnesian War, fell out of use by *ca.* 398 while the syntrierarchy remained in wide use. The best explanation for this is that wealthy Athenians were more willing to undertake *chorēgiai* than trierarchies. As we shall see, this may be due not only to cost considerations but also to the fact that *chorēgiai* were the instrument of choice among wealthy Athenians for displaying status and winning prestige.[55]

The relative attractiveness of the *chorēgia* to wealthy men does not mean, however, that it was always easy to recruit *chorēgoi*. Difficulties in recruiting *chorēgoi* for the comedies at the City Dionysia may lie behind the transfer of this responsibility, noted above, from the eponymous archon to the tribes sometime in the mid-fourth century ([Arist.] *Ath. Pol.* 56.3, with Rhodes 1981: 623–4).[56] Even the tribes, however, were not always able to produce candidates for *chorēgiai* by the appointed time: Demosthenes describes how in 349/8 he stepped forward under such circumstances to represent his tribe at the Dionysia as *chorēgos* for its men's dithyrambic chorus (21.13; cf. 21.15; Is. 5.36). Especially in

[54] Gabrielsen (1994: 225) seems to acknowledge this in his epilogue: "Extra manpower and funds had to be mobilized on several occasions through appeals for voluntary naval contributions (epidoseis)."

[55] If Athens' arrangements for festival liturgies tended to operate more smoothly than those for the trierarchy, this is due not so much to the city's superior administration of the former (as Dem. 4.35–7 claims) as to the different attitudes of the wealthy toward the two spheres of public service.

[56] In 390/89 B.C. the *archōn* may have had trouble recruiting *chorēgoi* for comedies at the City Dionysia (Platonius *apud* Meineke, *FCG* I.532). Davies (1981: 25) and Gabrielsen (1994: 262 n. 15) accept this tradition.

time of war when wealthy men were liable to *eisphorai* and trierarchies simultaneously, tensions could arise over festival liturgies. This may well be why the city reduced the number of some of these during the Peloponnesian War, as noted above, and why during the Social War (357–355 B.C.) Leptines won passage of a measure in 356/5 that abolished honorific exemptions from festival liturgies. Consistent with these glimpses of tensions concerning festival liturgies is the fact that our sources speak regularly of *antidosis* as a recourse in this sphere (Lys. 24.9; X. *Oec.* 7.3; Dem. 21.156) and treat it as routine that magistrates and courts have to deal with suits involving *antidosis* and *skēpsis* in connection with festival liturgies ([Arist.] *Ath. Pol.* 56.3; cf. [X.] *Ath. Pol.* 3.4).

This historical survey has attempted to trace, insofar as this is possible, the evolution of Athenian arrangements concerning liturgies and the *eisphora*, and to sketch out some of the social and political tensions associated with this. While the reforms introduced over time attest to the democracy's flexibility and ingenuity, they also point to the persistent challenges it faced as it sought to ensure that wealthy Athenians would fulfill their financial obligations.

That the city increasingly asserted its authority over the wealthy in the classical period is clear. In the 450s (?) the city took steps to ensure that the wealthy would fulfill their liturgical obligations by establishing the *antidosis* procedure and judicial review of exemption claims through *skēpsis*; by 428 it made the wealthy liable to the *eisphora*. It further tightened its control over liturgical fortunes in the fourth century by instituting *symmoriai* first for the *eisphora* (378/7 B.C.) and later for the trierarchy (358/7 B.C.). As the city extended its control over the wealthy, it also accommodated to some extent their concerns over fairness and equity; the pace of reform in this area was slow, however. While *antidosis* provided a rough mechanism for wealthy men to seek equity among their peers in the liturgical sphere, the principle that the wealthy should be liable to financial obligations in direct proportion to their wealth was not established for the *eisphora* until 378 and for the trierarchy until 340. For much of the classical period, the Athenian public may have been largely unsympathetic to complaints concerning inequity from men who were very wealthy compared to average citizens. The city's increased attention to equity in the fourth century may have arisen more from concern that the arrangements for the *eisphora* and trierarchy were not working well than from a desire to extend social justice to rich individuals. Consistent with this interpretation is the way the city made wealthy men collectively responsible for the city's needs. The *antidosis* procedure unambiguously made the rich men assigned liturgies responsible for finding substitutes from their class if they sought relief from service; the *symmoriai* for the *eisphora* and trierarchy made groups of wealthy men jointly responsible for their obligations.

In what follows, we turn from the often troubled history of Athens' arrangements for financial obligations to consider closely how wealthy Athenians viewed their civic obligations and what options they had as they determined whether or how to serve their city. The tensions apparent in the institutional history of the city's financial obligations suggest that we should take seriously the ancient evidence for attitudes and behavior among the wealthy at odds with patriotic ideals.

THE LIMITS OF *PHILOTIMIA*

To the extent that wealthy Athenians embraced or at least accepted their civic obligations, this was largely due to the appeal of the ideal of *philotimia*, which the city actively promoted.[57] According to this ideal, wealthy men were to compete zealously with each other in putting their financial resources to good use on behalf of the community; in exchange for this, they could expect to receive honor (*timē*) from the community and gratitude (*charis*), which could translate into a variety of civic benefits. The civic ideal of *philotimia* was potent: in keeping with the democratic ideology of citizenship (see Chapter 1), it appealed to individual self-interest by promising a personal reward for sacrifice on behalf of the community.

The appeal of this ideal, however, was limited by practical considerations, calculations, and concerns. If the prospect of reward for

[57] On *philotimia* and public service, see Davies 1981: 26; Whitehead 1983; 1993; Sinclair 1988: 188–90; Gabrielsen 1994: 48–9; Veligianni-Terzi 1997: 223 and *passim*; Wilson 2000: 144–97; cf. Veyne 1990: 71–83.

expenditure was enticing, wealthy men naturally weighed costs against rewards and did not always find the latter to counterbalance the former. Furthermore, the attraction of the ideal of *philotimia* could be greatly diminished by dissatisfaction with the arrangements governing financial obligations – in particular, the sense that these were unfair – and by cynicism concerning its relevance in the face of the increasingly compulsory nature of these obligations. Let us consider these diverse challenges to the ideal of *philotimia* and how the ancient sources present them.

Costs

Wealthy Athenians were acutely conscious of what they expended on behalf of the city and highly attuned to the impact this might have on their fortunes. Although an extraordinarily wealthy Athenian like Nicias could afford to be extravagant in his public expenditures without much concern over financial consequences (Plu. *Nic.* 3), most wealthy Athenians were aware that their resources were finite and that reckless expenditure might jeopardize the prestige and security that came with wealth.[58]

A client of Lysias provides a plausible glimpse into the private reckonings of the wealthy concerning their civic expenditures:

> My father in all his life spent more on the city than on himself and his family – twice the amount that we have now, as he often calculated in my presence. (19.9; cf. Isoc. 15.158)

That the speaker's father sometimes expanded on the subject of his costs is suggested by the speaker's itemization of these and tallying of their total cost later in his speech (19.57–9; cf. 29, with 42–3). Such reckonings were not, however, confined to the private sphere, as this public "disclosure" before an Athenian lawcourt attests. Indeed, litigants make it abundantly clear as they seek *charis* for their expenditures that they are intimately aware of the costs of public service. Another client of Lysias, for example, goes so far as to list in detail how much he

[58] On the dearth of evidence for reckless expenditure on liturgies, see note 69.

spent on each occasion for the city (21.1–5).[59] While litigants vary in the precision with which they speak of their expenditures, the pointedness with which they speak of these leaves no doubt that costs were very much on their minds.[60]

Cost-consciousness on the part of the wealthy is especially evident in their common characterization of public expenditure as "ruinous." Demosthenes, for example, asserts before a popular court that he regarded as utterly ruinous the prospect of carrying out the trierarchy his enemies sought to impose on him through *antidosis* (28.17).[61] Assertions concerning financial ruin were sufficiently familiar in the courts that one litigant quips, "no one ever blamed himself [for squandering his wealth]; on the contrary, he claims that the city has taken away his property" (Dem. 38.26; cf. 36.39). Theophrastus caricatures the political exploitation of this trope in his portrait of the Oligarch who walks about asking, "When shall we stop being ruined by liturgies and trierarchies?" (*Char.* 26.6; cf. Isoc. 15.160). The ubiquity of this figure, however, makes it clear that wealthy men of diverse political beliefs could regard financial obligations as daunting.

While the claim of wealthy men that their civic expenditures were ruinous need not have been valid to be historically significant for understanding their behavior (cf. Christ 1990: 152), this had at least some basis in reality (Davies 1981: 82–3; Millett 1991: 68–71; Gabrielsen 1994: 221–3). Liturgical costs could be very high, as we have seen, and cumulatively their impact on a liturgical fortune could be significant, especially when compounded by payment of the *eisphora*. Costs could easily exceed a wealthy man's income in a given year (Is. 6.38) or at least what was left from his income after he paid for deme liturgies (cf. Whitehead 1986: 150–2) and the costs of running

[59] While this individual may well be unusual in the magnitude and frequency of his expenditures (see Davies 1971: 592–3 and Todd 2000: 229–30), his cost-consciousness is not atypical.

[60] The frequent vagueness of litigants concerning the exact number and type of liturgies that they have performed and the amount they have paid in *eisphorai* (as in most of the passages cited in note 93) likely stems not from their ignorance of how much they have spent but from strategic considerations: this allows them to give the impression of extraordinary expenditure without itemization that might undercut this. On the rhetoric of self-presentation, see below in the text.

[61] Cf. Is. fr. 29 Thalheim; Dem. 18.102; 21.61; Antiph. fr. 202.

his household and maintaining an elite lifestyle (Is. 6.38; cf. Dem. 36.41).[62] Consistent with this is the fact that even very wealthy men sometimes borrowed money to meet their obligations.[63]

Meeting the costs of civic obligations must have been particularly challenging for less wealthy members of the liturgical class, for example, those with fortunes of three to four talents. Marginal liturgical fortunes might be depleted relatively quickly by heavy civic expenditure, and this could lead to individuals dropping out of the liturgical class. Indeed, this helps explain why membership in the liturgical class changed significantly over time in Athens.[64] While those who dropped out of the liturgical class for this reason were not literally impoverished, they might view their fall into the ranks of "poor men" – as Athenians often referred to those outside the liturgical class (Ober 1989: 194–6) – as tantamount to ruin.

Concerns among the wealthy about the costs of financial obligations were likely heightened by their uncertainty as to when these would arise and how much expense they might entail. Although the imposition of the *eisphora*, as an irregular tax, was particularly unpredictable, so too was selection to perform a liturgy. While a wealthy man could expect to perform some kind of liturgy within a several-year period, in a given year an individual who was not exempt did not know

[62] The annual income of a wealthy man's estate would depend on how much of this was in land, slaves, or cash, and on the rate of return on these (see Ste. Croix 1953: 49 n. 80; Sinclair 1988: 63 n. 70; Christesen 2003: 52). If we assume an average annual return on assets of 10% – which may be unrealistically high (cf. Millett 1991: 270 n. 25) – a five-talent estate might yield a half-talent of income per year, which might not be enough to cover the cost of a sole trierarchy.

[63] See e.g., Dem. 28.17; 47.54; [Dem.] 50.7, 13; Is. fr. 29 Thalheim; Davies 1981: 82–3; Millett 1991: 69–71. Borrowing, however, could stem from temporary problems with liquidity or be part of a strategy to create the appearance of indebtedness to avoid assignment to liturgies or *antidosis* challenges (see below in the text).

[64] Although Davies (1981: 80) plausibly identifies the division of large fortunes among numerous heirs over time as a major factor in families dropping out of the liturgical class, he underestimates the role of liturgical obligations in bringing this about because in his view *antidosis* should have prevented this (82–4). *Antidosis*, however, was probably not as effective as Davies and others have assumed in achieving a fair distribution of liturgical burdens among the wealth (see Christ 1990: 163 n. 75; and cf. below in the text); and even when it did achieve the transfer of a liturgy from a less wealthy man to a wealthier one, there was no guarantee that the new assignee would be able to sustain this expense without dropping out of the liturgical class.

whether he would be required to perform a liturgy and, if so, whether he would serve as *chorēgos* or trierarch; his costs could vary considerably depending on his assignment.

Individuals selected for a festival liturgy, as noted above, might have to pay as little as a few hundred drachmas or as much as several thousand drachmas, depending on the festival and the task involved. The costs of a trierarchy were also highly unpredictable. Actual costs depended on factors over which a trierarch might have little control, including the advance payments and bonuses required by officers and crew – whom he often had to recruit (Gabrielsen 1994: 108, 121) – and the length of the expedition involved; the city only provided sufficient money for provisions and pay for the crew for a short period and excess costs fell to the trierarch (*ibid.* 1994: 124). Most frightening of all perhaps was the liability of a trierarch for damage to, or loss of, his ship, if he was judged negligent for this; in the case of loss, he might be compelled to pay 5000 drachmas toward replacement of the ship (*ibid.* 136–9; 144–5).

As wealthy men reckoned up the costs of their civic obligations, they were conscious not only of financial costs but personal ones. One substantial personal risk was involvement in litigation arising from their performance of a public service. While a *chorēgos* might get entangled in litigation in a variety of ways (see e.g., Ant. 6; Dem. 21), a trierarch faced a greater chance of this especially when, after 358/7 B.C., he was required by the city to collect naval equipment from his predecessor (Dem. 47; Christ 1998b: 536–42). Trierarchic service carried with it additional challenges and risks. Recruitment of officers and crew could be difficult (Gabrielsen 1994: 108), and a trierarch might have to deal with desertion by crews on active duty ([Dem.] 50.11; Gabrielsen 1994: 122–4). Trierarchic service, moreover, might take a man away from home for long stretches of time and even cost him his life. In the fourth century these considerations prompted many wealthy men to hire agents to carry out their trierarchies, despite the additional cost (Gabrielsen 1994: 95–102).

The high costs, financial and personal, of civic obligations and the manifold uncertainties surrounding these must have been a source of considerable anxiety for many members of the liturgical class. If wealthy Athenians exaggerated the threat of "financial ruin" posed by these, they did so not only to manipulate their audiences but also because they viewed these with some unease. The fourth-century comic writer Antiphanes plausibly highlights civic obligations among the chief threats to a wealthy man's peace of mind, as one of his characters laments:

> Any mortal man who calculates that any possession is secure in life is way off the mark: for a war tax is sure to snatch away all he has; or a lawsuit will fall upon him and destroy him; or having served as general, he will find himself in debt; or having decked out his chorus in golden robes when selected as *chorēgos*, he will have to wear rags himself; or being named trierarch, he will hang himself; or sailing or walking somewhere he will be captured; or he will be slain by his slaves in his sleep. Nothing is certain, except what a man happens to spend with pleasure on himself each day. (fr. 202.1–10)

While this character comically takes anxiety to the level of paranoia, the basic concerns he lists, including those over civic obligations, were very much on the minds of wealthy Athenians. Like the other unhappy turns of fortune this character fears, the imposition of civic obligations was unpredictable and potentially hazardous (cf. X. *Smp.* 4.32; Christ 1990: 153–4).

Rewards

The extent to which a wealthy man viewed his financial obligations as costly and onerous depended not only on what they demanded of him but on his perception of the rewards that might accrue to him, in the form of honor and gratitude (*charis*) from the community, for his sacrifices. How wealthy Athenians perceived these rewards and their attractiveness depended on a host of factors.

Although the pursuit of honor was a common feature of Hellenic life, this was hardly ubiquitous.[65] Aristotle thus observes:

[65] Cf. Ober 1993: 145: "... in democratic Athens desire for outstanding honor remained a psychological condition (albeit a common one within elite status groups) rather than a generalized, definitive social value;" and *ibid.* 159 n. 69: "I tend to think that the aristocratic value of honor has been overgeneralized to a universal Athenian (or Greek) value."

> What constitutes happiness is a matter of dispute; and the popular account of it is not the same as that given by the philosophers. Ordinary people identify it with obvious and visible good, such as pleasure or wealth or honor – some say one thing and some another, indeed very often the same man says different things at different times. (*EN* 1095a22; cf. 1168b15; E. *Hipp.* 373–90; X. *Hier.* 7.1–4)

In Aristotle's view, in fact, "most men yearn more for gain than honor" (*Pol.* 1318b15; cf. *EN* 1121b12; Pl. *Lg.* 870a–b).[66] Even wealthy men, as Athenians recognized, might place a premium on acquiring more wealth (Solon fr. 13.71–3; S. fr. 354.1–5).

It was precisely because the pursuit of honor in the civic sphere could not be taken for granted that Athens did its best to foster this over alternate pursuits. For example, the Attic funeral orations for the state's war dead polemically reject alternatives to the pursuit of honor: "... among good men the acquisition of wealth and the enjoyment of the pleasures that go with living are scorned" (Dem. 60.2; cf. Th. 2.44). The city's honorific decrees for their part assert that *philotimia* is alive and well as a civic virtue, and insist that the city recognizes its debt of gratitude to its benefactors.[67]

To be sure, wealthy Athenians may have been especially drawn to the pursuit of honor because prestige competition was, as noted earlier, a traditional aristocratic activity, which the democracy harnessed within its liturgical system. If Athenian aristocrats were to some extent socially programmed to compete for honor, however, it is doubtful that many of them willingly depleted their fortunes in competition for it (cf. E. E. Cohen 1992: 199). In cases where liturgical expenditures eroded the fortunes of the wealthy and caused them to fall out of the liturgical class, we may reasonably suspect that the individuals involved did not actively seek out the expenditures in question but rather were compelled to

[66] Cf. E. *Ph.* 439–40, where Polyneices asserts: "Men honor property above all else; it has the greatest power in human life." For other instances of this commonplace sentiment, see Mastronarde 1994: 272.

[67] See e.g., *IG* II^2. 300.2–5; Whitehead 1983: 62–4; Rubinstein 2000: 217. Sinclair (1988: 190) astutely observes of the emergence of *philotimia* decrees in the 340s B.C., "It would seem, and not surprisingly, that the importance of philotimia and the notion of reciprocity were consciously or self-consciously emphasised when serious doubts had arisen among the well-to-do whether love of honour expressed in benefits to the polis still brought fitting rewards."

make them by the city. Wealthy Athenians were attuned to personal self-interest no less than other citizens and thus naturally sought to preserve the fortunes that made it possible for them to maintain their elite social status and to enjoy an aristocratic lifestyle.[68] Even those drawn strongly to augment their prestige through public expenditure had good reason not to throw caution to the winds, as a depleted fortune would hinder them from seeking prestige at a later date through further public expenditure. While some men may have spent recklessly in pursuit of political office or may simply have overestimated the ability of their fortunes to recover from their public expenditures, there is no reason to assume that carelessness was the norm.[69] A prudent way for a man to balance the competing pulls of financial self-preservation and pursuit of prestige was to seek to make public expenditures only from what he viewed as his surplus wealth. Thus, Xenophon's Socrates commends an industrious man who not only provides for himself, his family, and his herds, but "has so much to spare that he also often undertakes liturgies for the city" (*Mem.* 2.7.6; cf. Is. 7.39).

To the extent that a wealthy man was drawn to the pursuit of honor, he was naturally conscious that certain forms of public expenditure were more effective than others for this. A major consideration was the conspicuousness (*lamprotēs*) of the expenditure in question, that is, how visible it was to the public. The relative unpopularity of the *eisphora* among the wealthy, noted earlier, probably stemmed from the fact that, as a direct tax collected without fanfare, it provided

[68] It is a commonplace that wealth brings distinction and prestige, e.g., as in E. *Erec.* fr. 362.14–17: "Try though to have possessions; this bestows nobility and the means to make the best marriages. With poverty comes low reputation, even if one is wise, and low esteem in one's life." Cf. S. fr. 88; E. *HF* 633; Plu. *Cim.* 10.5 = Gorg. 82 fr. 20 D–K; Isoc. 15.159; Roisman 2005: 92; but note the more democratic perspective of S. fr. 835: "Even without wealth a man may acquire honors (*timai*)."

[69] Millett (1991: 67) argues, "The competitive *ethos* of liturgy-performance, combined with the peculiar mechanism of payment, encouraged people to indulge in expenditure far beyond their means" (cf. 1998: 251: "the competitive pressure to over-perform liturgies and other public services regularly resulted in the Athenian élite overreaching their often modest resources"). The evidence that Millett (1991: 67–71) cites to support this attests only to the heavy costs of public expenditure, not to willing overexpenditure on it; Millett (70) acknowledges that Apollodorus' zealous expenditure is a special case, because he – as the son of a former slave – was seeking to ingratiate himself with the city.

no immediate public recognition and acclaim (cf. Pritchett 1991: 5.480–2). While the performance of liturgies was, by contrast, typically visible to the public, liturgies varied widely in the extent to which they put a benefactor before the public's gaze.

The *chorēgia* at the City Dionysia was the most visible liturgy in Athens and thus the best vehicle for status display and prestige acquisition. Huge numbers of Athenians attended this festival, and a *chorēgos* was very much in the limelight before, during, and after the performance that he was sponsoring (Wilson 2000: 95–103). Victorious *chorēgoi* in the dithyrambic competitions, moreover, were publicly awarded prize tripods, which they often incorporated into the choregic monuments that they erected to ensure that their glory would not fade from public memory.[70] Other festival liturgies provided opportunities for public recognition and prestige, if typically on a smaller scale than those performed at the City Dionysia. The relative popularity of festival liturgies among the wealthy is likely due in large part to the immediate and considerable gratification they gave to their performers (cf. Lyc. 1.139–40).

The trierarchy, by contrast, was considerably less visible to the public and hence less effective as an instrument for winning prestige (Wilson 2000: 48).[71] Although the launching of a fleet could draw a large crowd – as when the Sicilian expedition left Athens in 415 (Th. 6.30) – a departing trierarch had to share the public stage with a host of other players including generals, other trierarchs, and crews; and once the fleet sailed, a trierarch moved beyond the direct view of a large public. Furthermore, while victorious *chorēgoi* in the dithyrambic contests routinely erected public monuments to their personal munificence, civic norms apparently discouraged successful trierarchs from doing the same: commemoration of military success in Athens usually took the form of publicly sanctioned monuments and these tended

[70] On this and other forms of "monumentalising victory" in the choregic sphere, see Wilson 2000: 198–262; cf. Millett 1998: 246–7.

[71] Gabrielsen (1994: 178) argues on the basis of Lyc. 1.139–40 that higher prestige attached to the trierarchy than to festival liturgies. This passage, however, is highly polemical, arguing contrary to common practice that appeals to *charis* should be based on trierarchies alone.

to honor collective more than individual efforts (see Chapter 3).[72] In general, the agonistic rivalry for prestige that was common in connection with *chorēgiai* did not figure prominently in the trierarchic sphere (Wilson 2000: 48–9). While the city sometimes encouraged trierarchs to compete to prepare their ships expeditiously by promising crowns to a distinguished few, this was not, as far as we know routine.[73]

Although a wealthy man could do relatively little about the public visibility of a financial obligation at the time he was fulfilling it, he could enhance its visibility after the fact by bringing it before the public. In addressing the courts or Assembly, for example, he could put his cumulative record on display and fashion an image of himself as civic benefactor that could advance his reputation. At this point, he could seek credit for his payment of the *eisphora*, which few had directly witnessed at the time he had submitted it, and for his performance of trierarchies, which had taken place beyond the view of a large public. A wealthy man's public representation of his benefactions was key not only to winning prestige, but to seeking *charis* in return for his sacrifices.

While some wealthy men may have embraced civic obligations because they were drawn to prestige as an end in itself, most who were attracted to public benefaction were conscious of the more tangible civic rewards that might go hand in hand with prestige. As Aristotle observes, "[most people] do not appear to value honor for its own sake but for something incidental to it" (*EN* 1159a20). In the case of wealthy Athenians, the prospect of civic prestige was enticing not simply because this raised their status relative to other citizens, but because this gave them a claim to public *charis*.

Specifically, wealthy men could seek to exploit the public's debt to them for their past benefactions in competitive politics and the lawcourts (Davies 1971: xvii–xviii; 1981: 92–7). Individuals could use their record of public services to gain elected political office, like that

[72] A trierarch could, however, commemorate his service through a dedication to a divinity: see Raubitschek 1949: no. 127 [extensively restored], erroneously cited as no. 27 by Gabrielsen 1994: 49; cf. Is. 5.41–2.

[73] This practice is only attested in the fourth century B.C. (Dem. 51.1, 6 [359 B.C.]; *IG* II^2 1629a.190–6 = Tod II.200 [325/4 B.C.]); Jordan (1975: 96), however, believes it dates back to the fifth century.

of general, or to exercise influence within the Assembly as public speakers (*rhētores*). Wealthy litigants could seek to capitalize on their benefactions by arguing or insinuating before popular courts that they deserved favorable treatment in return for their services to the *dēmos*.[74] As one litigant frankly puts it:

> My purpose in spending more than was enjoined upon me by the city was to raise myself the higher in your opinion, so that if any misfortune should befall me, I might defend myself better [in court]. (Lys. 25.13)

Such acknowledgements are sufficiently common (e.g., Lys. 20.31; *P. Ryl.* 3.489 col. 3 = Lys. fr. 9b Todd) that we may take them as evidence of how conscious wealthy Athenians were of the potential returns on what Davies (1971: xvii) aptly terms their "investment in public goodwill."

A wealthy Athenian's interest in investing in public *charis* through his expenditures depended very much, however, on his personal situation and outlook. Individuals who were politically ambitious had good reason to spend generously on the city to lay the groundwork for their advancement in public life (Plu. *Cim.* 10.5 = Gorg. 82 fr. 20 D–K; cf. Th. 6.16; Lys. 19.57). Not all members of the propertied class were drawn to politics, however; many preferred to remain inactive, and were happy to live quiet lives outside the public limelight (Carter 1986; cf. Gabrielsen 1994: 214–15). Even such men, however, might find it prudent to invest in public goodwill through benefactions, in case they found themselves defendants in lawsuits as wealthy men often did.[75] Individuals must have varied widely, however, in their concerns about future litigation and in their view of the need for investing in *charis* in anticipation of this.

How much a man might want to accumulate *charis* through benefaction also depended on how confident he was that the public would acknowledge and reward his sacrifices. While a wealthy man could assume that certain forms of public expenditure would win him

[74] It is primarily defendants who draw on *charis*: see Johnstone 1999: 94; Rubinstein 2000: 213, with n. 49. On the rhetoric of reciprocity in these contexts, see Millett 1998.

[75] Wealthy Athenians were much more likely than average citizens to become involved in litigation: see Christ 1998a: 32–4; 2002: 3–5.

immediate distinction because of their conspicuousness, he could not be sure that any of his expenditures would win him the tangible benefits of *charis* at some future date. Not without cause, then, do litigants appealing for *charis* express anxiety over whether their audiences will reward them for their sacrifices. Consider, for example, how one of Lysias' clients expresses his concerns:

> After so many dangers encountered on your behalf and after all the services that I have rendered to the city, I now request, not a gift from you for my reward, as others do, but that I not be deprived of my own property; for I consider it a disgrace to you also, to take it both with my will and against my will. I do not mind so much having to lose my possessions; but I could not put up with the outrage, and the impression that it must produce on those who shirk their liturgies – that while I get no credit (ἀχάριστα) for what I have spent on you, they prove to have been rightly advised in giving up to you no part of their own property. (21.11–12)

While this appeal and similar ones are without doubt manipulative, they also reflect a basic truth: it was inherently uncertain whether a wealthy man's investment in goodwill would bear fruit.

The uncertainty of public gratitude for benefactions was heightened by the fact that claims on public *charis* were problematic from a social perspective. Although most Athenians might agree that "a certain *charis*" (Dem. 38.25) was due to benefactors, what form this should take was open to debate.[76] This is especially evident in the courts where the proper scope of *charis* was regularly contested (Johnstone 1999: 94, 103). Prosecutors, for example, protest that past public expenditure is irrelevant to questions of guilt (e.g., Ant. 2.3.8); *charis* should not override the city's laws (e.g., Lys. 14.40); individuals acting as defense advocates (*synēgoroi*) should not be able to transfer the *charis* that is due to them personally to a defendant (Lyc. 1.139–40).[77] For their part, those seeking *charis* plea for what is

[76] It was also open to interpretation what level of civic benefaction merited a return of *charis*: while a man could seek credit for zealously doing whatever the city required him to do (Dem. 38.26), many wealthy men base their claims on having done more than was required of them (Lys. 7.31; 19.63; 21.5, 25.13; Is. 7.38; cf. Isoc. 15.145).

[77] On these and other rebuttals to *charis* claims, see Christ 1990: 155; Johnstone 1999: 98–100, 104–6; Rubinstein 2000: 212–20.

rightly due them (e.g., Lys. 3.47–8; 21.25); appeal to the self-interest of jurors, who can hope to benefit from future benefactions from them (Lys. 19.61–4; 21.12; cf. Dem. 28.24); and make veiled threats concerning how other wealthy men may react if they see the city is ungrateful to its benefactors (Lys. 21.12 [quoted above in the text]; cf. 18.23).[78] Ultimately, it was up to the jurors in each case to determine how to evaluate these competing positions and whether to reward benefactions.

While the persistence of *charis* claims in forensic oratory throughout the classical period suggests that these continued to have some power (Davies 1981: 95; Millett 1998: 237), the public's receptiveness to these may have diminished as democratic values and consciousness grew ever more sharp (Christ 1990: 155). Men outside the liturgical class, who dominated juries, had some reason to bristle at the claim of wealthy men to special treatment based on their public service (cf. Dem. 21.153); after all average men served the city too, and sometimes even "expended" their lives on its behalf.[79] From the late-fifth century on, in fact, the term *leitourgia* – which was originally confined to the public service of the wealthy – came also to be used more broadly of any service to the city (Lewis 1960: 181). Lycurgus (330 B.C.) challenges the very premise that *charis* is due to those performing festival liturgies, on the grounds that their conspicuous expenditures are made simply to enhance their reputations (1.139–40); Lycurgus was surely not the first Athenian to believe that aristocratic self-celebration did not merit democratic *charis*.

Developments in the institutions and practices involving the trierarchy in the fourth century may also have made it more difficult for the wealthy to lay claim to *charis* for trierarchic service. In particular, the

[78] Johnstone (1999: 95–101) observes that litigants often cite their liturgies as evidence of their good character instead of making these the basis of *charis* claims, and suggests that this may reflect the problematic nature of *charis* appeals. While there may be some truth to this, wealthy men who cite liturgies as evidence of good character may well be insinuating also that as good citizens and public benefactors they deserve favorable treatment from Athenian juries. Note, for example, how the assertion of good character on the basis of public services and an appeal for *charis* go hand-in-hand in Lys. 25.12–13.

[79] For the figure of "expenditure" of lives, see note 1.

establishment of naval *symmoriai* in 358/7 rendered such claims problematic. Because membership in these was mandatory, a wealthy man could have trouble laying claim to *charis* on this basis: after all, he had only done what the city had compelled him to do (Ober 1989: 241–2; Christ 1990: 155). Furthermore, because a trierarch's costs were now at least partly subsidized by those in his *symmoria*, his personal contribution toward expenses could be called into doubt (Dem. 21.155; cf. Is. 7.37). The public, moreover, had some reason to doubt that those claiming *charis* on the basis of trierarchic service had actually carried this out in person (Dem. 21.155), because the practice of hiring substitutes became common in the fourth century (Gabrielsen 1994: 95–102).

Although wealthy Athenians may have been concerned above all with the high costs and uncertain rewards of their financial obligations, they were also troubled by how these obligations were distributed and their compulsory aspect. These latter concerns could heighten a man's sensitivity to costs, raise his expectations of the rewards needed to counterbalance his expenditures, and profoundly affect his willingness to carry out his obligations.

Fairness

Athens' wealthy citizens could object to the fairness of their financial obligations on two grounds. First, the fact that the rich were subject to these while average citizens were not invited the complaint that they were carrying more than their fair share as a group. Second, quite apart from questions of fair treatment of the rich collectively, the distribution of obligations among wealthy men could appear unfair. Perceptions of inequities of either sort could lead to discontent and resistance to fulfilling financial obligations.

A striking feature of Athenian democracy is that it made a small percentage of citizens exclusively responsible for supporting the state financially (E. E. Cohen 1992: 194–5). This arrangement was broadly consistent with democratic ideology, which held that each man should contribute what he could to the city: the rich enjoyed extraordinary wealth and therefore could be called upon to share this with the city.[80] While other citizens could also have been required to contribute financially to the city in proportion to their level of wealth, Athenians chose not to take this course. This is due in part to the power of the *dēmos* to impose its will on a wealthy minority; as noted above, the *dēmos* gradually, but unmistakably, asserted its authority over the wealthy and their fortunes during the classical period. This arrangement also reflects, however, how Athenians perceived the distribution of wealth in their city: as observed earlier, they tended to view men as either "rich" or "poor." This social assumption probably influenced the formation of the liturgical system in the early years of the democracy; once this system was in place, it reinforced this impression of wealth distribution by fostering conspicuous public expenditure by wealthy men. When the *eisphora* was introduced later, it may have seemed natural to the Athenian public therefore to levy it exclusively on the rich.

If the process by which the rich came to be responsible exclusively for financial obligations under the democracy was a complex one and not simply a matter of the majority asserting its power over a minority, some wealthy men took the cynical view that this was class exploitation, pure and simple. Sources that are openly critical of the democracy voice this perspective most bluntly. The Old Oligarch, as noted above, asserts that the liturgical system makes the poor rich, and the rich poorer ([X.] *Ath. Pol.* 1.13; cf. Th. 8.63.4). Xenophon's Charmides advances a similar view, contrasting the position of a rich man and a poor one under the democracy: the rich man is constantly required to spend money on the city; the poor man is always getting money from it (*Smp.* 4.29–32, with Christ 1998a: 84–5; cf. *Oec.* 2.6–7; Pl. *R.* 564e). Isocrates voices similar sentiments in his *Antidosis* (354/3 B.C.). Still smarting from his assignment to a trierarchy through the *antidosis* procedure (15.4), he paints a bleak picture of the rich under the current democracy: "a man has to be ready to defend himself against being rich as if it were the worst of crimes" (15.160).[81] While these various

[80] On the "redistributive" character of this arrangement, see Ober 1989: 199–202; 1993: 146.

[81] Johnstone (2003: 249 n. 7) takes Isoc. 15.159–60 as an assertion, like 7.34–5, that wealthy men conceal their property due to fear of decisions from popular courts, and concludes

petulant assertions are colored by antipathy for democratic institutions, a wealthy man did not have to be a closet oligarch to see inequity in the city's arrangements involving financial obligations; it was hard to miss the fact that the rich paid a great deal while others paid nothing, especially if one was rich.

Not surprisingly, popular discourse in Athens did not encourage open complaints from the wealthy concerning the "soaking of the rich." Thus Demosthenes seeks to rally public hostility against his enemy Meidias by claiming that he crassly asserts in the Assembly and elsewhere, "We are the men who perform liturgies! We are the men who pay the *proeisphora* for you! We are the rich!" (21.153). If wealthy men were expected to address this division of civic responsibilities with some sensitivity in public settings, however, they make it abundantly clear that they are conscious of it. This imbalance, in fact, is the basis of their regular claim to be owed *charis* for their contributions to the city: because they contribute exceptionally to the city, they deserve special treatment from it in return.[82]

Although a wealthy man's expectation of *charis* could make him comfortable with his class' exclusive responsibility for financial obligations in the city, the taxation of a single segment of society encouraged class consciousness among the wealthy and, potentially, a sense of collective wrong. This could prove dangerous for the democracy, as it might lead to organized political opposition to majority rule. As noted above, a sense of inequity concerning the wartime financial obligations of the wealthy contributed to the oligarchic revolution of 411 B.C.; ancient political theorists, perhaps extrapolating in part from this episode, warned that civil strife (*stasis*) could result

therefore that Isocrates "associates hidden wealth with judicial decisions, not with excessive liturgies." In the case of 15.159–60, however, Isocrates may well have both judicial decisions and excessive liturgies in mind as causes of concealment of wealth, because the inspiration for his *Antidosis* is an Athenian jury's allegedly unfair imposition of a trierarchy on him in a trial arising in connection with *antidosis* (15.4).

[82] I am not convinced that, "While private *charis* created vertical, isolating links, public *charis* created horizontal links among ordinary Athenians" (Johnstone 1999: 107). On the hierarchical dimensions of the *charis* relationship and the tensions surrounding it in the courts, see Roisman 2005: 155–6. Cf. Anon. Iambl. 2.400.17–18 D–K: "it is not pleasant for men to honor another man – for they consider that they themselves are thereby deprived of something."

if the rich felt overburdened by their public obligations (Arist. *Pol.* 1304b20–1305a5; cf. [Arist.] *Rh. Al.* 1424a20–32). If, in fact, wealthy men did not league together again on this basis to overturn the city's constitution, a sense of class inequity may have been an important factor in the decision of some wealthy individuals to evade their obligations.

A wealthy man who was not troubled by the assignment of financial obligations exclusively to men of his class might still have deep concerns over how these obligations were distributed among the rich. Although such concerns probably surfaced early in the history of the liturgical system and contributed to the formation of rules concerning frequency of service and the establishment of the *antidosis* procedure, as noted above substantial reform in the area of equity came only late: the city finally and formally took into account the widely different degrees of wealth among the rich in 378 B.C. for the *eisphora*, and 340 B.C. for the trierarchy. For much of the classical period, the city's institutions provided little reassurance to a wealthy man that his share of financial obligations was a fair one that took into account his level of wealth (cf. Christ 1990: 154–5).

Even after the major fourth-century reforms of the *eisphora* and trierarchy, wealthy men had reason to be concerned about the equitable distribution of financial obligations. Because concealment of wealth was routine (see below), it continued to be difficult to ensure that the wealthiest men bore the largest share of expenses. Although a man assigned a liturgy could seek to have it transferred to a man he deemed wealthier through the *antidosis* procedure, this depended on a great deal of personal initiative on his part and there was no assurance that he would succeed; in many cases it must have been impossible to ferret out an opponent's concealed wealth (cf. Dem. 42.23). As noted above, *antidosis* was an effective mechanism from the perspective of the city, in that it helped to ensure that the requisite number of liturgists would be forthcoming. As a tool for individuals seeking equity, however, *antidosis* was much less effective: wealthy men were inclined to view it as another burden on them (Isoc. 8.128; 15.4; X. *Oec.* 7.3; cf. Dem. 28.17; Lys. 4.1–2) as much as a means of alleviating financial pressure (Dem. 42.25, 32) (Christ 1990: 160–8).

Compulsion

Although civic ideology emphasized the voluntary nature of expenditure on behalf of the city, rich men were under no illusion as to the ultimately compulsory nature of this. They regularly allude to the "necessity" (ἀνάγκη) of carrying out their obligations and refer to their duties as "commands/orders" (τὰ προσταττόμενα) from the city (Christ 1990: 156 n. 42). The latter figure, which evokes military service, invites equation of the compulsion on wealthy men with that operating on the city's conscripts. Just as compulsion on hoplites to serve was a point of tension in Athens, so too was the compulsion on the wealthy to carry out financial obligations.

While civic compulsion of free citizens was an inherently sensitive matter within the Athenian democracy, the specific form this took could shape the responses of individuals to it. The wealthy may have been especially sensitive to the compulsion upon them to serve the city financially because this came as an additional imposition on them: they could be conscripted as hoplites when not performing a liturgy. Furthermore, liturgical service loomed over the wealthy throughout their adult lives. Athenians were compelled to serve as hoplites only periodically, because the city's military enterprises were normally intermittent and call-up of the entire force was uncommon. Wealthy Athenians, however, were regularly called upon in time of peace and war to support the city financially, with only temporary respites from liturgies after recent service; and, while men became exempt from hoplite service at age sixty, there was apparently no upper age limit for liability to the trierarchy (Gabrielsen 1994: 87, 247 n. 29). In the case of trierarchic service, moreover, the wealthy could claim that their lives were at stake as they, like hoplites, faced danger (e.g., Lys. 21.11, 24; Isoc. 18.58–62). The compulsion upon wealthy men to serve the city could also entangle them in open-ended activities, for example, the collection of the *eisphora* from reluctant peers after the establishment of the *proeisphora* (cf. [Dem.] 50.9) or the retrieval of naval equipment from deadbeat trierarchs (Dem. 47.19–22), and lead to interpersonal conflict and litigation (Lys. XLIII Thalheim; Dem. 47; cf. Dem. 42). Even when the city was not currently requiring service of them, there was some public expectation that they should preserve their fortunes for the city's benefit: litigants do not hesitate to rebuke one another for squandering liturgical fortunes on private extravagances (Is. 5.43, with 41; fr. 22 Thalheim; Aeschin. 1.96–7; cf. Gabrielsen 1986: 108). In light of the far-reaching implications of this compulsion and its omnipresence in the lives of the wealthy, it comes as no surprise that wealthy men sometimes viewed it as irksome and intrusive.

The most extreme reaction to this compulsion upon the wealthy is found, not surprisingly, in the writings of ardent critics of the democracy. Xenophon, for example, characterizes this compulsion as "slavery" in his *Symposium*. His Charmides expands ironically on the benefits of his (alleged) fall from wealth to poverty under the democracy (4.29–32): under the democracy the rich man is a slave (4.32; 4.29; cf. 4.31) because of the city's financial demands upon him (4.30); to join the ranks of the poor is therefore to gain freedom (4.29, 31) and tyrannical power over the rich (4.32). Later, the wealthy Callias employs the same imagery, when he congratulates Antisthenes, a man of slender means (4.34), on the grounds that "the city does not lay its commands on you (ἐπιτάττουσα) and treat you as a slave" (4.45).

While public discourse did not invite this sort of barbed social commentary on the "slavery" of the rich, wealthy men do not entirely avoid the subject before popular audiences. Consider, for example, how a wealthy litigant pursuing an *antidosis* claim speaks of his need for a respite from public service:

> For, if I had been your household slave (οἰκέτης) and not a citizen, seeing my industry and my goodwill toward you, you would have given me respite from my expenditures and would have turned to one of those who was running away from his duty (ἐπὶ τὸν δραπετεύοντα τῶν ἄλλων).[83] (Dem. 42.32; cf. 25)

This speaker deftly makes his point that even a slave deserves a respite from hard work while at the same time distancing himself, through

[83] For an evader of civic duties as a δραπέτης, which is a common term for a runaway slave (Hdt. 6.11.2; S. fr. 63), see Din. 1.82; Aeschin. 3.152; cf. Ar. *Ach.* 1187; X. *HG* 2.4.16. Individuals are frequently accused of "running away" from their duties; for the use of ἀποδιδράσκω in this context, see Isoc. 18.48; Lys. 16.17; Dem. 21.165; [Dem.] 50.65; Aeschin. 3.161, 167, 226, 253; Din. 1.81–2); for διαδιδράσκω and cognates, see Ar. *Ach.* 601; *Ra.* 1014; cf. *Lys.* 719.

the counterfactual condition, from the blunt assertion that the city has enslaved him and other men of his class.[84]

That the compulsion upon the wealthy to serve the city was a matter of some sensitivity is also clear in Demosthenes' *Second Olynthiac* (349/8 B.C.). As Demosthenes works to unify Athenians against the menace posed by Philip of Macedon, he exhorts the *dēmos* not "to force (ἀναγκάζεσθαι) some men to serve as trierarchs, to pay the *eisphora*, and to go on expeditions," while others "have no other public toil (συμπονεῖν) than to condemn these men"; otherwise, "there will always be some aggrieved group who will fail you, and then it will be your privilege to punish them instead of the enemy" (2.30). While Demosthenes stops short of framing the problem in explicit class terms of rich and poor, his warning is clear: exercise restraint in making demands upon wealthier Athenians and do not expect them to toil alone for the city (cf. 2.31; Th. 8.48.1, 63.4).

CHOICES AND STRATEGIES

Although concerns about financial obligations figured in the decision of some wealthy men to league together in political opposition to democratic rule in 411 B.C., this extreme form of resistance was exceptional. More commonly, wealthy Athenians may have collaborated to influence the democratic institutions governing financial obligations; this would help explain some features of the reforms surveyed earlier that take into account the interests of wealthy men. Different groups of wealthy men, however, might well pursue different agendas: for example, Demosthenes asserts that very rich Athenians banded together to oppose his trierarchic reform of 340 B.C., which sought to provide relief to less wealthy members of the liturgical class (18.103–4).

While wealthy men had good reason to collaborate in lobbying for arrangements that were favorable to them, we know little concerning such alliances. We are in a much better position to assess individual responses to financial obligations. It remains to examine some of the

[84] For the hostile claim that democratic citizens in general regard the compulsion to carry out civic duties as slavery, see Pl. *R.* 562d, 563d; cf. *Lg.* 698a–b; Arist. *Pol.* 1310a30; Plu. *Pyrrh.* 16.2.

tactics to which the wealthy had recourse and the efficacy of these. It was very much in the interest of a wealthy man to engage in advanced planning concerning the disposition of his property; and to make prudent choices when obligations were being assigned, when he carried out liturgies, and when he represented his services to the public afterward. Strategic behavior was in the interest not only of shameless dodgers but of prudent patriots.

Concealment of Property

Concerns over financial obligations had a significant impact on the choices that wealthy men made concerning the public visibility of their wealth. Concealment of wealth was fundamental for a man to have some control over when or whether he was liable to public service and over the extent of his liability to the *eisphora*. Concealment was achievable through a wide range of devices and nearly impossible for the city to control, and appears to have been extremely common (Gabrielsen 1986; 1994: 53–60; Christ 1990: 158–60; E. E. Cohen 1992: 191–207).

Consider, for example, how a client of Lysias seeks credit for his father because he did not conceal his property (*ca.* 410 B.C.):

> Although he might well (ἐξὸν) have concealed his wealth and deprived you of his service, he chose rather that you should have knowledge of it, so that even if he should wish to be unscrupulous, it would not be possible, but he would instead have to pay the war tax and perform liturgies. (20.23)

This passage is of interest not only in its assumption that honesty in this sphere is something to boast of (cf. Isoc. 18.59–60; Lys. 18.7; Is. 7.39–40), but also in its portrayal of how tempting it was to conceal property: this was a real possibility for the rich and largely a matter of choice (cf. Dem. 28.1–4).[85]

[85] The charge of concealment is commonplace: see e.g., Is. 11.47; Dem. 14.25; 42.23; 45.66; Aeschin. 1.101; Ste. Croix 1953: 34, with n. 17; Johnstone 2003: 249 n. 4 (collecting 25 passages from the orators). While concealment may have intensified in the fourth century, it was probably common in the fifth century as well, *contra* Isoc. 7.34–5 (cf. Gabrielsen 1986: 104–5). Johnstone (2003: 249) points out that litigants link concealment of wealth not only to the desire to evade taxes but to other antisocial motivations, including "escaping the adverse consequences of legal judgments (fines to the state or compensation to the prosecutor)."

Wealth could be concealed through a large number of devices suited to an individual's preferences and the nature of his wealth (Is. 5.43, cf. Is. 7.42, Dem. 42.2, 19, 30; Gabrielsen 1986: 108). Cash was ideal for concealing, because it was nearly impossible for outsiders to keep track of in classical Athens (Ar. *Ec.* 601–3). It could be buried in the ground (cf. Gabrielsen 1986: 109; Johnstone 2003: 255 n. 39) or, better, deposited in a bank (esp. Isoc. 17.2–11), where it could be shielded from public view and earn a return, which was also untraceable.[86] Indeed, the growth of banks in Athens may be due in no small part to the fact that bankers helped depositors conceal their wealth (E. E. Cohen 1992: 201–7; cf. Shipton 1997: 416–17, 422).[87] Although most citizen fortunes were based on land and slaves, a wealthy man could convert these assets into cash in proportion to his aversion to financial obligations (Gabrielsen 1986: 108).

While real property was more difficult to conceal from public view than cash, prudent decisions could reduce outside knowledge even of land holdings. In Attica, a wealthy man could seek to hold land in several demes and thus make it harder for others to keep track of it (but cf. [Dem.] 50.8). The fewer leases and other public transactions in which he was involved in connection with these, the easier it was to conceal them from the public (Gabrielsen 1986: 105). Wealthy men's holdings outside of Attica, which were often considerable, must have been largely invisible to the public (*ibid.* 112, with 112 n. 39). When real property could not be concealed in any of these ways, a wealthy man could reduce the appearance of his landed wealth by borrowing large sums of money secured by his land and posting stone markers (*horoi*) on his property recording this debt. Although wealthy men may have borrowed sometimes because they were genuinely short of cash, for example, for their public obligations, this also might allow them to

[86] Although concealment of money in private banks could be risky if a banker was dishonest (as the speaker of Isoc. 17 claims of Pasio), bankers had a strong financial interest in maintaining a reputation for personal honesty (cf. E. Cohen 1992: 24–5, 62–7). Although concealment of wealth, in general, carried with it a variety of risks (see Johnstone 2003: 262–7; cf. Todd 1990: 170–1), this does not appear to have deterred Athenians much from engaging in it.

[87] Individuals could also avail themselves of legal "tax shelters" for their cash, by investing in the city's silver mines (Dem. 42.18, 23) or in property in Athenian cleruchies (Dem. 14.16); cf. Gabrielsen 1994: 87–90.

look less well-off than they actually were; a property dotted with *horoi* might discourage city officials who were assigning liturgies or wealthy men who were seeking rivals for *antidosis* from troubling its owner (cf. Dem. 42.5, 9, 28; Gabrielsen 1986: 104, with n. 17; 1994: 89–90).

To conceal family wealth in the form of cash or land, it was essential for wealthy men to take care in how they passed this on to their heirs, whom the city was likely to call upon to fulfill financial obligations (Gabrielsen 1994: 60–7). A wealthy man could help his heirs conceal wealth by passing on cash and real property outside of a written will because the public might well gain knowledge of this document (Gabrielsen 1986: 106). While a man whose children were still minors might feel compelled to rely upon guardians to carry out this sensitive operation after his death (Dem. 27.55), a man with grown sons might prefer to turn over concealed wealth to them directly while he was still alive. In fact, an aging man might divide his visible wealth as well among his grown sons (cf. Dem. 47.34–5, with MacDowell 1978: 91–2), with an eye to protecting his family's fortune from state impositions: if the portions that his sons received were small enough, they might not be liable to liturgies and the *eisphora*.[88] Division of property among heirs may often have led to fortunes dropping out of the liturgical class (Davies 1981: 74–7); to the extent a man could speed this along in his own lifetime, this would help keep wealth in the hands of his family members.[89]

It was virtually impossible for the city to stop wealthy citizens from concealing their wealth. It had no central land registry to help it keep track of a wealthy man's land holdings (Gabrielsen 1986: 112–13). Banks, which assisted in the concealment of cash, were not subject to audit. The assessment (*timēma*) that a wealthy man submitted in connection with the *eisphora* after 378 B.C. was a self-assessment and hence inherently unreliable (Is. 7.39; cf. Pl. *R.* 343d; *Lg.* 754d–e).

88 There would be an especially strong incentive to adopt this strategy, if, as Gabrielsen suggests (1994: 64), "insofar as a household remained undivided, all adult males with an ownership share, including the co-ownership of father and son, became individually liable."

89 Adoption might also be exploited to control estate size and liability to civic demands: see Is. 11.44–50 (denying resort to this strategy); cf. Gabrielsen 1986: 107–8; Davies 1971: 88.

While the city could have made concealment more difficult by instituting reforms in any of these areas, it did not. The city's inaction may reflect the fact that the task of policing concealment would have been a daunting one for its bureaucracy. The city, moreover, was insulated from some of the most serious consequences of concealment. In the liturgical sphere, the city's agents simply assigned liturgies to those who plausibly had the resources to carry these out and left it to them, if they objected, to seek to transfer their burdens to others through *antidosis*. In the case of the *eisphora*, according to my reconstruction the city levied the tax before 378 as a fixed amount due from each wealthy man, and thus sidestepped the problem of evaluating net worth; after 378 when the city required wealthy men to submit assessments of their wealth within the *symmoriai*, underreporting by a symmory member increased the tax burden of his fellow members – because each group was responsible for a fixed sum – and did not affect the city's total revenues.

Assignment of Financial Obligations

While concealment of wealth could reduce a man's chance of being assigned a liturgy, in most cases it probably did not eliminate this possibility. It was very much to his advantage, therefore, to be familiar with the procedures surrounding the assignment of liturgies and to develop strategies for protecting or advancing his interests in light of these.

One option for a wealthy man was to seek to influence the assignment process through his personal connections. Because initial assignment to financial obligations involved discretion on the part of state officials, personal influence with these individuals could be extremely useful. The power of wealthy men to get personal favors granted here – as in the sphere of conscription (see Chapter 2) – was likely considerable, especially when those being approached were cronies, as may often have been the case. For example, the generals, who selected trierarchs, were frequently themselves members of the liturgical class (Davies 1981: 122–4; cf. Gabrielsen 1994: 213–15) and linked to many of their peers socially and politically; it was natural in these circumstances that favors would be sought and granted (cf. Lys. 29.3–4).

Favoritism could take many forms: a general could pass over an individual who was eligible for the trierarchy; endorse a contrived exemption before a lawcourt considering a *skēpsis* (cf. Lys. 15.1–5); allow a man who could afford a sole trierarchy to divide costs with a syntrierarch; or assign a new ship to a trierarch to reduce his costs of maintaining it (cf. Ar. *Eq.* 912–18).[90] While generals had good reason to be discreet in granting favors to avoid prosecution at their end-of-year judicial scrutinies (*euthynai*), they had considerable latitude to help their friends.

In the absence of personal connections to exploit, a wealthy man who anticipated that he might be assigned a liturgy – for example, because he was manifestly very rich – could put himself forward as a candidate. By embracing what was in his view inevitable anyway, he could enhance his prestige as a volunteer benefactor of the city and build a foundation for future claims to *charis* from the community.[91]

Voluntarism could be advantageous for other reasons as well, however. It allowed a wealthy man to choose the form of his benefaction, considering its visibility, expense, and any risks involved. Festival liturgies, as noted above, were relatively attractive to the wealthy, because they entailed high public visibility, costs that could be controlled, and no risk of mortality. To be sure, a festival liturgist received only a one-year respite from public service upon completion of his task, while a trierarch received a two-year break; his expenditure, however, might well be less than half of that of a trierarch, especially if he carried out one of the less expensive festival liturgies or economized in carrying out one of the more costly ones. An individual seeking assignment to a festival liturgy could present himself to the appropriate official at the start of the civic year before being nominated as trierarch. As far as we know, officials filled their liturgical rosters as they saw fit, without consulting or negotiating with others who were seeking candidates for other liturgies.[92] While a man who

[90] Jordan (1975: 68–70) argues that the generals assigned ships to trierarchs in the fifth century; Hamel (1998a: 31 n. 91; cf. Cawkwell 1984: 338; Gabrielsen 1994: 74) doubts this was so. By at least the 370s ships were assigned by lot to trierarchs (see Gabrielsen 1994: 80–4).

[91] For boasts of voluntarism, see e.g., Lys. 21.5; 29.4; Dem. 18.99; 19.230; 21.13, 156; 45.85.

[92] When the generals and archons came into office simultaneously in mid summer (Rhodes 1981: 537), they made the naming of liturgists a priority: the incoming generals sought

carried out *chorēgiai* and shunned the trierarchy might be subject to criticism (cf. Is. 5.36), this was not illegal and could conceivably be defended on the grounds of prior experience and success.[93]

Although voluntarism was presumably common in the sphere of festival liturgies, it was probably less routine in the case of the trierarchy – given the disincentives involved – and rare in connection with the costly and inglorious *eisphora*. If a man was assigned to a financial obligation against his will, his options depended on the nature of the duty. As noted above, if he was assigned to pay the *eisphora*, he had no legal recourse to seek release from this; he therefore had either to pay or take his chances on not complying (cf. Ar. *Lys.* 652–5; Dem. 22.44). If a man was assigned a liturgy, however, he could seek release by advancing the legal claim (*skēpsis*) that he was exempt from it, which would lead to a judicial hearing; or he might seek through the *antidosis* procedure to transfer his burden to a wealthier man. Strategic considerations came into play in both cases.

An initial question for a man assigned to a liturgy was whether to advance a claim to exemption based on any of the recognized grounds. If a man was not averse to service, he might choose not to assert an

to fill the ranks of trierarchs right away (cf. [Dem.] 50.23, with Jordan 1975: 66); and the new eponymous archon (and presumably also the *archōn basileus*) sought straightaway to name festival liturgists ([Arist.] *Ath. Pol.* 56.3, with Rhodes 1981: 623; Wilson 2000: 51).

The statement of Dem. 20.19 (355 B.C.) that "the richest men, since (when?) they serve as trierarchs, are always exempt from *chorēgiai*" (οἱ μὲν τοίνυν πλουσιώτατοι τριηραρχοῦντες ἀεὶ τῶν χορηγιῶν ἀτελεῖς ὑπάρχουσιν) is often construed to mean that the city sought to channel the wealthiest men into the trierarchy (thus MacDowell 1990: 374; Hansen 1991: 113; cf. Rhodes 1982: 4; but cf. Gabrielsen 1994: 177, with 261 n. 11). This passage, however, does not explicitly claim that this is so, and note how [Arist.] *Ath. Pol.* 56.3 speaks of the "richest of all Athenians" (ἐξ ἁπάντων Ἀθηναίων τοὺς πλουσιωτάτους) serving as *chorēgoi* for tragedies at the Dionysia. Contrary to modern assumptions that the naming of trierarchs should have been a priority for Athenians (see e.g., Gabrielsen 1994: 178) and much to the frustration of some ancient commentators who objected to festival liturgies as wasteful (see Arist. *Pol.* 1309a14–19, 1320b4; frr. 88–9 Rose; Plu. *Mor.* 349a–b = Dem. Phal. fr. 136 Wehrli; cf. Isoc. 7.53–5), Athenians did not privilege naval arrangements over festival ones (cf. Dem. 4.35–7).

93 Although litigants make the most of the fact that they have provided comprehensive support to the city through the triad of trierarchies, *chorēgiai*, and *eisphorai* (Ant. 2.2.12; Lys. 7.31; 19.29, 57; 21.1–5; Is. 5.41; Dem. 18.257; cf. Lys. 25.12; Is. 7.38), they can claim credit on the basis of festival liturgies alone ([And.] 4.42) or in combination with *eisphorai* (Is. 7.40).

exemption to which he was entitled.[94] The normal practice, however, was probably to make the most of exemptions, including those giving temporary respite for recent service – only the very wealthy could afford not to take advantage of such exemptions. Consistent with this is the fact that claims of continuous service are relatively infrequent and individuals who claim to have ignored exemptions boast of this as if their behavior was exceptional (Isoc. 18.59–60; Lys. 21.5; Is. 7.38; cf. Lys. 19.29; Is. 5.41).

While a man might seek to evade liturgical service through a false claim of exemption, it was probably much harder to win release from liturgies through illicit claims of exemption than to escape hoplite service in this way (see Chapter 2). First, claims of physical disability, which conscripts likely abused with some success, would not automatically disqualify a wealthy man from liturgical service: after all, he could at least finance the liturgy in question and hire an agent to execute it in his place.[95] Second, as noted above, officials apparently could not grant these and other claims to exemption on their own authority, as the generals could when conscripting hoplites; rather, they were obliged to bring these before a popular court, which scrutinized the grounds claimed for exemption. The city had good reason to exercise more control here than in the sphere of conscription, as it was drawing on a much smaller pool of candidates for liturgical service and lax administration of exemptions would have led to a shortfall in liturgists.

If a man seeking release from liturgical assignment did not have a plausible basis for claiming an exemption, therefore, it was in his interest to force one of his peers to assume this through *antidosis*. Success in this depended above all on competitive acumen and shrewdness (Christ 1990: 164–8). While the city encouraged wealthy men to compete with one another in a prestige contest (*agōn*) in performing their financial obligations admirably, they were involved in a less public

[94] For example, a very wealthy man might fear public ridicule for pressing the "letter of the law" (cf. Lys. 21.5) on his entitlement to a respite due to recent service; so too, a man who had performed one of the less expensive festival liturgies in the previous year might be embarrassed to claim exemption on this basis.

[95] For the weak and aged sometimes serving as trierarchs, see e.g., Lys. fr. 35 Thalheim; Dem. 21.165; Gabrielsen 1994: 91, 97, with 247 n. 29, 188–9.

contest to transfer their assignments to others and to avoid being saddled with others' obligations; sharp players, anticipating their involvement in *antidosis*, concealed their wealth from public view as much as possible. In initiating the *antidosis* procedure, a wealthy man had first to identify an attractive target to challenge: an ideal opponent had considerable visible wealth; was inexperienced in the *antidosis* procedure and litigation in general; was strongly attached to his property and thus averse to an actual exchange (this could be used against him in court as evidence of his superior wealth); and reluctant to appear before a popular court due to personal or political reasons. In executing each stage of the procedure, shrewd self-presentation improved a man's chances of success: a challenger did well to give the impression from the start that he was willing to pursue the procedure all the way to court if necessary and that he would gladly exchange property (though few would genuinely wish to do so); and, once in court, it was in his interest to portray himself as a patriot who normally embraced public service, while casting his opponent as a shameless dodger (Dem. 42; Christ 1990: 166–7).

To all appearances, wealthy men frequently had recourse to the *antidosis* procedure (Christ 1990: 163–4). There seems to have been little stigma attached to participation in *antidosis* (Christ 1990: 164): an individual who sought relief through this procedure naturally claimed this was only fair given his circumstances (Dem. 42.3–4); a man assigned a liturgy in this way could protest after the fact that he had been taken advantage of (cf. Dem. 21.78–80; Isoc. 15.4–5). Our sources treat *antidosis* as a routine step in the assignment of liturgies ([Arist.] *Ath. Pol.* 56.3, 61.1; cf. [X.] *Ath. Pol.* 3.4) and speak often of it.[96] Wealthy litigants and their popular audiences, moreover, are intimately familiar with it (e.g., Lys. 24.9). The apparent frequency of the *antidosis* procedure confirms that public service was unattractive in the eyes of many.

[96] The numerous ancient testimonia are collected in Gabrielsen 1987a: 10 n. 9, with additions in Christ 1990: 163 n. 78. In light of the number of testimonia and their treatment of *antidosis* as routine, Gabrielsen (1987a: 29) is overcautious in stating, "It is not possible to infer anything about the frequency with which the *antidosis* procedure was employed."

Performing a Liturgy

Whether a wealthy man undertook a liturgy voluntarily or reluctantly, he faced a series of choices in carrying it out that could affect his total costs and the rewards to which he might lay claim. For example, at the outset he had to decide how actively to be involved in carrying out a liturgy. It was tempting to delegate much or all of the service component of a liturgy to a hired agent. *Chorēgoi* regularly relied upon agents to carry out the supervision and training of their choruses (Wilson 2000: 81–4), and trierarchs in the fourth century often hired substitutes to sail in their place (Gabrielsen 1994: 95–102). There was some risk involved, however, in delegating authority, as a liturgist could be held accountable for actions carried out in his name. A *chorēgos* might be held responsible for harm to a chorister at the hands of those assisting him (Ant. 6; cf. Gagarin 1997: 220–5); a trierarch who remained at home was ultimately liable for damage to or loss of the ship due to negligence on the part of his agent (Gabrielsen 1994: 99). A wealthy man who hired a substitute to serve in his place as trierarch, moreover, could find it difficult to lay claim to *charis* for such a trierarchy, as noted above.[97]

A further question for liturgists was how much to spend in carrying out their tasks. Because liturgies (except for the *proeisphora*) did not entail fixed costs, a man could choose, on the one hand, to spend extravagantly as an investment in prestige and power or, on the other hand, to spend the bare minimum to get the task done (cf. Lys. 7.31; Is. 7.38; Isoc. 15.5). Those choosing the latter course, however, had reason to proceed with a degree of caution to avoid drawing negative attention. Skimping on a *chorēgia*, for example, could be risky, because marked stinginess, for example in the form of an ill-clad chorus, would be immediately visible to a large public (Eup. fr. 329); and a man's failure to place well with his chorus could be cast against him later by his enemies (Is. 5.36; cf. Plu. *Mor.* 349a–b = Dem. Phal. fr. 136 Wehrli).[98] Skimping on a trierarchy, if taken to an extreme, might lead

[97] By contrast, the reliance of *chorēgoi* on agents does not appear to have drawn criticism, presumably because this was the norm and they – unlike trierarchs relying upon substitutes – were present in a supervisory capacity.

[98] Cf. Thphr. *Char.* 22.2 (on skimping in commemorating a choregic victory).

to more than public embarrassment: trierarchs were liable to judicial review (*euthynai*) at the end of their service (Aeschin. 3.19), and gross shortcomings might lead to prosecution and, as noted earlier, large fines for neglect or loss of ships.[99]

Whatever strategy a liturgist adopted, it made sense – unless he was extremely rich and planned to remain so – to monitor and control his costs. Nothing prevented a *chorēgos*, for example, from discreetly recycling costumes from his own previous *chorēgia* or that of a friend or relative. Trierarchs could even seek to offset their costs through active profit-making strategies. On campaign, they could engage in piracy and looting against the enemy (Dem. 21.167; 24.11–14; Gabrielsen 1994: 100). More surprisingly, on returning to Athens trierarchs apparently often held on to their ship's state-owned equipment (Dem. 47.25, 28; 22.63) to reap private profit from it (Gabrielsen 1994: 153–8). Had the naval officials who were responsible for this equipment not themselves been involved in similar sharp practices, it might have proven easier for the city to control this (*ibid.* 149–53).[100]

Representation of Public Service

Whatever strategies a wealthy Athenian adopted concerning concealment of property, assignment to liturgies, and performance of them, he had good reason to put the best public face upon his citizenship. Arguably, the most critical decision that a wealthy man made concerning his public benefactions was how he would represent – or misrepresent – them to others. The wealthy enjoyed considerable license to portray their benefactions as they saw fit, as their claims could be difficult, if not impossible, to contradict. The best evidence for the malleability of claims concerning public services comes from extant forensic oratory.

Concealment of property was inherently secretive, and claims concerning it, therefore, extremely difficult for Athenian juries to evaluate.

99 Hansen (1991: 111) posits on the basis of Aeschin. 3.19 that all liturgists were liable to *euthynai*, but this passage speaks only of the judicial review of trierarchs; Wilson (2000: 170, with 359 n. 62) rightly rejects *euthynai* in connection with the *chorēgia*.

100 Gabrielsen (1994: 153) observes in connection with the retention of equipment by officials, "in more than a few cases the amount of equipment involved is so large that the withholder must have needed a private storehouse to accommodate it."

To be sure, litigants sometimes cite their performance of liturgies as sufficient proof that they have not concealed property from the city (cf. Lys. 20.23; Is. 7.40–1); but this only proves that enough of their property was visible that they were sometimes obliged to carry out liturgies, not that they refrained entirely from concealment. A client of Isaeus goes so far as to list his holdings in detail before a jury to contradict a charge that he was concealing property; while such itemization could give the impression of veracity, a jury had no way to know if this was a full disclosure (11.44–50, with Davies 1971: 88).

Whatever the circumstances under which a man came to undertake a liturgy, he could later cast his service as voluntary and seek credit on this basis. If he accepted without protest a liturgy assigned to him by an official, there was little to keep him from asserting later that he had been a zealous benefactor; he might well believe this was so, in fact, as he had not sought to win release through *skēpsis* or *antidosis*. Even if a man had unsuccessfully sought release through these legal channels or had been forced through *antidosis* to assume another man's burden, he might not acknowledge this later if he believed that the public was not aware of his reluctance. There was, as far as we know, no permanent public record of the outcome of cases involving *skēpsis* and *antidosis*, and after a lapse of time few men might recall the circumstances under which a liturgist had come to perform a public service.[101] Still, there was some risk that a man who brazenly lied about how he came to perform a particular liturgy might be publicly exposed, for example, by a personal enemy who had ferreted out information concerning this (cf. Dem. 21.156, 160–7). This may help explain why litigants often group together their past services and cite them collectively as evidence of their willingness to serve the city (see above, note 93): if one of these turned out to have been performed only under duress, a speaker could still save face by maintaining the basic truth of his generalization.[102]

[101] It serves Demosthenes (21.80) to pretend this is not so, as he relates to his audience how his enemies plotted to stick him with a trierarchy: "This happened a long time ago, but still I expect some of you remember it; for at the time the whole city knew about the proposal for *antidosis* and this plot and the bullying." On appeals to "common knowledge," see Ober 1989: 148–51.

[102] Some speakers, even after speaking of their own assignment to a liturgy ἐξ ἀντιδοσέως, go on later in the same speech to seek credit for their many liturgies as if these were

The fact that wealthy men in boasting of their services include their payment of *eisphorai* along with their liturgies as evidence of their willingness to serve the community is noteworthy: their payment of the *eisphora* was compulsory, and so too probably were many of the liturgies that they cite in the same breath.

While wealthy men could mislead their audiences concerning the circumstances under which they came to be liturgists, they were also free to exaggerate how often and how extravagantly they had performed liturgies (see above, note 93). It is noteworthy that litigants invoking liturgical records do not normally substantiate their claims with witness testimony or evidence.[103] There was, in fact, no public record of their cumulative liturgies or the amount they had spent on each. Although a determined individual could perhaps track down and collate information concerning a man's *chorēgiai* and trierarchies, it could be exceedingly difficult to refute a wealthy man who spoke collectively of his "many" *chorēgiai* and trierarchies and his generosity in carrying these out.

On the one hand, the malleability of liturgical records meant that there was little to prevent wealthy Athenians from misrepresenting – in part, if not in whole – their benefactions to the public. On the other hand, this may have made Athenian audiences wary of such assertions, and have contributed, along with the factors discussed earlier, to a reluctance to recognize the legitimacy of claims to *charis* based on public service. If the public could not be sure of the scope of its "debt" to its self-proclaimed benefactors, it naturally would hesitate to repay this debt from the public bank of gratitude.

This survey of some of the options available to wealthy men as they responded to their various financial obligations to the city suggests that, while they were to some extent constrained by civic regulations and institutions, they had considerable flexibility in protecting or pursuing

all voluntary: see Dem. 21.78–80 and 21.154–6; Lys. 3.20 and 3.47; Isoc. 15.4–5 and 15.145; all discussed by Gabrielsen 1987a: 37–8; cf. 1994: 95.

[103] Note, for example, how a client of Lysias simply asserts that "the entire city bears witness" to his excellent record as a performer of liturgies and payer of *eisphorai* (7.30–3). As Johnstone (1999: 96) points out, "Statements about liturgies were not objectively more factual or known in a different way than other kinds of claims a litigant might make."

their interests within or outside of these parameters. Depending upon their attitudes toward their financial obligations, the wealthy could avail themselves of a wide range of choices and strategies in advance of and at the time of assignment to an obligation, during its execution, and after its completion. This was true not only of those seeking to evade their obligations altogether, but also of individuals who were, to varying degrees, prepared to comply in meeting the city's requirements of them. The obligation to support the city financially had far-reaching implications for the private and public lives of wealthy citizens; that they responded self-consciously and often shrewdly to this came as no surprise to Athenians and should come as no surprise to us.

The Athenian democracy throughout its history grappled with the problem of how to ensure that wealthy citizens would meet their financial obligations to the city. The institutional history of the arrangements governing liturgies and the *eisphora* attests both to the city's creativity in meeting this challenge and to the continuing tensions between the city and the wealthy over these obligations. Wealthy men likely varied widely in the way they viewed these costly duties and in the way they responded to them. At one extreme, artful dodgers cynically did their best to evade these altogether; at the opposite extreme, zealous patriots embraced them. The majority of wealthy Athenians, however, probably fell somewhere between these two extremes, cognizant of the city's needs but also of the threat expenditures on the city could pose to their personal fortunes.

While the behavior of wealthy citizens reflects their special situation as members of a class that was exclusively responsible for financial obligations, their civic behavior has much in common with that of citizens liable for hoplite service, who likewise varied in their willingness to respond to the call to duty. In both cases, individual self-interests prompted some to act strategically within or outside the city's institutions to evade service. In each case, evasion might be achieved through manipulation of exemptions – though there was more scope for this in the area of conscription – or through influence with officials. Although both draft evasion and tax dodging were at odds with civic ideology, those engaging in these behaviors may have found some justification in the democratic ideology of citizenship, which stressed the compatibility of individual and group interests: if individuals could not reconcile the two in the case of the duties they were called upon to perform, they may not have felt obliged to perform them.

At the same time, however, differences emerge between draft evasion and tax evasion in Athens, which help explain why the latter was apparently more prevalent than the former. While the call to employ martial valor for fatherland did not rouse all Athenians equally, it was a potent one in a culture that placed a high premium on manly courage; this may have induced many to carry out their obligation to serve as hoplite. By contrast, the call to spend money on the city, notwithstanding the ideology of *philotimia*, may immediately have run up against cynicism and pragmatism: after all, this entailed certain personal sacrifice – money spent on the city was directly subtracted from that available for private consumption – whereas military service, if a man survived it, might "cost" him relatively little. Thucydides' Pericles astutely observes in analyzing the financial resources of Sparta and its allies that farmers are more ready to risk their lives than their money in war, as they trust they will survive battle but are not confident that their fortunes will survive intact if subject to taxation (1.141.5). The same observation may hold true for Athenians, many of whom were farmers.

The frequency with which citizens were called upon to carry out each type of obligation may also have affected how individuals responded to each. Conscription may have been tolerable to many because the call to serve as hoplite was intermittent and could be viewed as a discrete and finite demand with no immediate prospect for repetition. By contrast, by the late-fifth century wealthy men could expect to be liable to liturgies regularly and to the *eisphora* with some frequency. Their ever-present liability to financial obligations likely increased their perception of these as burdensome, and encouraged them to adopt long-term strategies for protecting their fortunes from these. To the extent that Athenians dodged hoplite service, this was likely *ad hoc* and not the result of years of planning. By contrast, wealthy Athenians had to plan well in advance to shield their fortunes from civic obligations: tax evasion was a way of life.

CONCLUSION

The picture of the Athenian citizen that emerges from this study is neither bleak nor altogether reassuring. Democratic Athens, like other historic states, faced persistent challenges as it sought to ensure that its citizens would carry out their civic obligations. Although the bond between citizen and city was generally strong, Athenian citizens responded individually and diversely to their civic duties. In particular, concerns over person and property could, and did, lead to evasion and underperformance of civic obligations. Just as Athenians were prepared to act shrewdly to protect or advance their personal interests in their relations with one another, so too were they ready to do so in their relations with the city. The nature and intensity of the difficulties that arose as a result, however, varied in the different spheres of civic duty, and the city's responses to these challenges differed accordingly.

The conflict between citizen and state was especially salient in the area of financial obligations. Notwithstanding social pressures on the wealthy to be benefactors of their city, they were deeply concerned about depleting their fortunes through performance of liturgies and payment of the *eisphora* and therefore actively sought to defend their personal interests. Wealthy Athenians routinely concealed their wealth from the view of the city and of their rich peers, who might seek to transfer liturgies to them through *antidosis*. The troubled history of the *eisphora* and trierarchy attests to the ongoing struggle between the wealthy and the city over financial obligations.

Although the conflict between citizen and city over conscription is less pronounced in our sources than that over financial obligations, draft evasion was tempting and possible for Athenians. To be sure, martial and civic ideals may have inspired many Athenians to embrace military service. There were, however, many reasons why an Athenian might not want to serve as hoplite – not least, fear for his life – and numerous ways in which he could avoid service. Although the rich and powerful in Athens, as in other societies, were best positioned to evade conscription through personal influence, average conscripts had options as well, including fabricating grounds for exemption or simply not appearing at muster. In light of these motivations and opportunities for draft evasion, we ought to take seriously the Athenian concerns over this that are voiced in oratory, comedy, and even tragedy. It would be a mistake to assume too high a level of compliance, especially in light of the rather lax arrangements that were in place for much of the classical period under conscription by *katalogos*.

Although citizens who complied with conscription and went out on campaign fulfilled a fundamental obligation of their citizenship, not all of them proved able to fulfill the further obligation of serving honorably and shunning cowardice. While few citizens went out on an expedition intending to fall short of civic expectations of courage, the rigors of campaign could strain their resolve and on the battlefield citizens often chose survival over the self-sacrifice that was hailed in patriotic oratory. Of particular interest is the common phenomenon of group flight by routed troops. Whether flight was deemed honorable – as a necessity brought on by fortune – or ignoble was open to dispute and contestation after the fact. Individual and group alike had a vested interested in putting the best face possible on martial behavior in the immediate aftermath of battle and on returning home to Athens.

Athenians were all too conscious of the fragility of good citizenship. They, like other Greeks, were cynical about human nature and inclined to believe that individuals will pursue their narrow personal interests unless constrained or persuaded to do otherwise. Athenians' experience of bad citizenship in its different forms must have confirmed the validity of this general perspective for them. How they responded to the problem of bad citizenship within a democratic framework is significant for our understanding of Athenian democracy.

In keeping with their democratic values, Athenians preferred to regard good citizenship as a voluntary and rational choice for free citizens rather than as an imposition upon them. Consistent with this was their preference for persuasion over compulsion in eliciting good citizenship and discouraging its opposite. Indeed, Athenian public discourse in its diverse forms and venues provided a potent instrument for exhorting citizens to embrace good citizenship and to reject its dark alternative. Athenians recognized, however, that as a practical matter civic duties had to be compulsory if they were to be carried out reliably. The city thus made various officials responsible for administering civic duties; developed procedures and regulations concerning them; and gave the popular lawcourts ultimate jurisdiction over cases arising in connection with them. Although there was no mistaking the civic authority that lay behind these measures, the city sought to avoid the appearance of despotism over its citizens and therefore relied largely on private persons rather than state agents to pursue those shirking their obligations and to initiate litigation against them.

If persuasion and compulsion each played a role in ensuring that citizens would perform their civic duties, the city's reliance on each varied in the different areas of civic obligation. In the case of financial obligations, while the city persisted throughout the classical period in extolling the virtues of voluntary civic benefaction, compulsion came to play a larger role in the system over time. Although the trierarchy may have been a largely voluntary office at its inception, it evolved in the fifth century into an unmistakably compulsory obligation as wealthy individuals came to regard it as burdensome and sought to avoid it; the continuing aversion of many wealthy men to the trierarchy and the evasive tactics that they adopted eventually led the city to establish naval *symmoriai* in 358/7 B.C. to constrain them to perform their obligations. While the *chorēgia* kept its veneer of voluntarity through its history, compulsion lurked beneath the surface, and there are some signs in the fourth century that the city had to assert its authority to ensure it would have a sufficient number of individuals to perform festival liturgies. The *eisphora* made no pretense of voluntarity through its history; the city recognized that the rich would not like handing over money directly to it and therefore made payment of the *eisphora* compulsory from its inception. Collection of this unpopular tax, however, proved challenging for the city; there are hints of this late in the Peloponnesian War, and difficulties in the early-fourth century led the city to extract payment of the tax by establishing *symmoriai* in 378/7 B.C. and the *proeisphora* at the same time or not much later. The general trend toward compelling the rich to fulfill their financial obligations attests to the fact that the city viewed bad citizenship here as a major threat that called for strict measures; it may also reflect the willingness of the *dēmos* to wield civic authority against the city's wealthy minority.

In the case of hoplite service, while the city regularly exhorted citizens to risk their lives willingly on the battlefield for the common good, as a practical matter it relied upon conscription throughout the classical period to fill its hoplite ranks. Although the city altered the way conscription was carried out in the fourth century when it adopted conscription by age groups, the basic compulsion to serve if called upon remained unchanged. Throughout the history of conscription, however, conscripts could seek exemptions on numerous grounds, and these were apparently freely used and probably abused as well. Because the city had a much larger pool of citizens to draw on for hoplite service than for financial obligations, it could afford to be more flexible here in granting release from service and thereby avoid the appearance of rigidity.

Although compulsion was conspicuous in the conscription of hoplites and even more so in the imposition of financial obligations on the rich, the city treaded more softly in enforcing the obligation of citizen-soldiers to serve honorably and without cowardice on campaign. Athenians appear to have been reluctant to exercise compulsion here, relying instead on public discourse to exhort citizens to act with courage and, by the fourth century if not earlier, on the *ephēbeia* to equip young men with the skills and values conducive to this. Because the question of hoplite performance was a highly sensitive one for the city, it tended to overlook deficiencies in this. This is particularly true of the city's response to the humiliation of groups of its hoplites in routs; their ignominy and the city's embarrassment over this were willed into oblivion. Although individual cowardice, especially when it involved radical deviation from group behavior, could lead to legal prosecution, this was apparently uncommon. Much more frequently, cowardice cropped up as a subject in public discourse, where individuals who were prominent in public life could find their battlefield behavior brought under public scrutiny by their political rivals; this allowed Athenians to reflect both on the character of their leaders and the otherwise largely taboo subject of citizen cowardice.

Athenian democracy's ongoing engagement, institutional and ideological, with bad citizenship attests both to the challenges it posed and to the flexibility, and often ingenuity, of the democracy in responding to these. If bad citizenship, rooted as it was in personal self-interests, was a problem that could never be entirely solved, the democracy showed itself able to address challenges – if not always swiftly or entirely successfully – and to do so without violating basic democratic values and understandings of citizenship. While the city could have controlled bad citizenship more than it did through aggressive and coercive action, the cost would have been high for the individual and perhaps for the city too because rigidity on its part might have led to more rather than less citizen resistance to civic obligations.

Although many features of Athens' encounter with bad citizenship are peculiar to it and its cultural context, it is perhaps reassuring for citizens of modern democracies to see that in this ancient democracy citizenship was not free of tensions and civic obligations were a subject of controversy and conflict. If Athenians throughout the classical period grappled with the problem of preserving individual freedom while requiring citizens to carry out civic duties, their modern counterparts continue to confront the same challenge.

BIBLIOGRAPHY

Adeleye, G. 1983. "The Purpose of the *Dokimasia*." *GRBS* 24: 295–306.

Allen, D. S. 2000a. *The World of Prometheus: The Politics of Punishing in Democratic Athens*. Princeton.

Allen, D. S. 2000b. "Changing the Authoritative Voice: Lycurgus' *Against Leocrates*." *ClAnt* 19: 5–33.

Amemiya, T. 2005. "Comment on Davies." In Manning and Morris, eds. (2005), 157–60.

Anderson, M. J. 1997. *The Fall of Troy in Early Greek Poetry and Art*. Oxford.

Andreades, A. M. 1933. *A History of Greek Public Finance*. Vol. 1. Cambridge, MA.

Andrewes, A. 1981. "The Hoplite *Katalogos*." In G. S. Shrimpton and D. J. McCargar, eds., *Classical Contributions: Studies in honor of Malcolm Francis McGregor*, 1–3. Locust Valley, NY.

Austin, C. 1968. *Nova Fragmenta Euripidea in papyris reperta*. Berlin.

Baldwin, B. 1967. "Medical Grounds for Exemptions from Military Service at Athens." *CP* 62: 42–3.

Balot, R. K. 2001a. *Greed and Injustice in Classical Athens*. Princeton.

Balot, R. K. 2001b. "Pericles' Anatomy of Democratic Courage." *AJP* 122: 505–25.

Balot, R. K. 2004a. "Free Speech, Courage, and Democratic Deliberation." In Sluiter and Rosen, eds. (2004), 233–59.

Balot, R. K. 2004b. "Courage in the Democratic *Polis*." *CQ* n.s. 54: 406–23.

Balot, R. K. 2004c. "The Dark Side of Democratic Courage." *Social Research* 71: 73–106.

Bartlett, J. 1980. *Familiar Quotations*. E. M. Beck. ed., Boston.

Bassi, K. 2003. "The Semantics of Manliness in Ancient Greece." In Rosen and Sluiter, eds. (2003a), 25–58.

Boedeker, D. and K. A. Raaflaub, eds. 1998. *Democracy, Empire, and the Arts in Fifth-Century Athens*. Cambridge, MA.

Boegehold, A. and A. Scafuro, eds. 1994. *Athenian Identity and Civic Ideology*. Baltimore.

Bond, G. W. 1963. *Euripides: Hypsipyle*. Oxford.

Bowersock, G. W. and E. C. Marchant, eds. and trans., 1968. *Xenophon: Scripta Minora*. Vol. 7. Cambridge, MA.

Bowie, A. M. 1997. "Tragic Filters for History: Euripides' *Supplices* and Sophocles' *Philoctetes*." In Pelling, ed. (1997a), 39–62. Oxford.

Bradeen, D. W. 1969. "The Athenian Casualty Lists." *CQ* n.s. 19: 145–59.

Bradeen, D. W. 1974. *Inscriptions: The Funerary Monuments*. The Athenian Agora Vol. 17. Princeton.

Bradford, A. 1994. "The Duplicitous Spartan." In A. Powell and S. Hodkinson, eds., *The Shadow of Sparta*, 59–86. London.

Brun, P. 1983. *Eisphora – Syntaxis – Stratiotika*. Annales Littéraires de l'Université de Besançon, no. 284. Paris.

Buckler, J. 1972. "A Second Look at the Monument of Chabrias." *Hesperia* 41: 466–74.

Bugh, G. R. 1988. *The Horsemen of Athens*. Princeton.

Burckhardt, L. A. 1996. *Bürger und Soldaten: Aspekte der politischen und militärischen Rolle athenischer Bürger im Kriegswesen des 4. Jahrhunderts v. Chr.* Stuttgart.

Burke, E. M. 1992. "The Economy of Athens in the Classical Era: Some Adjustments to the Primitivist Model." *TAPA* 122: 199–226.

Cairns, D. L. 1993. *Aidōs: The Psychology and Ethics of Honour and Shame in Ancient Greek Literature*. Oxford.

Camp, J. M. 1986. *The Athenian Agora: Excavations in the Heart of Classical Athens*. London.

Carey, C., ed. 1989. *Lysias: Selected Speeches*. Cambridge.

Carey, C., trans. 2000. *Aeschines*. The Oratory of Classical Greece Vol. 3. Austin.

Carey, C. and R. A. Reid, eds. 1985. *Demosthenes: Selected Private Speeches*. Cambridge.

Carter, L. B. 1986. *The Quiet Athenian*. Oxford.

Cartledge, P. 1996. "Comparatively Equal." In Ober and Hedrick, eds. (1996), 175–85.

Cartledge, P. 1998. "The *machismo* of the Athenian Empire – or the reign of the *phaulus?*" In L. Foxhall and J. Salmon, eds., *When Men were Men: Masculinity, power and identity in classical antiquity*, 54–67. London.

Cartledge, P. 2002a. "The Political Economy of Greek Slavery." In P. Cartledge, E. E. Cohen, and L. Foxhall, eds., *Money, Labour and Land: Approaches to the economies of ancient Greece*, 156–66. London.

Cartledge, P. 2002b. "The Economy (Economies) of Ancient Greece." In W. Scheidel and S. von Reden, eds., *The Ancient Economy*, 11–32. New York.

Cartledge, P. and F. D. Harvey, eds. 1985. *Crux: Essays Presented to G. E. M. de Ste. Croix on his 75th birthday*. London.

Cawkwell, G. L. 1984. "Athenian Naval Power in the Fourth Century." *CQ* n.s. 34: 334–45.

Cawkwell, G. L. 1989. "Orthodoxy and Hoplites." *CQ* n.s. 39: 375–89.

Chambers, J. W. II. 1975. *Draftees or Volunteers: A Documentary History of the Debate over Military Conscription in the United States, 1787–1973*. New York.

Christ, M. R. 1990. "Liturgy Avoidance and *Antidosis* in Classical Athens." *TAPA* 120: 147–69.

Christ, M. R. 1998a. *The Litigious Athenian*. Baltimore.

Christ, M. R. 1998b. "Legal Self-Help on Private Property in Classical Athens." *AJP* 119: 521–45.

Christ, M. R. 2001. "Conscription of Hoplites in Classical Athens." *CQ* n.s. 51: 398–422.

Christ, M. R. 2002. Review of Rubinstein 2000. *BMCR*. Online. <http://ccat.sas.upenn.edu/bmcr/2002/2002-04-01.html>.

Christ, M. R. 2003. Review of Hesk 2000. *CP* 98: 92–7.

Christ, M. R. 2004. "Draft Evasion onstage and offstage in Classical Athens." *CQ* n.s. 54: 33–57.

Christ, M. R. forthcoming. "The Evolution of the *Eisphora* in Classical Athens." *CQ*.

Christensen, J. and M. H. Hansen. 1983. "What is *Syllogos* at Thukydides 2.22.1?" *C&M* 34: 17–31.

Christesen, P. 2003. "Economic Rationalism in Fourth-Century BCE Athens." *G&R* 50: 31–56.

Cohen, D. 1995. *Law, Violence and Community in Classical Athens*. Cambridge.

Cohen, D. 1997. "Democracy and Individual Rights in Athens." *ZRG* 114: 27–44.

Cohen, D., ed. 2002. *Demokratie, Recht und soziale Kontrolle im klassischen Athen*. Schriften des Historischen Kollegs Kolloquien 49. Munich.

Cohen, E. A. 1985. *Citizens and Soldiers: The Dilemmas of Military Service*. Ithaca.

Cohen, E. E. 1992. *Athenian Economy and Society. A Banking Perspective*. Princeton.

Collard, C., ed. 1975. *Euripides: Supplices*. 2 vols. Groningen.

Collard, C., M. J. Cropp, and K. H. Lee, eds. and trans. 1997. *Euripides: Selected Fragmentary Plays*. Vol. 1. Warminster.

Connor, W. R. 1994. "The Problem of Athenian Civic Identity." In Boegehold and Scafuro, eds. (1994), 34–44.

Cox, C. A. 1998. *Household Interests: Property, Marriage Strategies, and Family Dynamics in Ancient Athens*. Princeton.

Craik, E. M. 1999. "Mantitheus of Lysias 16: Neither Long-Haired nor Simple-Minded." *CQ* n.s. 49: 626–8.

Cropp, M. J., ed. and trans. 1988. *Euripides: Electra*. Warminster.

David, E. 1989. "Laughter in Spartan Society." In A. Powell, ed., *Classical Sparta: Techniques Behind Her Success*, 1–25. Norman and London.

Davies, J. K. 1967. "Demosthenes on Liturgies: A Note." *JHS* 87: 33–40.

Davies, J. K. 1971. *Athenian Propertied Families*. Oxford.

Davies, J. K. 1981. *Wealth and the Power of Wealth in Classical Athens*. New York.

Davies, M. 1989. *The Epic Cycle*. Bristol.

Deslauriers, M. 2003. "Aristotle on *Andreia*, Divine and Sub-Human Virtues." In Rosen and Sluiter, eds. (2003a), 187–211.

Détienne, M. and J.-P. Vernant. 1978. *Cunning Intelligence in Greek Culture and Society*. Trans. by J. Lloyd. Hassocks, Sussex.

Develin, R. 1989. *Athenian Officials 684–321 B.C.* Cambridge.

Diggins, J. P. 1984. *The Lost Soul of American Politics: Virtue, Self-Interest, and the Foundation of Liberalism*. New York.

Dodds, E. R. 1959. *Plato: Gorgias*. Oxford.

Dorjahn, A. 1940. "Demosthenes' Reply to the Charge of Cowardice." *PhQ* 19: 337–42.

Dover, K. J. 1972. *Aristophanic Comedy*. Berkeley.

Dover, K. J. 1974. *Greek Popular Morality in the Time of Plato and Aristotle*. Berkeley.

Durkin, J. T., ed. 1945. *John Dooley, Confederate Soldier: His War Journal*. Georgetown.

Ehrenberg, V. 1951. *The People of Aristophanes: A Sociology of Old Attic Comedy*. Oxford.

Ellis, J. R. 1976. *Philip II and Macedonian Imperialism*. London.

Elster, J. 2002. "Norms, Emotions and Social Control." In D. Cohen, ed. (2002), 1–13.

Euben, J. P., J. R. Wallach, and J. Ober, eds. 1994a. *Athenian Political Thought and the Reconstruction of American Democracy*. Ithaca.

Euben, J. P. 1994b. "Introduction." In Euben, Wallach, and Ober, eds. (1994a), 1–26.

Evans, J. K. 1988. "Resistance at Home: The Evasion of Military Service in Italy during the Second Century B.C." In T. Yuge and M. Doi, eds., *Forms of Control and Subordination in Antiquity*, 121–40. Leiden.

Evans, R. J. 1999. "Displaying Honourable Scars: A Roman Gimmick." *AClass* 42: 77–94.

Farrar, C. 1992. "Ancient Greek Political Theory as a Response to Democracy." In J. Dunn, ed., *Democracy: The Unfinished Journey, 508 B.C. to A.D. 1993*, 17–39. Oxford.

Farrar, C. 1996. "Gyges' Ring: Reflections on the Boundaries of Democratic Citizenship." In M. Sakellariou, ed., *Colloque International Démocratie Athénienne et Culture*, 109–36. Athens.

Finley, M. I. 1981. "The Athenian Empire: A balance sheet." In *idem*, *Economy and Society in Ancient Greece*, R. Saller and B. Shaw, eds., 41–61. London.

Foley, H. P. 2001. *Female Acts in Greek Tragedy*. Princeton.

Forrest, A. 1989. *Conscripts and Deserters: The Army and French Society During the Revolution and Empire*. Oxford.

Forsdyke, S. 2001. "Athenian Democratic Ideology and Herodotus' *Histories*." *AJP* 122: 329–58.

Foxhall, L. 1993. "Farming and fighting in ancient Greece." In J. Rich and G. Shipley, eds., *War and Society in the Greek World*, 134–45. London.

Freeman, K., trans. 1948. *Ancilla to the Pre-Socratic Philosophers*. Cambridge, MA.

Gabrielsen, V. 1986. "ΦΑΝΕΡΑ and ΑΦΑΝΗΣ ΟΥΣΙΑ in Classical Athens." *C&M* 37: 99–114.

Gabrielsen, V. 1987a. "The *Antidosis* Procedure in Classical Athens." *C&M* 38: 7–38.

Gabrielsen, V. 1987b. "The *Diadikasia*-Documents." *C&M* 38: 39–51.

Gabrielsen, V. 1994. *Financing the Athenian Fleet: Public Taxation and Social Relations*. Baltimore.

Gabrielsen, V. 2002. "The Impact of Armed Forces on Government and Politics in Archaic and Classical Greek Poleis: A Response to Hans van Wees." In A. Chaniotis and P. Ducrey, eds., *Army and Power in the Ancient World*, 83–98. Stuttgart.

Gagarin, M., ed. 1997. *Antiphon: The Speeches*. Cambridge.

Gantz, T. 1993. *Early Greek Myth*. 2 vols. Baltimore.

Gill, C., N. Postlethwaite, and R. Seaford, eds. 1998. *Reciprocity in Ancient Greece*. Oxford.

Goldhill, S. 1990. "The Great Dionysia and Civic Ideology." In Winkler and Zeitlin, eds. (1990), 97–129.

Goldhill, S. 1999. "Programme notes." In Goldhill and Osborne, eds. (1999), 1–29.

Goldhill, S. 2000. "Civic ideology and the problem of difference: the politics of Aeschylean tragedy, once again." *JHS* 120: 34–56.

Goldhill, S. and R. Osborne, eds. 1999. *Performance Culture and Athenian Democracy*. New York.

Goldsworthy, A. K. 1997. "The *Othismos*, Myths and Heresies: The Nature of Hoplite Battle." *War in History* 4.1: 1–26. Online. <http://www.warinhistory.com/>.

Gomme, A. W. 1956. *A Historical Commentary on Thucydides*. Volume II. Oxford.

Gregory, J. 2002. "Euripides as Social Critic." *G&R* 49: 145–62.

Grene, D., trans. 1987. *The History: Herodotus*. Chicago.

Griffin, J. 1998. "The Social Function of Attic Tragedy." *CQ* n.s. 48: 39–61.

Griffith, J. G. 1977. "A Note on the First Eisphora at Athens." *AJAH* 2: 3–7.

Guthrie, W. K. 1971. *The Sophists*. Cambridge.

Hamel, D. 1998a. *Athenian Generals: Military Authority in the Classical Period*. Mnemosyne Supplement 182. Leiden.

Hamel, D. 1998b. "Coming to Terms with λιποτάξιον." *GRBS* 39: 361–405.

Hansen, M. H. 1975. *Eisangelia: The Sovereignty of the People's Court in Athens in the Fourth Century B.C. and the Impeachment of Generals and Politicians*. Odense.

Hansen, M. H. 1976. *Apagoge, Endeixis and Ephegesis against Kakourgoi, Atimoi and Pheugontes: A Study in the Athenian Administration of Justice in the Fourth Century B.C.* Odense.

Hansen, M. H. 1985. *Demography and Democracy: The Number of Athenian Citizens in the Fourth Century B.C.* Herning.

Hansen, M. H. 1991. *The Athenian Democracy in the Age of Demosthenes.* Oxford.

Hansen, M. H. 1993. "The Battle Exhortation in Ancient Historiography. Fact or Fiction?" *Historia* 42: 161–80.

Hansen, M. H. 1996. "The Ancient Athenian and the Modern Liberal View of Liberty as a Democratic Ideal." In Ober and Hedrick, eds. (1996), 91–104.

Hansen, M. H. 2001. "The little grey horse: Henry V's speech at Agincourt and the battle exhortation in ancient historiography." *C&M* 52: 95–114.

Hansen, M. H. 2003. "Lysias 14 and 15. A note on the γραφὴ ἀστρατείας." In G. W. Bakewell and J. P. Sickinger, eds., *Gestures: Essays in Ancient History, Literature, and Philosophy Presented to Alan L. Boegehold*, 278–9. Oxford.

Hanson, V. D. 1989. *The Western Way of War: Infantry Battle in Classical Greece.* New York.

Hanson, V. D., ed. 1991. *Hoplites: The Classical Greek Battle Experience.* London.

Hanson, V. D. 2000. "Hoplite Battle as Ancient Greek Warfare: When, where, and why?" In van Wees, ed. (2000a), 201–32.

Hanson, V. D. 2001. *Carnage and Culture: Landmark Battles in the Rise of Western Power.* New York.

Harrison, A. R. W. 1968–71. *The Law of Athens.* 2 vols. Oxford.

Harvey, F. D. 1985. "*Dona Ferentes*: Some Aspects of Bribery in Greek Politics." In Cartledge and Harvey, eds. (1985), 76–117.

Heath, M. 1999. "Sophocles' *Philoctetes*: A Problem Play?" In J. Griffin, ed., *Sophocles Revisited*, 137–60. Oxford.

Hedrick, Charles W., Jr. 1994. "The Zero Degree of Society: Aristotle and the Athenian Citizen." In Euben, Wallach, and Ober, eds. (1994a), 289–318.

Heinaman, R. 2004. "Why justice does not pay in Plato's *Republic*." *CQ* n.s. 54: 379–93.

Henderson, J. 1990. "The *Demos* and the Comic Competition." In Winkler and Zeitlin, eds. (1990), 271–313.

Henderson, J. 1991. *The Maculate Muse: Obscene Language in Attic Comedy*². Oxford.

Henderson, J. 2000. "Pherekrates and the women of Old Comedy." In D. Harvey and J. Wilkins, eds., *The Rivals of Aristophanes: Studies in Athenian Old Comedy*, 135–50. London.

Herman, G. 1998. "Reciprocity, Altruism, and the Prisoner's Dilemma: The Special Case of Classical Athens." In Gill, Postlethwaite, and Seaford, eds. (1998), 199–225.

Hesk, J. 2000. *Deception and Democracy in Classical Athens.* Cambridge.

Heynen, C. and R. Krumeich. 1999. "Sophokles: Unsicheres." In Krumeich, Pechstein, and Seidensticker, eds. (1999), 388–98.

Hobbs, A. 2000. *Plato and the Hero: Courage, Manliness and the Impersonal Good.* Cambridge.

Holmes, S. 1990. "The Secret History of Self-Interest." In Mansbridge, ed. (1990a), 267–86.

Hornblower, S. 1991. *A Commentary on Thucydides: Volume I: Books I–III.* Oxford.

Hornblower, S. 2000. "The *Old Oligarch* (Pseudo-Xenophon's *Athenaion Politeia)* and Thucydides. A Fourth-Century Date for the *Old Oligarch.*" In P. Flensted-Jensen, T. H. Nielsen, and L. Rubinstein, eds., *Polis & Politics: Studies in Ancient Greek History*, 363–84. Copenhagen.

Hunter, V. 1994. *Policing Athens: Social Control in the Attic Lawsuits, 420–320 B.C.* Princeton.

Jackson, A. H. 1991. "Hoplites and the Gods: The Dedication of Captured Arms and Armour." In Hanson, ed. (1991), 228–49.

Johnstone, S. 1999. *Disputes and Democracy: The Consequences of Litigation in Ancient Athens.* Austin.

Johnstone, S. 2003. "Women, Property, and Surveillance in Classical Athens." *ClAnt* 22: 247–74.

Jones, N. F. 1999. *The Associations of Classical Athens: The Response to Democracy.* Oxford.

Jordan, B. 1975. *The Athenian Navy in the Classical Period.* University of California Publications: Classical Studies Vol. 13. Berkeley.

Jordan, B. 2001. "Metic Trierarchs." *AHB* 15: 131–4.

Kallet, L. 1998. "Accounting for Culture in Fifth-Century Athens." In Boedeker and Raaflaub, eds. (1998), 43–58.

Kallet-Marx, L. 1989. "The Kallias Decree, Thucydides, and the Outbreak of the Peloponnesian War." *CQ* n.s. 39: 94–113.

Kannicht, R. and B. Snell, eds. 1981. *Tragicorum Graecorum Fragmenta.* Vol. 2. Göttingen.

Kapparis, K. A., ed. 1999. *Apollodoros 'Against Neaira' [D. 59].* Berlin.

Kassel, R. and C. Austin, eds. 1983–. *Poetae Comici Graeci.* 8 vols. Berlin.

Kerferd, G. B. 1981. *The Sophistic Movement.* Cambridge.

Knox, R. A. 1985. "'So Mischievous a Beaste'? The Athenian *demos* and its treatment of its politicians." *G&R* 32: 132–61.

Konstan, D. 2000. "Altruism." *TAPA* 130: 1–17.

Kovacs, D., ed. and trans. 1994–2002. *Euripides.* 6 vols. Cambridge, MA.

Krentz, P., ed. and trans. 1989. *Xenophon: Hellenika I–II.3.10.* Warminster.

Krentz, P. 1991. "The *Salpinx* in Greek Warfare." In Hanson, ed. (1991), 110–20.

Krentz, P. 1994. "Continuing the *othismos* on *othismos.*" *AHB* 8: 45–9.

Krentz, P. 2000. "Deception in Archaic and Classical Greek Warfare." In van Wees, ed. (2000a), 167–200.

Krentz, P. 2002. "Fighting by the Rules: The Invention of the Hoplite Agôn." *Hesperia* 71: 23–39.

Kromayer, J. and G. Veith. 1928. *Heerwesen und Kriegführung der Griechen und Römer.* Handbuch der Altertumswissenschaft IV 3.2. Munich.

Krumeich, R., N. Pechstein, and B. Seidensticker, eds. 1999. *Das griechische Satyrspiel.* Texte zur Forschung Band 72. Darmstadt.

Kurke, L. 1991. *The Traffic in Praise: Pindar and the Poetics of Social Economy.* Ithaca.

Kurke, L. 1992. "The Politics of ἁβροσύνη in Archaic Greece." *CA* 11: 91–120.

Lanni, A. 2004. "Arguing from 'Precedent': Modern Perspectives on Athenian Practice." In E. M. Harris and L. Rubinstein, eds., *The Law and the Courts in Ancient Greece*, 159–71. London.

Lateiner, D. 1995. *Sardonic Smile: Nonverbal Behavior in Homeric Epic.* Ann Arbor.

Lazenby, J. 1991. "The Killing Zone." In Hanson, ed. (1991), 87–109.

Leigh, M. 1995. "Wounding and Popular Rhetoric at Rome." *BICS* 40: 195–216.

Lendon, J. E. 2005. *Soldiers & Ghosts: A History of Battle in Classical Antiquity.* New Haven.

Lewis, N. 1960. "*Leitourgia* and Related Terms." *GRBS* 3: 175–84.

Lipsius, J. H. 1905–15. *Das attische Recht und Rechtsverfahren.* 3 vols. in 4. Leipzig.

Lloyd-Jones, H., ed. and trans. 1994–1996. *Sophocles.* 3 vols. Cambridge, MA.

Loomis, W. T. 1998. *Wages, Welfare Costs and Inflation in Classical Athens.* Ann Arbor.

Loraux, N. 1986. *The Invention of Athens. The Funeral Oration in the Classical City.* Trans. by A. Sheridan. Cambridge, MA.

Loraux, N. 1995. *The Experiences of Tiresias: The Feminine and the Greek Man.* Trans. by P. Wissing. Princeton.

Loraux, N. 1998. *Mothers in Mourning, with the essay Of Amnesty and Its Opposite.* Trans. by C. Pache. Ithaca.

Low, P. 2002. "Cavalry Identity and Democratic Ideology in early fourth-century Athens." *PCPhS* 48: 102–19.

Ludwig, P. W. 2002. *Eros and Polis: Desire and Community in Greek Political Theory.* Cambridge.

Luginbill, R. D. 1994. "*Othismos*: The Importance of the Mass-Shove in Hoplite Warfare." *Phoenix* 48: 51–61.

Lyttkens, C. H. 1997. "A Rational-Actor Perspective on the Origin of Liturgies in Ancient Greece." *Journal of Institutional and Theoretical Economics* 153: 462–84.

MacDowell, D. M., ed. 1962. *Andokides: On the Mysteries.* Oxford.

MacDowell, D. M., ed. 1971. *Aristophanes: Wasps.* Oxford.

MacDowell, D. M. 1978. *The Law in Classical Athens.* Ithaca.

MacDowell, D. M. 1982 [1989]. "Athenian Laws about Choruses." In F. J. Nieto, ed., *Symposion 1982: Vorträge zur griechischen und hellenistischen Rechtsgeschichte*, 65–77. Cologne.

MacDowell, D. M. 1983. "Athenian Laws about Bribery." *RIDA* 30: 57–78.

MacDowell, D. M. 1986a. *Spartan Law.* Edinburgh.

MacDowell, D. M. 1986b. "The Law of Periandros about Symmories." *CQ* n.s. 36: 438–49.

MacDowell, D. M., ed. and trans. 1990. *Demosthenes: Against Meidias (Oration 21).* Oxford.

MacDowell, D. M. 1994. "The case of the Rude Soldier (Lysias 9)." In G. Thür, ed., *Symposion 1993: Vorträge zur griechischen und hellenistischen Rechtsgeschichte*, 153–64. Cologne, Weimar, and Vienna.

MacDowell, D. M. 2005. "The Athenian Procedure of *Dokimasia* of Orators." In M. Gagarin and R. Wallace, eds., *Symposion 2001: Vorträge zur griechischen und hellenistischen Rechtsgeschicht*, 79–87. Vienna.

Manning, J. G. and I. Morris, eds. 2005. *The Ancient Economy: Evidence and Models*. Stanford.

Mansbridge, J. J., ed. 1990a. *Beyond Self-Interest*. Chicago.

Mansbridge, J. J. 1990b. "The Rise and Fall of Self-Interest in the Explanation of Political Life." In Mansbridge, ed. (1990a), 3–22.

Manville, P. B. 1990. *The Origins of Citizenship in Ancient Athens*. Princeton.

Markle, M. M. 1985. "Jury Pay and Assembly Pay at Athens." In Cartledge and Harvey, eds. (1985), 265–97.

Mastronarde, D. J. 1994. *Euripides: Phoenissae*. Cambridge.

McGlew, J. F. 2002. *Citizens on Stage: Comedy and Political Culture in the Athenian Democracy*. Ann Arbor.

Meier, C. 1990. *The Greek Discovery of Politics*. Trans. by D. McLintock. Cambridge, MA.

Meier, C. 1993. *The Political Art of Greek Tragedy*. Trans. by A. Webber. Baltimore.

Meiggs, R. 1972. *The Athenian Empire*. Oxford.

Meiggs, R. and D. Lewis, eds. 1969. *A Selection of Greek Historical Inscriptions to the end of the fifth century B.C.* Oxford.

Mendelsohn, D. 2002. *Gender and the City in Euripides' Political Plays*. Oxford.

Michelakis, P. 2002. *Achilles in Greek Tragedy*. Cambridge.

Michelini, A. N. 1994. "Political Themes in Euripides' *Suppliants*." *AJP* 115: 219–52.

Migeotte, L. 1992. *Les Souscriptions Publiques dans les Cités Grecques*. Hautes Études du Monde Gréco-Romain 17. Geneva.

Millender, E. G. 2002. "Νόμος Δεσπότης: Spartan Obedience and Athenian Lawfulness in Fifth-Century Thought." In V. B. Gorman and E. W. Robinson, eds., *Oikistes: Studies in Constitutions, Colonies, and Military Power in the Ancient World, offered in honor of A. J. Graham*, 33–59. Leiden.

Miller, W. I. 2000. *The Mystery of Courage*. Cambridge, MA.

Miller, W. I. 2002. "Weak Legs: Misbehavior before the Enemy." In D. Cohen, ed. (2002), 15–35.

Millett, P. 1991. *Lending and Borrowing in Ancient Athens*. Cambridge.

Millett, P. 1998. "The Rhetoric of Reciprocity in Classical Athens." In Gill, Postlethwaite, and Seaford, eds. (1998), 227–53.

Monoson, S. 1994. "Citizen as *Erastes*: Erotic Imagery and the Idea of Reciprocity in the Periclean Funeral Oration." *Political Theory* 22: 253–76.

Moreno, A. 2003. "Athenian Bread-Baskets: The Grain-Tax Law of 374/3 B.C. Re-interpreted." *ZPE* 145: 97–106.

Morris, I. 1994. "The Athenian Economy Twenty Years After *The Ancient Economy*." *CP* 89: 351–66.

Morris, I. and J. G. Manning. 2005. "Introduction." In Manning and Morris, eds. (2005), 1–44.

Moskos, C. C. and J. W. Chambers II, eds. 1993. *The New Conscientious Objection: From Sacred to Secular Resistance*. Oxford.

Müller, C. W. 1990 [1993]. "Euripides' *Philoctetes* as a political play." In A. H. Sommerstein, S. Halliwell, J. Henderson, and B. Zimmermann, eds., *Tragedy, Comedy and the Polis: Papers from the Greek Drama Conference, Nottingham, 18–20 July 1990*, 241–52. Bari.

Müller, C. W. 1997. *Philoktet: Beiträge zur Wiedergewinnung einer Tragödie des Euripides aus der Geschichte ihrer Rezeption*. Stuttgart and Leipzig.

Nauck, A., ed. 1964. *Tragicorum Graecorum Fragmenta*², with *Supplementum* by B. Snell. Hildesheim.

Nesselrath, H.-G. 1990. *Die attische Mittlere Komödie: Ihre Stellung in der antiken Literaturkritik und Literaturgeschichte*. Untersuchungen zur antiken Literatur und Geschichte Band 36. Berlin.

Ober, J. 1985. *Fortress Attica: Defense of the Athenian Land Frontier, 404–322 B.C.* Mnemosyne Supplement 84. Leiden.

Ober, J. 1989. *Mass and Elite in Democratic Athens: Rhetoric, Ideology, and the Power of the People*. Princeton.

Ober, J. 1993. "The *Polis* as a Society: Aristotle, John Rawls and the Athenian Social Contract." In M. H. Hansen, ed., *The Ancient Greek City-State* (Historisk-filosofiske Meddelelser 67), 129–60. Copenhagen.

Ober, J. 1996. "The Rules of War in Classical Greece." In *The Athenian Revolution: Essays on Ancient Greek Democracy and Political Theory*, 53–71. Princeton.

Ober, J. 1998. *Political Dissent in Democratic Athens: Intellectual Critics of Popular Rule*. Princeton.

Ober, J. and C. Hedrick, eds. 1996. *Dēmokratia: A Conversation on Democracies, Ancient and Modern*. Princeton.

Ober, J. and B. S. Strauss. 1990. "Drama, Political Rhetoric, and the Discourse of Athenian Democracy." In Winkler and Zeitlin, eds. (1990), 237–70.

Olson, S. D. 1991a. "Politics and the Lost Euripidean *Philoctetes*." *Hesperia* 60: 269–83.

Olson, S. D. 1991b. "Anonymous Male Parts in Aristophanes' *Ecclesiazusae* and the Identity of the ΔΕΣΠΟΤΗΣ." *CQ* n.s. 41: 36–40.

Olson, S. D., ed. 1998. *Aristophanes: Peace*. Oxford.

Olson, S. D., ed. 2002. *Aristophanes: Acharnians*. Oxford.

Osborne, R. 1991. "Pride and prejudice, sense and subsistence: exchange and society in the Greek city." In J. Rich and A. Wallace-Hadrill, eds., *City and Country in the Ancient World*, 119–45. London.

Ostwald, M. 1986. *From Popular Sovereignty to the Sovereignty of Law: Law, Society, and Politics in Fifth-Century Athens*. Berkeley.

Ostwald, M. 1996. "Shares and Rights: 'Citizenship' Greek Style and American Style." In Ober and Hedrick, eds. (1996), 49–61.

Patterson, C. B. 1981. *Pericles' Citizenship Law of 451–50 B.C.* New York.

Patterson, C. B. 1998. *The Family in Greek History*. Cambridge, MA.

Paulsen, T. 1999. *Die Parapresbeia-Reden des Demosthenes und des Aischines: Kommentar und Interpretationen zu Demosthenes, or. XIX, und Aischines, or. II.* Trier.

Pearson, L. 1962. *Popular Ethics in Ancient Greece*. Stanford.

Pélékidis, C. 1962. *Histoire de l'éphébie attique des origines à 31 avant Jésus-Christ.* Paris.

Pelling, C., ed. 1997a. *Greek Tragedy and the Historian*. Oxford.

Pelling, C. 1997b. "Conclusion." In Pelling, ed. (1997a), 213–35.

Piepenbrink, K. 2001. *Politische Ordnungskonzeptionen in der attischen Demokratie des vierten Jahrhunderts v. Chr.* Historia Einzelschriften 154. Stuttgart.

Pierce, K. F. 1998. "Ideals of Masculinity in New Comedy." In L. Foxhall and J. Salmon, eds., *Thinking Men: Masculinity and its Self-Representation in the Classical Tradition*, 130–47. London.

Pomeroy, S., ed. and trans. 1994. *Xenophon, Oeconomicus. A Social and Historical Commentary*. Oxford.

Pouncey, P. R. 1980. *The Necessities of War: A Study of Thucydides' Pessimism*. New York.

Pritchard, D. M. 1998. "'The Fractured Imaginary': Popular Thinking on Military Matters in Fifth Century Athens." *AH* 28: 38–61.

Pritchett, W. K. 1971–1991. *The Greek State at War: Parts I–V.* Berkeley.

Pritchett, W. K. 1994. "The General's Exhortation in Greek Warfare." In *Essays in Greek History*, 27–109. Amsterdam.

Pritchett, W. K. 2002. *Ancient Greek Battle Speeches and a Palfrey*. Amsterdam.

Raaflaub, K. A. 1994. "Democracy, Power, and Imperialism in Fifth-Century Athens." In Euben, Wallach, and Ober, eds. (1994a), 103–46.

Raaflaub, K. A. 1996. "Equalities and Inequalities in Athenian Democracy." In Ober and Hedrick, eds. (1996), 139–74.

Raaflaub, K. A. 2001. "Father of All, Destroyer of All: War in Late Fifth-Century Athenian Discourse and Ideology." In D. McCann and B. S. Strauss, eds., *War and Democracy: A Comparative Study of the Korean War and the Peloponnesian War*, 307–56. Armonk, NY.

Raaflaub, K. A. 2004. *The Discovery of Freedom in Ancient Greece*. Trans. by R. Franciscono. Chicago.

Rademaker, A. 2003. "'Most Citizens are Europrōktoi Now:' (Un)manliness in Aristophanes." In Rosen and Sluiter, eds. (2003a), 115–25.

Radt, S., ed. *Tragicorum Graecorum Fragmenta*. Vol. 3: Aeschylus, 1985, and Vol. 4: Sophocles, 1977. Göttingen.

Raubitschek, A. E. 1949. *Dedications from the Athenian Akropolis: A Catalogue of the Inscriptions of the Sixth and Fifth Centuries B.C.* Cambridge, MA.

Reinmuth, O. W. 1971. *The Ephebic Inscriptions of the Fourth Century B.C.* Mnemosyne Supplement 14. Leiden.

Rhodes, P. J. 1981. *A Commentary on the Aristotelian Athenaion Politeia.* Oxford.

Rhodes, P. J. 1982. "Problems in Athenian *Eisphora* and Liturgies." *AJAH* 7: 1–19.

Rhodes, P. J., ed. and trans. 1988. *Thucydides: History II.* Warminster.

Rhodes, P. J. 2003. "Nothing to do with Democracy: Athenian Drama and the *Polis*." *JHS* 123: 104–19.

Rhodes, P. J. and R. Osborne, eds. 2003. *Greek Historical Inscriptions 404–323 BC.* Oxford.

Roberts, J. T. 1982. *Accountability in Athenian Government.* Madison, WI.

Roisman, J. 2003. "The Rhetoric of Courage in the Athenian Orators." In Rosen and Sluiter, eds. (2003a), 127–43.

Roisman, J. 2004. "Speaker-Audience Interaction in Athens: A Power Struggle." In Sluiter and Rosen, eds. (2004), 261–78.

Roisman, J. 2005. *The Rhetoric of Manhood: Masculinity in the Attic Orators.* Berkeley.

Romilly, J. de. 1992. *The Great Sophists in Periclean Athens.* Trans. by J. Lloyd. Oxford.

Rosen, R. M. and I. Sluiter, eds. 2003a. *Andreia: Studies in Manliness and Courage in Classical Antiquity.* Mnemosyne Supplement 238. Leiden.

Rosen, R. M. and I. Sluiter. 2003b. "General Introduction." In Rosen and Sluiter, eds. (2003a), 1–24.

Rosivach, V. J. 2001. "Manpower and the Athenian Navy in 362 B.C." In R. W. Love et al., eds., *New Interpretations of Naval History*, 12–26. Annapolis.

Rosivach, V. J. 2002. "*Zeugitai* and Hoplites." *AHB* 16: 33–43.

Rothwell, K. S. 1990. *Politics and Persuasion in Aristophanes' Ecclesiazusae.* Mnemosyne Supplement 111. Leiden.

Rubinstein, L. 2000. *Litigation and Cooperation: Supporting Speakers in the Courts of Classical Athens.* Historia Einzelschriften 147. Stuttgart.

Rusten, J. S., ed. 1989. *Thucydides: The Peloponnesian War, Book II.* Cambridge.

Sagan, E. 1991. *The Honey and the Hemlock. Democracy and Paranoia in Ancient Athens and Modern America.* Princeton.

Saïd, S. 1998. "Tragedy and Politics." In Boedeker and Raaflaub, eds. (1998), 275–95.

Ste. Croix, G. E. M. de. 1953. "Demosthenes' TIMHMA and the Athenian Eisphora in the Fourth Century B.C." *C&M* 14: 30–70.

Salkever, S. G. 1991. "Women, Soldiers, Citizens: Plato and Aristotle on the Politics of Virility." In C. Lord and D. K. O'Connor, eds., *Essays on the Foundations of Aristotelian Political Science*, 165–90. Berkeley.

Samons, L. J. II. 2004. *What's Wrong with Democracy? From Athenian Practice to American Worship.* Berkeley.

Scafuro, A. 1997. *The Forensic Stage: Settling Disputes in Graeco-Roman New Comedy*. Cambridge.

Schein, S. 2001. "Herakles and the Ending of Sophokles' *Philoktetes*." *SIFC* 19: 38–52.

Scheurer, S. and S. Kansteiner. 1999. "Sophokles: Amphiareos." In Krumeich, Pechstein, and Seidensticker, eds. (1999), 236–42.

Schofield, M. 1996. "Sharing in the Constitution." *Review of Metaphysics* 49: 831–58.

Schwertfeger, T. 1982. "Der Schild des Archilochos." *Chiron* 12: 253–80.

Seaford, R. 2000. "The Social Function of Attic Tragedy: A Response to Jasper Griffin." *CQ* n.s. 50: 30–44.

Seager, R. 2001. "Xenophon and Athenian Democratic Ideology." *CQ* n.s. 51: 385–97.

Sealey, R. 1984. "The *Tetralogies* ascribed to Antiphon." *TAPA* 114: 71–85.

Sekunda, N. V. 1992. "Athenian Demography and Military Strength 338–322 BC." *ABSA* 87: 311–55.

Severyns, A., ed. 1963. *Recherches sur la Chrestomathie de Proclus*. Vol. 4. Paris.

Shaw, B. 1991. "The Paradoxes of People Power." *Helios* 18: 194–214.

Shay, J. 1994. *Achilles in Vietnam: Combat Trauma and the Undoing of Character*. New York.

Shay, J. 2002. *Odysseus in America: Combat Trauma and the Trials of Homecoming*. New York.

Shipton, K. M. W. 1997. "The Private Banks in Fourth-Century B.C. Athens: A Reappraisal." *CQ* n.s. 47: 396–422.

Shipton, K. M. W. 2001. "Money and the Élite in Classical Athens." In A. Meadows and K. Shipton, eds., *Money and its Uses in the Ancient Greek World*, 129–44. Oxford.

Sinclair, R. K. 1988. *Democracy and Participation in Athens*. Cambridge.

Sluiter, I. and R. M. Rosen, eds. 2004. *Free Speech in Classical Antiquity*. Mnemosyne Supplement 254. Leiden.

Smoes, E. 1995. *Le courage chez les Grecs, d'Homère à Aristote*. Cahiers de Philosophie Ancienne no. 12. Brussels.

Snell, B., ed. 1971. *Tragicorum Graecorum Fragmenta*. Vol. 1. Göttingen.

Sommerstein, A. H., ed. and trans. 1980. *Acharnians*. Warminster.

Sommerstein, A. H., ed. and trans. 1981. *Knights*. Warminster.

Sommerstein, A. H., ed. and trans. 1982. *Clouds*. Warminster.

Sommerstein, A. H., ed. and trans. 1983. *Wasps*. Warminster.

Sommerstein, A. H., ed. and trans. 1985. *Peace*. Warminster.

Sommerstein, A. H., ed. and trans. 1987. *Birds*. Warminster.

Sommerstein, A. H., ed. and trans. 1990. *Lysistrata*. Warminster.

Sommerstein, A. H., ed. and trans. 1994. *Thesmophoriazusae*. Warminster.

Sommerstein, A. H.. 1996a. "How to Avoid Being a Komodoumenos." *CQ* n.s. 46: 327–56.

Sommerstein, A. H., ed. and trans. 1996b. *Frogs.* Warminster.

Sommerstein, A. H., ed. and trans. 1998. *Ecclesiazusae.* Warminster.

Sommerstein, A. H., ed. and trans. 2001. *Wealth.* Warminster.

Sommerstein, A. H. 2002. *Indexes* [to Sommerstein's editions of 1980–2001]. Warminster.

Spence, I. G. 1993. *The Cavalry of Classical Greece: A Social and Military History with Particular Reference to Athens.* Oxford.

Stanford, W. B. 1963. *The Ulysses Theme: A Study in the Adaptability of a Traditional Hero.* Oxford.

Stanley, P. V. 1993. "Release from Liturgical Service in Athens." *Laverna* 4: 26–44.

Storey, I. C. 1989. "The 'Blameless Shield' of Kleonymos." *RhM* 132: 247–61.

Storey, I. C. 2003. *Eupolis: Poet of Old Comedy.* Oxford.

Strauss, B. S. 1985. "The Cultural Significance of Bribery and Embezzlement in Athenian Politics: The Evidence of the Period 403–386 B.C." *AW* 11: 67–74.

Strauss, B. S. 1986. *Athens after the Peloponnesian War: Class, Faction and Policy 403–386 B.C.* Cornell.

Strauss, B. S. 1993. *Fathers and Sons in Athens.* Princeton.

Strauss, B. S. 1996. "The Athenian Trireme, School of Democracy." In Ober and Hedrick, eds. (1996), 313–25.

Strauss, B. S. 2000. "Perspectives on the Death of Fifth-Century Athenian Seamen." In van Wees, ed. (2000a), 261–83.

Sullivan, J. 2002. "'Second' Thoughts on Aiskhines 3.252." *G&R* 49: 1–7.

Tatum, J. 2003. *The Mourner's Song: War and Remembrance from the Iliad to Vietnam.* Chicago.

Taylor, C. 2001a. "Bribery in Athenian Politics Part I: Accusations, Allegations, and Slander." *G&R* 48: 53–66.

Taylor, C. 2001b. "Bribery in Athenian Politics Part II: Ancient Reaction and Perceptions." *G&R* 48: 154–72.

Taylor, M. C. 2002. "Implicating the *Demos*: A Reading of Thucydides on the Rise of the Four Hundred." *JHS* 122: 91–108.

Thomsen, R. 1964. *Eisphora: A Study of Direct Taxation in Ancient Athens.* Humanitas III. Copenhagen.

Tod, M. N. 1948. *A Selection of Greek Historical Inscriptions: Vol. II: From 403 to 323 B.C.* Oxford.

Todd, S. C. 1990. "The Use and Abuse of the Attic Orators." *G&R* 37: 159–78.

Todd, S. C. 1993. *The Shape of Athenian Law.* Oxford.

Todd, S. C., trans. 2000. *Lysias.* The Oratory of Classical Greece Vol. 2. Austin.

Tritle, L. A. 2000. *From Melos to My Lai: War and Survival.* London.

Usher, S., ed. and trans. 1993. *Demosthenes: On the Crown.* Warminster.

Velho, G. 2002. "Les déserteurs des armées civiques en grèce ancienne, ou la négation du modèle du citoyen-soldat." *LEC* 70: 239–56.

Veligianni-Terzi, C. 1997. *Wertbegriffe in den attischen Ehrendekreten der Klassischen Zeit.* Heidelberger althistorische Beiträge und epigraphische Studien 25. Stuttgart.

Veyne, P. 1990. *Bread and Circuses: Historical Sociology and Political Pluralism.* Trans. by B. Pearce. London.

Voegelin, W. 1943. *Die Diabole bei Lysias.* Basel.

Wallace, R. W. 1989. "The Athenian *Proeispherontes.*" *Hesperia* 58: 473–90.

Wallace, R. W. 1994. "Private Lives and Public Enemies: Freedom of Thought in Classical Athens." In Boegehold and Scafuro, eds. (1994), 127–55.

Wallace, R. W. 1996. "Law, Freedom, and the Concept of Citizens' Rights in Democratic Athens." In Ober and Hedrick, eds. (1996), 105–19.

Wallace, R. W. 1998a. "Unconvicted or Potential 'Atimoi' in Ancient Athens." *Dike* 1: 63–78.

Wallace, R. W. 1998b. "The Sophists in Athens." In Boedeker and Raaflaub, eds. (1998), 203–22.

Wallace, R. W. 2004. "The Power to Speak – and not to Listen – in Ancient Athens." In Sluiter and Rosen, eds. (2004), 220–32.

Wankel, H. 1976. *Rede für Ktesiphon über den Kranz.* 2 vols. Heidelberg.

Wankel, H. 1982. "Die Korruption in der rednerischen Topik und in der Realität des klassischen Athen." In W. Schuller, ed., *Korruption im Altertum*, 29–47. Munich and Vienna.

Webster, T. B. L. 1967. *The Tragedies of Euripides.* London.

Webster, T. B. L., ed. 1970. *Sophocles: Philoctetes.* Cambridge.

Wees, H. van, ed. 2000a. *War and Violence in Ancient Greece.* London.

Wees, H. van. 2000b. "The Development of the Hoplite Phalanx: Iconography and Reality in the Seventh Century." In van Wees, ed. (2000a), 125–66.

Wees, H. van. 2001. "The Myth of the Middle-Class Army: Military and Social Status in Ancient Athens." In T. Bekker-Nielsen and L. Hannestad, eds., *War as a Cultural and Social Force: Essays on Warfare in Antiquity*, 45–71. Copenhagen.

Wees, H. van. 2004. *Greek Warfare: Myths and Realities.* London.

Wheeler, E. L. 1991. "The General as Hoplite." In Hanson, ed. (1991), 121–70.

Whitehead, D. 1977. *The Ideology of the Athenian Metic.* Cambridge Philological Society Supplement Vol. 4. Cambridge.

Whitehead, D. 1983. "Competitive Outlay and Community Profit: φιλοτιμία in Democratic Athens." *C&M* 34: 55–74.

Whitehead, D. 1986. *The Demes of Attica 508/7–ca. 250 B.C.: A Political and Social Study.* Princeton.

Whitehead, D. 1988. "ΚΛΟΠΗ ΠΟΛΕΜΟΥ: Theft in Ancient Greek Warfare." *C&M* 39: 43–53.

Whitehead, D. 1991. "Norms of Citizenship in Ancient Greece." In A. Molho, K. Raaflaub, and J. Emlen, eds., *City States in Classical Antiquity and Medieval Italy*, 135–54. Ann Arbor.

Whitehead, D. 1993. "Cardinal Virtues: The Language of Public Approbation in Democratic Athens." *C&M* 44: 37–75.

Wilkins, J. 1990. "The state and the individual: Euripides' plays of voluntary self-sacrifice." In A. Powell, ed., *Euripides, Women, and Sexuality*, 177–94. London.

Williams, B. 1993. *Shame and Necessity*. Sather Classical Lectures 57. Berkeley.

Willink, C. W., ed. 1986. *Euripides: Orestes*. Oxford.

Wilson, P. 2000. *The Athenian Institution of the Khoregia: The Chorus, the City and the Stage*. Cambridge.

Winkler, J. J. 1990. *The Constraints of Desire: The Anthropology of Sex and Gender in Ancient Greece*. New York.

Winkler, J. and F. Zeitlin, eds. 1990. *Nothing to Do with Dionysos? Athenian Drama in Its Social Context*. Princeton.

Wissmann, J. 1997. *Motivation und Schmähung: Feigheit in der Ilias und in der griechischen Tragödie*. Drama: Beiträge zum antiken Drama und seiner Rezeption Beiheft 7. Stuttgart.

Wohl, V. 2002. *Love among the Ruins: The Erotics of Democracy in Classical Athens*. Princeton.

Wolpert, A. 2002. *Remembering Defeat: Civil War and Civic Memory in Ancient Athens*. Baltimore.

Worman, N. 2002. *The Cast of Character: Style in Greek Literature*. Austin.

Worthington, I. 1992. *A Historical Commentary on Dinarchus: Rhetoric and Conspiracy in Later Fourth-Century Athens*. Ann Arbor.

Yunis, H. 1996. *Taming Democracy: Models of Political Rhetoric in Classical Athens*. Ithaca.

Yunis, H., ed. 2001. *Demosthenes: On the Crown*. Cambridge.

Zeitlin, F. 1990. "Thebes: Theater of Self and Society." In Winkler and Zeitlin, eds. (1990), 130–67.

Ziolkowski, J. E. 1981. *Thucydides and the Tradition of Funeral Speeches at Athens*. New York.

INDEX OF ANCIENT CITATIONS

AELIAN (AEL.)
De natura animalium (NA)
4.1: 129n82, 129n83
Varia Historia (VH)
13.12: 55
AESCHINES (AESCHIN.)
1.28–9: 121n67
1.28–32: 42, 62n46
1.96–7: 82
1.101: 191n85
1.134: 62n46
2.79: 50n17
2.94–5: 53, 54n25, 55n28
2.148: 47, 134n93
2.167: 48, 134n93
2.167–9: 47, 48, 52, 58n37
2.169: 25, 134
2.170: 134
2.177: 50n17, 56, 58n36
3.1: 135
3.7: 99, 135
3.19: 200, 200n99
3.70: 137
3.82: 50n17
3.148: 58n37, 135, 136n97
3.151: 136n97
3.152: 129, 134, 136n97, 137, 189n83
3.154: 107n44
3.155: 136n97
3.159: 56n31, 135, 136n97
3.160: 136n97
3.161: 136n97, 189n83
3.163: 136n97, 137
3.167: 136n97, 189n83
3.170: 136n97
3.175: 119, 124, 126n79, 127n79, 136, 136n97
3.175–6: 43n68, 62, 64n53, 89, 119
3.176: 121
3.181: 136n97
3.183: 114
3.183–5: 113
3.183–7: 113
3.186: 113, 114
3.187: 113, 136n97
3.212: 136n97
3.214: 136n97
3.226: 136n97, 137, 189n83
3.231: 136n97
3.240: 34n55
3.243: 114, 136n97
3.244: 134, 136n97
3.244–5: 137
3.247: 136n97, 140
3.250–1: 34n55
3.251: 30n45
3.252: 55, 136n98
3.253: 56n31, 135, 136n97, 189n83
AESCHYLUS (A.)
Agamemnon (A.)
212–13: 71n65
228–47: 71
437–44: 143n1
808–9: 80
841–2: 68
1223–5: 66n55, 80
1625–7: 66n55, 80

Eumenides (Eu.)
696–9: 43n68, 64n53, 124n71
Myrmidons (Myrm.): 72
Seven against Thebes (Th.)
10–20: 26n29
268–70: 101
415–16: 26n29
ALCAEUS (ALC.)
fr. 428a: 106n41, 107n41
ANACREON (ANACR.)
fr. 381b: 106n41, 107n41
ANDOCIDES (AND.)
1.73–6: 123
1.74: 62, 118n64, 119, 121
1.132: 150
2.17–18: 114n54
4.42: 196n93
ANDROTION (ANDROT.)
FGrH 324 F 38: 78n83
ANONYMOUS AUTHORS
Adespota Tragica (adesp. tr.)
fr. 450: 106
Anonymus Iamblichi (Anon. Iambl.)
2.400.17–18 D-K: 186n82
ANTIPHANES (ANTIPH.)
fr. 202: 173n61
fr. 202.1–10: 176
ANTIPHON (ANT.)
2.1.10: 20
2.2.12: 148n11, 162n43, 196n93
2.3.8: 182
6: 175, 199
fr. 1 Thalheim: 20
ANTIPHON THE SOPHIST (ANT. SOPH.)
87 fr. 44 D-K: 18
87 fr. 56 D-K: 131n87
87 fr. 57 D-K: 55
APOLLODORUS (APOLLOD.)
Bibliotheca (Bibl.)
3.6.2: 67, 67n58
3.7.2: 67n58
3.10.8–9: 67n58
Epitome (Epit.)
5.11: 79
APOSTOLIUS (APOSTOL.)
14.14: 129n83
ARCHILOCHUS (ARCHIL.)
fr. 5: 106n41, 107n41
ARISTOPHANES (AR.)
Acharnians (Ach.)
392: 160n41
572–625: 39n63
598–609: 56, 136n96
601: 189n83
676–702: 39n63
692–702: 116n58
1129: 120n66
1187: 189n83
Birds (Av.)
288–90: 129n82
450: 93n14
638–9: 97
1364–9: 49
1473–81: 129n82
1556–8: 58n37, 129n83
Clouds (Nu.)
353–4: 129n82
362: 106
672–80: 107n42, 129n82
685–93: 48n10, 56n31, 58n37, 136n96
Ecclesiazusae (Ec.): 23, 48
197–8: 165
205–7: 33
233–4: 82
307–10: 33
380–2: 33
455–7: 32
590–729: 32
601–3: 192
678–80: 89n3
681–93: 33
730–876: 32
746–876: 24
750–3: 33
769–70: 33
769–72: 37
777–8: 33
786–8: 33
794–5: 33
797–8: 33
812–22: 33
834: 33
855: 33
859: 33
872–4: 33
1027: 160n41

Frogs (Ra.)
190–2: 55
1014: 24, 189n83
1014–17: 47
1065–6: 24, 39, 163
Knights (Eq.): 23, 24, 35n57
368: 58n37, 61, 120n66
442–4: 58n37, 61
716–18: 34n55
797: 24
912–18: 163, 195
923–6: 149, 162n43, 163
1218–23: 34n55
1330: 24
1369–72: 57, 58n37, 129n82
Lysistrata (Lys.): 48
589–90: 30, 143n1
638–48: 26
640–1: 30n46
648: 30n46
651: 82
651–5: 30, 143n1, 196
654–5: 24, 162n43, 163
719: 189n83
Peace (Pax)
395: 129n84
444–6: 129n82
674–8: 129n82
1172–90: 39n63, 99, 131n87
1179–84: 52
1180–1: 57
1183–4: 93n14
1295–1304: 129n82
Thesmophoriazusae (Th.)
443–8: 51
824–9: 107
832–9: 89n3
Wasps (V.): 23
15–27: 129n82
235–9: 116n58
592: 129n82
655–724: 24
666–85: 34n55, 50
821–3: 129n82
1029–37: 24
1060–90: 116n58
1114–21: 24, 45n2, 47
Wealth (Pl.)
904: 160n41
907–19: 33
Fragments (fr.)
84: 129n84
ARISTOTLE (ARIST.)
Nicomachean Ethics (EN)
1095a22: 51, 177
1103b18: 90n5
1104b3: 90n5
1104b30: 19n11
1107b: 104n35
1108b24–5: 89n4
1115a-b: 104n35
1115a- 1117b: 89n4
1115a30–2: 91n7
1116a17–22: 124n71, 124n74
1116a20: 89n3
1116b2: 124n73
1119a27–31: 90n5
1121b12: 177
1134b: 23n23
1142a: 24n25
1150b10: 55
1159a14: 24n25
1159a20: 180
1160a10: 24n26
1163a1: 15, 19n11, 24n25, 51
1167a27: 31n49
1167b10: 37
1168b10: 22n19, 24n25
1168b15: 177
Poetics (Poet.)
1448a: 23
Politics (Pol.)
1263a30: 29n43
1263b1: 24n25
1267b4: 23n23
1270b32: 43n69
1271b13: 163n45
1304b20–1305a5: 187
1309a14–19: 195n92, 196n92
1309a18–21: 157n35
1310a30: 190n84
1318b15: 23n23, 177
1320b4: 195n92, 196n92
1337a25: 25n27
Rhetoric (Rh.)
1358b: 21

1371b19: 24n25
1399a: 35, 151
1401b16–21: 72
1416a28–35: 160n41
Fragments (fr.)
88–9: 195n92, 196n92
PS.-ARISTOTLE ([ARIST.])
Constitution of Athens (Ath. Pol.)
25: 161
25.2: 160
26.4: 17
27.4: 160
29.5: 1n1, 2n1, 164
49.4: 55n26
53.4: 52, 53n23, 54n23
53.5: 53n23, 54n23
53.7: 52
55.3: 1n1, 2n1
56.3: 150, 152, 153, 153n25, 159n38, 169, 170, 195n92, 196n92, 198
57.1: 150
58.1: 28n38
61.1: 150, 153n25, 198
Rhetoric to Alexander (Rh. Al.)
1424a20–32: 187
ATHENAEUS (ATH.)
Deipnosophistae
1.17c: 71n67

CRATINUS (CRATIN.)
fr. 290: 160n41

DEMADES (DEMAD.)
fr. 28 Burtt: 137n100
fr. 83.2: 28n37, 64n51
DEMETRIUS OF PHALERON (DEM. PHAL.)
fr. 136 Wehrli: 195n92, 196n92, 199
DEMOCRITUS (DEMOCR.)
68 fr. 181 D-K: 43
68 fr. 269 D-K: 125n76
DEMOSTHENES (DEM.)
1.6: 166n50
2.24: 166n50
2.27: 166n50
2.30: 36, 68, 190
2.31: 166n50, 190
3.17: 107
3.30: 130
3.33–4: 25
3.36: 130, 139
4.7: 36, 166n50
4.35–7: 169n55, 195n92, 196n92
8.21–3: 134n92, 166n50
8.21–4: 36
8.68–70: 138
9.36–40: 130
9.74: 36
10.28: 1n1, 2n1, 36
10.40: 29n44
10.45: 25
13.21–3: 114n54
14.7–8: 131
14.15: 33, 36
14.16: 53n23, 54n23, 151, 151n20, 152, 154, 192n87
14.17: 168
14.19: 147n9, 148n9
14.25: 191n85
14.27: 147n9, 148n9
15.32: 99, 121, 122
15.32–3: 139
18.62: 139n104
18.66: 143n1
18.68: 139, 140
18.96–7: 64n52
18.99: 195n91
18.102: 173n61
18.102–8: 168
18.103: 168
18.103–4: 190
18.104: 168n52
18.114: 107
18.116: 107n44
18.117: 107
18.129: 134
18.138: 139n104
18.173: 138, 139, 139n104
18.192: 139n104
18.192–4: 140
18.193: 139, 140
18.194: 131, 139
18.197: 139, 139n104
18.205: 26, 64n52
18.208: 125n76
18.212: 138, 139
18.217: 139n104
18.221: 139, 139n104
18.245: 43, 137, 138, 139

18.246: 139
18.248: 136, 138
18.249–50: 136
18.257: 196n93
18.262: 137
18.277: 139n104
18.285–6: 134
18.303–4: 139
18.304: 138, 139n104
18.310: 139n104
18.320: 139, 139n104
19.9: 139
19.113: 58n37, 134
19.124: 53, 54n25, 55n28, 58
19.230: 195n91
19.257: 62n46
19.282: 134
19.284: 62n46
20: 152n22
20.8: 152
20.18: 149, 151, 152
20.19: 152, 152n23, 195n92, 196n92
20.20: 151
20.28: 151, 152, 154
20.40: 153n26
21: 175
21.13: 134, 169, 195n91
21.15: 53n23, 54n23, 54n25, 169
21.58–60: 57, 60, 62
21.59: 61
21.61: 173n61
21.78–80: 132, 198, 201n102, 202n102
21.79: 153n26
21.80: 201n101
21.95: 47
21.103: 53n23, 54n23, 57n32, 60, 93n14, 119, 121, 133, 134n93
21.106: 132
21.110: 58n37, 133
21.133: 133
21.153: 183, 186
21.154: 151
21.154–6: 201n102, 202n102
21.155: 152, 168n52, 184
21.156: 170, 195n91, 201
21.160–6: 56, 133
21.160–7: 151n21, 201
21.161: 168
21.162–4: 45n2
21.164: 133
21.165: 189n83, 197n95
21.166: 53n23, 54n23
21.167: 200
21.202–3: 132
21.203: 134n92
22.4: 196
22.44: 166
22.47–56: 41
22.51: 63, 122
22.63: 200
23.196–8: 114n54
24.11–14: 200
24.24: 63
24.103: 62
25: 121n67
26: 121n67
27.37: 151
27.55: 193
28.1–4: 191
28.17: 153, 153n25, 153n26, 173, 174n63, 187
28.24: 183
36.39: 173
36.41: 174
36.54: 20
38.25: 182
38.26: 173, 182n76
39.8: 149
39.16: 53n23, 54n23
39.16–17: 57, 60
39.17: 59, 60n39
42: 188, 198
42.1: 160n41
42.2: 192
42.3–4: 149n15, 198
42.5: 149, 193
42.9: 193
42.14: 149
42.18: 192n87
42.19: 153n26, 192
42.23: 187, 191n85, 192n87
42.25: 1n1, 2n1, 149n15, 187, 189
42.27: 153n26
42.28: 193
42.30: 192
42.32: 187, 189
45.66: 191n85
45.85: 195n91

47: 175, 188
47.19–22: 188
47.25: 200
47.28: 200
47.34–5: 193
47.54: 174n63
51.1: 180n73
51.6: 180n73
51.11: 61n45
54.3–5: 91n9
54.44: 1n1, 2n1, 46n4
57.64: 115n56
58: 121n67
58.43: 55n28
60.1: 64n52
60.2: 32n50, 177
60.4: 26
60.8: 83
60.17–18: 126n79, 127n79
60.18: 64n51, 126
60.21: 125n76
60.25–6: 42, 64n52
60.26: 29n40, 126n79, 127, 127n79
60.27–8: 64n52
60.28: 28n37, 125
60.29: 71n64, 83
60.32: 29
60.33: 28n38
60.36: 28n38
60.37: 64n52

Prooemia (Prooem.)
41.2: 166n50
50.1: 131

PS.-DEMOSTHENES ([DEM.])
50.6–7: 45n2
50.7: 174n63
50.8: 149n14, 150n16, 192
50.9: 152, 188
50.11: 175
50.13: 174n63
50.14–16: 95
50.22–3: 61n45
50.23: 195n92, 196n92
50.65: 189n83
59.27: 53n23, 54n23, 57n32, 60, 61, 62, 62n48

DINARCHUS (DIN.)
1.12: 129, 135, 138, 138n102
1.69: 148
1.71: 128
1.80–1: 135
1.80–2: 136, 138n102
1.81–2: 189n83
1.82: 66n55, 81, 101, 189n83

DIO CHRYSOSTOM (D.CHR.)
Orationes (Or.)
52.2: 73n70
52.11: 74
52.11–13: 73
52.13: 73, 74
52.14: 74
52.16: 75n73
59.2: 73
59.3: 73, 74
59.4: 74
59.5: 74

DIODORUS SICULUS (D.S.)
11.81.4–5: 59
11.81.5–6: 94
11.84.4: 49n14
12.16.1–2: 48n10, 107n42, 122n69
12.47.3: 129n83
13.47.7: 162n43
13.52.5: 162n43
13.64.4: 162n43
16.86.4: 104, 135
16.87.1: 137n100
16.88.1: 136n98
16.88.1–2: 118n63
18.10.2: 52n21

DIOGENES LAERTIUS (D.L.)
2.53: 56n30

EUPOLIS (EUP.)
Astrateutoi: 48
Taxiarchoi: 96n18
fr. 35: 58n37, 129n83
fr. 46: 48
fr. 272: 96n18
fr. 300: 162n43
fr. 329: 199
fr. 352: 129n82
fr. 394: 129n84

EURIPIDES (E.)
Andromache (Andr.)
682–3: 80
693–8: 114n54
693–705: 118

968–70: 79
Electra (El.)
377–8: 103
1020–3: 71
Hecuba (Hec.)
130–40: 79
306–16: 80
400–2: 89n3
Helen (Hel.)
98–9: 70n61
395–6: 80
999: 22
Heracles (HF)
165–9: 22n21
191–2: 99
633: 178n68
Heraclidae (Heracl.)
1–4: 22
1–8: 66n56
500–6: 71n64
694: 66n55
700–1: 59n38, 66, 81
722–3: 59n38, 66
826–7: 26n29
Hippolytus (Hipp.)
373–90: 19n11, 177
925–31: 38n62, 39n62
Iphigenia at Aulis (IA)
67: 68
395: 68
514: 71n67
818: 72n69
825: 71n67
1386–7: 82
Iphigenia among the Taurians (IT)
24–5: 70, 79
359–71: 71
361–71: 70
852: 70
1386–7: 71
Medea (Med.)
85–6: 21
516–19: 38n62, 39n62
Orestes (Or.)
647–8: 80
923–4: 81
925–9: 81
Phoenician Women (Ph.)
439–40: 22, 177n66
499–525: 22
745–7: 83n97, 104n35
962–76: 82n93
997– 1005: 71n64
999– 1005: 82n92
Skyrioi: 69–70, 71, 72, 78, 78n84, 78n86, 82, 84
Suppliant Women (Supp.)
161–2: 83, 104n35
232–7: 50
304–5: 84
314–23: 84
342–5: 84
355–7: 84
391: 84
393–4: 84
481–2: 49
509–10: 83n97
510: 84, 104n35
650–730: 103n33
775–7: 143n1
850–6: 103
913–14: 84
Fragments (fr.)
360.14–15: 82
360.22–31: 83
360.22–37: 71n64
362.14–17: 178n68
452: 22
459: 22n21
682–4: 69
683a: 69, 70, 72
787: 38n60
788–9: 74
794: 22n20, 74
796: 74
798–9: 74
880: 70n62
885: 70n62
Hypsipylē fr. 1.V.15 Bond: 67
Telephus fr. 727c10–23K: 71n67, 72n69
Hypotheses (Hyp.)
Philoctetes
254–8: 74
265–6: 74
Skyrioi
11–20: 69
20–2: 69
22–6: 69

PS.-EURIPIDES ([E.])
Rhesus (Rh.)
896–901: 82
934–5: 82
976–7: 82n91

GORGIAS (GORG.)
82fr. 6.17–18 D-K: 28n37, 64
82fr. 8 D-K: 104n35
82fr. 11.16 D-K: 90n5, 100
82fr. 20 D-K: 178n68, 181
82fr. 23 D-K: 39

HARPOCRATION (HARP.)
διάγραμμα: 147
HERMIPPUS (HERMIPP.)
fr. 46: 66n55
fr. 47.1–4: 130
HERODOTUS (HDT.)
1.60.3: 35n56
1.87.4: 82n93
4.84: 63n49, 82n93
5.27: 63n49
5.78: 27, 64n51
6.11.2: 189n83
6.92.3: 115n57
6.117: 115
7.31: 122
7.38–9: 63n49, 82n93
7.99: 63n49
7.104.4–5: 63
7.108: 63n49
7.226: 97
7.227: 97n19
7.229: 55
7.230: 59n38
9.74: 115n57
9.75: 115n57
9.80–1: 115
HESIOD (HES.)
Ehoiai
frr. 196–204: 67n58
HIPPOCRATES (HP.)
Airs, Waters, Places (Aer.)
16: 27n34, 63n49, 64n51
HOMER (HOM.)
Iliad (Il.): 72
1.220: 77
2.721–5: 73
4.297–309: 98
5.529–32: 100
9: 75, 78n86
9.225–306: 72
9.262–99: 79n89
11.330–2:, 82n91, 82n93
13.278–86: 97
13.663–70: 85n99
15.561–4: 100
17.760–1: 106
23.296–9: 85n99
24.396–400: 85n99
Odyssey (Od.)
1.226: 30n45
3.262–4: 80
11.508–9: 78
13.291–5: 38n62, 39n62
HYGINUS (HYG.)
Fabulae (Fab.)
73: 66
96: 69
HYPERIDES (HYP.)
6.15: 64, 64n52
6.24: 28n37, 29n40, 64n51
6.40: 64n52
fr. A.4 Burtt: 126n79, 127n79

INSCRIPTIONS
IG I² 1085 = *ML* 51= Fornara 101: 52n21
IG I³ 52= *ML* 58: 162n44, 163
IG I³ 254: 160n41
IG II² 244.12–13: 148
IG II² 300.2–5: 177n67
IG II² 505.14–17: 148
IG II² 1496: 22–5: 107
IG II² 1496.28–39: 107
IG II² 1629a.190–6 = Tod II.200: 180n73
ML 78 fr. c: 148n12, 162n43
Tod II.204.6–8 = Rhodes and Osborne 88.1.6–8: 91
Tod II.204.6–11= Rhodes and Osborne 88.1.6–11: 88
ISAEUS (IS.)
3.66: 20
4.27–8: 1n1, 2n1, 55
4.27–9: 46n4
4.29: 1n1, 2n1

5.35–7: 154n29
5.36: 169, 196, 199
5.37: 165
5.37–8: 168
5.38: 93n14
5.41: 189, 196n93, 197
5.41–2: 180n72
5.43: 189, 192
5.46: 1n1, 2n1, 46n4
6.38: 173, 174
7.37: 184
7.38: 152, 158n37, 182n76, 196n93, 197, 199
7.39: 178, 193
7.39–40: 191
7.40: 143, 196n93
7.40–1: 201
7.41: 47
7.41–2: 1n1, 2n1
7.42: 192
10.20: 68
11.44–50: 193n89, 201
11.47: 191n85
fr. 22 Thalheim: 189
fr. 29 Thalheim: 173n61, 174n63
ISOCRATES (ISOC.)
4.77: 125
4.83: 29n40, 64n52
4.94–5: 126
4.124: 63n49
7.24–5: 34n53
7.34–5:, 185n81, 186n81, 191n85
7.53–5: 195n92, 196n92
8.77: 130
8.128: 168, 187
8.133: 20
15.4: 185, 185n81, 186n81, 187
15.4–5: 198, 201n102, 202n102
15.5: 199
15.145: 154, 182n76, 201n102, 202n102
15.158: 172
15.159: 178n68
15.159–60: 185n81, 186n81
15.160: 173, 185
17: 192n86
17.2–11: 192
17.41: 147, 148
17.49: 148
18.47: 1n1, 2n1
18.47–8: 46n4, 55
18.48: 189n83
18.58–62: 188
18.59–60: 191, 197
18.60: 164
20.14: 38n62, 39n62

LUCIAN
Timon (Tim.)
51: 53n23, 54n23
LYCURGUS (LYC.)
1: 136n98
1.37: 53n23, 54n23
1.43: 55
1.46: 125n77
1.48–9: 28n37, 64n51
1.49: 64n52, 125n76
1.51: 114
1.53: 26, 26n32, 55
1.73: 62
1.74: 89n3, 124n74
1.77: 89
1.83–9: 35n56
1.86: 64n52
1.101: 71n64, 83
1.129: 62, 62n47
1.129–30: 63, 124, 126n79, 127n79
1.130: 43n68, 64n53, 124
1.131: 95
1.133: 25n27, 26n32
1.139–40: 179, 179n71, 182, 183
1.143: 29, 64n52
1.147: 46n4
fr. 75 Sauppe: 118n63
LYSIAS (LYS.)
2.7–10: 83
2.9: 28n38
2.14: 28n37, 64n51
2.17: 26
2.18: 28n37
2.22: 64n51
2.23: 29n40
2.25: 126
2.41: 63n49
2.56: 28n37
2.58: 118, 125n76
2.62: 64n52
2.79: 64n52
2.80: 28n38

3.20: 201n102, 202n102
3.44–5: 95
3.45: 59n38
3.47: 201n102, 202n102
3.47–8: 183
4.1: 153n26, 160n40
4.1–2: 187
6.46: 1n1, 2n1, 46n4
7.30–3: 202n103
7.31: 182n76, 196n93, 199
9.4: 51, 52, 53, 53n23, 54n23
9.5–6: 61
9.15: 51, 53n23, 54n23
10.1: 106n41, 107n41, 121n67
10.3: 121n67
10.9: 106n41, 107n41, 120
10.12: 120
10.27–8: 113
10.28: 106n41, 107n41
12.20: 151
13.7–12: 95
13.12: 95n17
14: 60, 60n40, 60n41
14.2: 61
14.5: 59, 60, 105, 119, 120n66
14.5–7: 89
14.7: 58
14.8: 58
14.12: 46, 61
14.14: 46, 53n23, 54n23, 54n24, 57, 58
14.14–15: 53n23, 54n23
14.15: 43n68, 59, 64n53, 123, 126n79, 127n79
14.17: 59
14.40: 182
14.45: 46
15: 60, 60n40, 60n41
15.1–2: 59, 119
15.1–5: 195
15.1–6: 58, 61
15.5–6: 57
15.7: 58n35
15.8: 46, 58
15.9: 46, 61
15.12: 61
16: 121n67
16.3–5: 55
16.13: 47, 53n23, 54n23, 58, 58n35
16.15: 98n23, 99, 104, 108, 117
16.15–16: 98, 105
16.15–17: 128n80
16.16: 109
16.17: 128, 189n83
18.7: 191
18.23: 183
19.9: 172
19.29: 172, 196n93, 197
19.42–3: 172
19.43: 148n11
19.57: 181, 196n93
19.57–9: 172
19.61–4: 183
19.63: 182n76
19.64: 20
20.23: 1n1, 2n1, 36, 47, 164, 191, 201
20.31: 181
21.1–5: 146, 154n29, 173, 196n93
21.2: 152, 158n37
21.3: 148n11, 162n43, 164
21.5: 152, 158n37, 182n76, 195n91, 197, 197n94
21.11: 188
21.11–12: 154n29, 182
21.12: 164, 183
21.20: 46n4, 57n32
21.24: 188
21.25: 154n29, 183
24: 55n26
24.9: 153n26, 170, 198
25.8: 20
25.10: 20
25.12: 196n93
25.12–13: 154n29, 183n78
25.13: 181, 182n76
28.3–4: 165
28.7–8: 95n16
29.3–4: 194
29.4: 195n91
29.9: 165
30.26: 46n4
30.27–9: 55
31: 121n67
31.5: 25n27
31.5–14: 55
32.24: 151
fr. 9b Todd (= *P. Ryl.* 3.489 col.3): 181
fr. 35 Thalheim: 163, 197n95
title XLIII Thalheim: 188

MENANDER (MEN.)
Dyscolus (Dys.)
718–22: 23n24
Monostichoi (Mon.) (Jaekel)
407: 22n19

PAUSANIAS (PAUS.)
1.3.2: 114
1.3.3–5: 113
1.15.1–3: 113
1.15.4: 113
1.29.4: 114n55
1.29.11–12: 114n55, 118n63
PHILOSTRATUS THE YOUNGER (PHILOSTR. MIN.)
Imagines (Im.)
1b: 78, 79
2f: 78, 79
PHRYNICUS COMICUS (PHRYN. COM.)
fr. 21: 129n83
PINDAR (PI.)
Isthmian Odes (I.)
7.35–6: 98n23
PLATO (PL.)
Apology (Ap.)
19e-20a: 18
28d-e: 99
28e: 106n39
30b: 24n26
Crito (Cri.)
50e: 26n29
51b: 26n29
51c: 25n27
Gorgias (Grg.)
447a: 59n38
471d-472a: 23n23
482e: 19
483b-d: 19
498a: 101n28
522d-e: 24n26
522e: 126
527b: 24n26
Laches (La.)
181b: 106, 116
197b: 89n4, 104n35
Laws (Lg.)
643e: 29
698a-b: 190n84
731d-e: 19, 22n19, 24n25
754d-e: 25n27, 193
762b-d: 93n14, 95n17
780a: 43n69
780b: 63
804d: 26n29
831c: 19
870 a–b: 23n23, 177
874e-875b: 23n23
918c-d: 23n23
942a-b: 104
942a5–945b2: 118n64
943a-c: 62
943c: 115n56
943d: 95n17
943d-945a: 107n43
944d-e: 107n42
944e-945a: 122n69
955b-c: 43n69, 63
Menexenus (Mx.)
236d: 28n38
238c: 28n37
239a: 28n37
239a-b: 28n37, 64n51
239b: 64, 83
246b4–5: 126
246d2–3: 126
247c2–3: 126
249a: 51
249a6-b2: 107n44
249b3–6: 28n38
Protagoras (Prt.)
313c-e: 18
326b-c: 92
327b: 24n26
Republic (R.)
343d: 37, 193
361a-b: 40n64
365c: 19
369b-c: 24n26
424a: 29n43
505b: 23n23
548a-b: 43n69
555b-562a: 19
556d: 132n88
557b: 43n69, 63
557e: 43n69, 63, 123
561d-e: 63
562d: 190n84
563d: 190n84

564e: 185
565a: 34n53, 34n55
580e: 23n23
586a-b: 19
Symposium (Smp.)
219e-220b: 96, 115
220d-e: 96n18, 111, 115
221a-c: 96n18, 106, 115, 117
PLATONIUS
apud Meineke, *FCG* I.532: 169n56
PLUTARCH (PLU.)
Lives:
Agesilaus (Ages.)
30.2: 122
30.2–3: 122
30.3–4: 122
37.6: 25
Alcibiades (Alc.)
16.1–2: 103n34
17.5–6: 53n23, 54, 54n23, 55
29.1–2: 109, 116n59
32: 113
Alexander (Alex.)
41.9: 55
Aratus (Arat.)
28: 110
29.5: 97n21
Aristides (Arist.)
12.1: 98n23
25.2–3: 17
Artaxerxes (Art.)
14: 122n69
Cimon (Cim.)
7: 113
7–8.1: 113
8.1: 113, 114
10.5: 178n68, 181
Cleomenes (Cleom.)
9.1: 42
Demosthenes (Dem.)
20.2: 103n34, 135n95
24.2–5: 140
25.5: 55n28
Dion
30.7: 105
Nicias (Nic.)
3: 172
6.5: 110
7.2: 130
8.1: 130n86
13.7–8: 53n23, 54, 54n23, 55
16.8: 97
17.4: 125n76
21.2–4: 97
21.9: 104, 106
28.5: 103n34
Pelopidas (Pel.)
2.3: 115
Pericles (Per.)
7.1: 130n85
9.2–3: 35n57
10.1: 130n85
12: 17
18.2: 49
33.6: 129
37.2–5: 17
38: 110
Phocion (Phoc.)
8.1: 130
9.2: 130
9.5: 132
10.2: 53n23, 54n23, 55, 58n37, 132
12.3: 94, 95, 121
23.2: 134n92
24.4: 53n23, 54n23
25.2: 99
Pyrrhus (Pyrrh.)
16.2: 63, 190n84
Solon (Sol.)
5: 24n26
30: 35n56
Themistocles (Them.)
3: 110
Timoleon (Tim.)
25.5: 94
Moralia (Mor.)
34d: 69
72e: 69
74a: 72
185f6–186a3: 94
187c: 115
210f: 55n27
217c: 55n27
234e: 55n27
240f-242b: 82n94
349a-b: 195n92, 196n92, 199
PS.-PLUTARCH ([PLU.])
Moralia (Mor.)

840c: 140
845f: 135n95
846a: 136
POLLUX (POLL.)
6.151: 95
8.40: 95
8.115: 72, 93
POLYBIUS (PLB.)
6.26.4: 59
6.36–8: 59
6.38: 105n37
POLYEUCTUS
fr. 1 Baiter-Sauppe: 137n100
PROCLUS (PROCL.)
Chrestomathia (Chr.)
119–21 Severyns (*Cypria*): 68
144–6 Severyns (*Cypria*): 72, 73
211–13 Severyns (*Little Iliad*): 73
211–18 Severyns (*Little Iliad*): 75
217–18 Severyns (*Little Iliad*): 79
277–8 Severyns (*Sack of Ilium*): 79

QUINTUS SMYRNAEUS (Q.S.)
6.81–2: 79
6.84–92: 79
7.170–4: 78
7.193–212: 79
7.213–18: 79
7.235–393: 79
7.242–52: 79

SOLON
fr. 13.71–3: 23n23, 177
SOPHOCLES (S.)
Achaiōn Sullogos: 71–72
Ajax (Aj.)
1073–6: 124n72
1364–8: 23
1366: 22
Antigone (Ant.)
435–40: 22
Odysseus Mainomenos: 68, 76
Oedipus at Colonus (OC)
309: 21
Philoctetes (Ph.)
58: 79
60–1: 78
68: 75n74
69: 78
72–3: 76
72–4: 68, 76
80: 77
87–8: 77
95: 77
111: 22, 22n20, 77
113: 75n74
114: 76, 79
114–15: 78
133: 77
243: 78
343–4: 78
343–53: 76, 78, 79
349: 79
378: 79
379: 76n76
592–4: 77
610–13: 75n74
839–42: 75n74
915: 77n81
922–3: 77n81
969–70: 76, 76n77
981–98: 77
985: 75n74
989–90: 77n81
1025: 68
1025–7: 76
1055–60: 75n74
1226–7: 77
1263– 1408: 77
1296: 75n74
1305–6: 131n87
1332: 77
1334–5: 78
1339–40: 77n81
1343: 77
1363: 79
1368–9: 76n77
1373: 77n81
1392: 77
1409–44: 76
1415: 77, 77n81
1423–4: 77
1425–9: 77
1433–5: 78
1439: 77n81
1445–7: 77
1447: 77
1448: 77n82

1465: 77
1466–8: 77
Skyrioi: 75, 78, 82
Sundeipnoi: 72
Fragments (fr.)
63: 189n83
88: 178n68
113: 66
144: 68, 71, 93
305: 70n63
354.1–5: 22n20, 177
554: 45, 79
555: 79
555b: 79
557: 78n84, 79
566: 72
724: 131n87
835: 178n68
963: 132n88
SUDA
α 2092 (ἀνασύνταξις): 149
δ 319: 129n83

THEOPHRASTUS (THPHR.)
Characters (Char.)
22.2: 199n98
25.4: 102
25.5–6: 102
26.6: 173
THEOPOMPUS COMICUS (THEOPOMP. COM.)
Stratiōtides: 48
fr. 56: 48n12
fr. 57: 48n12
THEOPOMPUS HISTORICUS (THEOPOMP. HIST.)
FGrH 115 F 93: 117
THUCYDIDES (TH.)
1.17: 27n34
1.70.3: 50
1.70.6: 64n51
1.74.1–2: 64n51
1.75: 17
1.75–6: 18
1.75.1: 64n51
1.75.5: 30
1.104: 157
1.107: 161
1.109–10: 157
1.141.5: 49, 204
1.141.7: 36
1.144.3: 30
1.144.4: 130
2.14: 30n47, 31n47
2.21.3: 130
2.34: 28
2.35: 28n38
2.36.4: 64n51
2.37.1: 28n37
2.37.2: 25
2.37.3: 43n68, 64n53
2.39: 42, 124
2.39.4: 64, 64n52
2.40.1–2: 32n50
2.40.2: 38n60
2.40.2–3: 83n97, 126n79, 127n79
2.40.3: 104n35
2.40.4: 126
2.42.4: 64, 64n52, 125, 126, 126n79, 127n79
2.43.1: 29, 64, 64n52, 86, 126n79, 127n79
2.43.1–2: 29
2.43.2: 28, 127
2.43.4: 28n37, 126
2.43.6: 126
2.44: 32n50, 177
2.44.3: 83
2.46: 28n38, 127
2.46.1: 27n34, 30, 51
2.53: 31
2.59: 31
2.60.2–5: 30
2.60.3: 30
2.63.1: 25n27
2.65.6–13: 31
2.79: 104, 106, 129n83
2.79.7: 99
3.16.1: 58
3.19.1: 148, 161, 162, 162n43
3.44: 21n18
4.27.5: 130
4.77: 71n67
4.95: 98
4.96: 104
4.96.4: 103n33
4.96.6–8: 106
4.96.8–9: 106
4.101.2: 99
4.134: 110

5.10: 104
5.10.5: 100
5.10.7–10: 106n39
5.10.8: 100
5.10.9: 99, 129n84
5.34.2: 122
5.71.1: 100
5.72.4: 100
5.74.3: 99
6.9.2: 31
6.13.1: 131
6.15.2: 50n17
6.16: 181
6.24: 49
6.24.3: 49
6.26.2: 49
6.30: 179
6.31.3: 49
6.43: 49n15
7.43–5: 104
7.44.1: 103
7.45: 106
7.57.2: 53n23, 54n23
7.69.2: 27n34
7.80.3: 100
8.24.2: 49n15
8.48.1: 31, 162n43, 164, 190
8.48.3: 18n6
8.48.5–6: 157
8.63.1: 162n43
8.63.4: 31, 164, 185, 190
TYRTAEUS (TYRT.)
fr. 10: 126n78
fr. 10.16: 105n36
fr. 11: 126n78
fr. 11.10–14: 105
fr. 11.11–16: 102n31, 103n32
fr. 11.17–18: 106
fr. 12.15–19: 98n23

XENOPHON (X.)
Anabasis (An.)
3.1.37: 99
3.2.19: 58
3.4.46–9: 96n18
5.8.4: 91n9
5.8.13: 95n16
Constitution of the Lacedaimonians (Lac.)
9.1–2: 100
9.3–4: 123
9.4–6: 122
11.8: 98n23
Cynegeticus (Cyn.)
13.11: 132n88
Cyropaedia (Cyr.)
6.2.11: 71n67
6.3.25: 98
6.3.27: 98
De equitandi ratione (Eq.)
1.1: 115n56
De equitum magistro (Eq. Mag.)
1.10: 61
1.11–12: 49n14
2.6: 99
5.9: 35n56
8.20: 100
Hiero (Hier.)
1.9: 23n23
2.15–16: 110, 115
7.1–4: 177
8.8–9: 59
9.3: 41n67
9.7: 59, 166n50
Historia Graeca = Hellenica (HG)
1.2.5: 95n16
1.2.7–9: 104
1.2.15: 109, 116n59
2.4.16: 101, 189n83
3.2.17: 100
4.2.9–23: 104, 107
4.2.14: 167
5.4.17: 107n43
6.2.1: 166n50
6.3.11: 24n26
6.4.13: 101
6.4.17: 52n21
7.2.4: 110
7.5.24: 104
7.5.26: 110
Memorabilia (Mem.)
1.6.13: 18
2.7.6: 178
3.1.8: 98
3.1.10: 98n23
3.4.1: 52, 57, 58n37, 115
3.4.11: 100
3.5.19–21: 95n16
3.9.1: 92

3.9.4: 24n26
3.10.5: 38n62, 39n62
3.12.1–3: 132n88
Oeconomicus (Oec.)
2.6–7: 185
7.3: 160n41, 170, 187
Poroi: 59
Symposium (Smp.)
2.14: 58n37, 129n83
4.29–32: 185, 189
4.32: 176
4.34: 189
4.45: 189
PS.-XENOPHON ([X.])
Constitution of Athens (Ath. Pol.)
1.13: 20n16, 161, 185
1.16–17: 17
2.17: 50
2.19: 18
3.4: 147, 153n25, 159n38, 160n41, 170, 198
3.5: 60n42

GENERAL INDEX

Achilles, 39n63, 48, 66n57, 69–71, 72, 72n69, 75, 78, 78n84, 78n86, 79, 79n87, 79n89, 80, 82, 82n91, 84
adeia, 163
Adrastus, 50, 66–7, 83, 84
Aegisthus, 80–1
Aeschines, 46n4, 54n25, 58n37, 113, 123, 133–41
Aeschylus, 67n58, 73
Aethra, 83–4
Agamemnon, 51, 68, 69n59, 71n65, 72, 80–1, 112
agōn, 91, 197. *See also* competition
Agora, 52, 53, 93n14, 113–14
Ajax, 22
Alcibiades, 76n78, 95–6, 105, 110, 116n59, 130
Alcibiades, the younger, 46, 58, 60, 61, 123
altruism, 17n2
Amphiaraus, 66–7
Amynias, 48n10, 56n31, 58n37
andreia, 91–111, 125. *See also* courage
antidosis, 13, 41n66, 152, 153, 153n25, 155, 159–60, 161, 170–1, 173, 174n64, 185, 187, 189, 193, 194, 196, 197–8, 201–2
Antiphon, 20
Antisthenes, 58n37, 189
Apollodorus, 178n69
apragmōn, 38n60
Aratus
aretē, 125, 127
Argos, 70, 83
aristeia, 110–11
Aristides, 60, 62
Aristogeiton, 55, 58n37
Aristophanes, 23–4, 32–4, 39, 47, 50, 67n58, 163–4
Aristotle, 23n23, 24, 37
Assembly, 18, 19, 21, 23, 24, 30–2, 33, 35, 39, 40, 50, 52, 113, 116, 122, 130, 134n92, 148, 149, 168, 180, 181, 186
astrateia, 46, 60n41. *See also* draft evasion; *graphē astrateias*
ateleia, 151
Athenian civic ideology. *See* ideology, Athenian civic
atimia, 61–2, 62n46, 62n48, 120, 121–3
Attic funeral orations. *See* funeral orations, Attic
Aulis, 69n59, 70–1

bad citizenship
  in its cultural context, 4, 9–10
  definition of, 3n5
  and free-riders, 34
  gossip about, 117n61
  gradations of, 9
  as ideological and practical challenge, 1, 4, 14, 16, 40
  as integral to citizen experience, 4, 7
  as inversion of citizen ideals, 2, 4, 4n8, 10, 42
  legal actions concerning,. 3, 5, 10, 41, 43
  motives and opportunities for, 8–9
  and mutual distrust, 37–8

bad citizenship (*cont.*)
as a neglected topic, 4–5
"otherness" of, 8
private initiative and control of, 41–2
and self-interest, 5–6, 15, 144, 203, 205–9
and share-holding, 34, 37
social concern over, 3
sources concerning, 6–7
types of, 5–6
See also cowardice; draft evasion; self-interest; shrewdness; tax evasion
banks, 145, 192, 193
Bdelycleon, 24
Boeotus, 60
Boule. *See* Council
"braggart soldier," 116
Brasidas, 100
bribery, 34n55, 57, 57n33, 74. *See also* personal influence
Bush, G. W., 58n37

Callias, 189
cavalry, 2n2, 47, 53, 57–8, 58n35, 58n37, 106, 116, 133, 151n21
evasion of, 45n2
Chaeronea, 55, 56n31, 104, 107, 118n63, 123, 129, 131, 134–40
Charidemus, 107
charis, 13, 128n80, 157, 171, 172, 176, 179n71, 180–4, 186, 199
in the lawcourts, 180–1, 182–4
in politics, 180–1
social concern over, 182–4, 202
Charmides, 185, 189
Charondas, 122n69
chorēgia, chorēgiai, 13, 53, 57n32, 132, 133, 143, 144, 146, 175
assignment to, 149–51
costs of, 146, 175
under the early democracy, 156
in the fourth century, 169–70
magistrates as administrators of, 149–51
number of, 156
during the Peloponnesian War, 163, 164
skimping on, 199–200
and status display, 157, 169, 179, 180
temporary exemption from, 152, 158, 195
visibility of, 179, 195
and voluntarism, 157
See also liturgies; *synchorēgia*
choregic monuments, 40, 179
Cinesias, 57n32
citizenship
and financial support of the city, 1, 143
formal obligations of, 1–2
ideology of, 9–10, 15–16, 24–34, 40–4, 122–4, 126, 171
law of 451/0 B.C., 17
and military service, 1, 26n29
norms and ideals of, 2, 42
as performance, 38–40
and politicians, 128, 139–40
and reciprocity, 9, 15–16, 24–34
and self-interest, 15–16, 24–34, 35–40, 171
self-presentation of, 38–40
and share-holding, 9, 25, 25n27, 29, 34, 37
strategies of, 35–40
varying obligations of, 2, 34, 143–4
women and, 30, 32
See also bad citizenship; ideology, Athenian civic
citizenship, bad. *See* bad citizenship
Cleisthenes, 156
Cleon, 24, 58n37, 117, 117n60, 129n84, 130, 163
Cleonymus, 58n37, 106n41, 107n41, 129, 129n82, 129n84
Cleophon, 95n17
cleruchs, 53n23, 54n23, 152
Clinton, W. J., 58n37
Clytemnestra, 51, 80–1
competition, 19n12, 36, 40, 91, 92, 111, 112, 141, 145, 151, 156–7, 177, 178n69, 180
compulsion, 10, 15–16, 40–4, 63, 64, 65, 67, 67n58, 68, 70, 71, 73n70, 74, 76, 77, 80, 85–6, 146, 158, 161, 167, 184, 188–90, 205–9
concealment of wealth, 36, 145, 166, 187, 191–4, 198, 200–1
frequency of, 191

limited measures against, 193–4
methods of, 192–3
conscription
of hoplites, 2, 10–11, 40, 49, 52–3
of rowers, 2n2, 45n2
Corinthian War, 165
Council, 54n25, 56, 107, 168
courage, 11–13, 28n36, 49, 64, 83, 84, 91, 114–16, 125, 126n79, 127n79, 128, 130, 138, 141, 204. *See also* cowardice
courts. *See* lawcourts
cowardice, 3, 5, 11–13, 27, 42, 62n47, 80, 83, 83n97, 205–9
and abandonment of one's shield, 90n5, 106–7, 118n64, 120, 121n67, 129, 130n86, 136n99
atimia as legal penalty for, 121–3, 142
in Attic funeral orations, 125–8
before battle, 96–9
in battle, 99–103, 104
on campaign, 91–111
as conceptual category, 89–90
contestable nature of, 89, 92, 111
degrees of, 89
and Demosthenes' career, 132–41
and desertion on campaign, 94–5
and desertion of the ranks in battle, 105
and draft evasion, 93–4
as effeminate, 107, 107n42, 122n69, 129
and fear, 89–90, 100–1
and generals, 92, 93–5, 96–7, 98, 99, 104, 105, 117–18, 119, 120, 128–32
and hardship on campaign, 95–6
of individual and group, 92–3
and morale, 99, 102
as a neglected topic, 88
and panic, 92, 100
and politicians, 118, 121, 125, 128–41
and position in the ranks, 98, 101–2
prosecution for, 60, 112, 117, 118–21, 124, 142
in public discourse, 112, 124–41
in a rout, 103–9, 116–17, 141
and scapegoating, 129, 141
and self-presentation, 91, 92
slanderous claims of, 120, 136n99
as social concern, 88, 124
as subjective category, 89, 111
and temperament, 92
and volition, 89–90, 125, 126
See also courage; *lipotaxion*
Creon, 82n92, 82n93
Ctesiphon, 134–5

deception. *See* shrewdness
decimatio, 105n37
Deidamia, 69–70, 79
"delayers," 59n38
Delian League, 157
Demades, 137n100
demarch, 57n34, 149
demes, 52, 57n34, 149, 173, 192
democracy. *See* Assembly; citizenship; compulsion; *dēmos*; equality; freedom; free speech; lawcourts; persuasion
Democritus, 43
dēmos, 18n6, 20, 24, 28, 31, 113, 128, 138, 151, 157, 159–60, 161, 164, 181, 185, 190
Demosthenes, 13, 36, 36n58, 46n4, 56n31, 58n37, 119, 121, 123, 129, 131, 132–41, 151n21, 169, 186, 190
desertion
on campaign, 94–5
frequency of, 95
motives for, 95
opportunities for, 95
prosecution for, 95
of the ranks in battle, 42, 59
See also lipotaxion
despotēs, 26n29, 63
diadikasia, 153, 153n25, 159n38, 165n48, 166n48
Dieneces, 96
Dikaiopolis, 56
Diodorus Siculus, 7
Diodotus, 21n18
Diomedes, 69, 74
Diotimus, 107
dokimasia
for cavalry, 47, 58
for Council, 107
rhētorōn, 62n46, 121n67

draft evasion, 3, 5, 10–11, 36, 37, 39n63, 40, 42, 136, 205–9
  atimia as legal penalty for, 61–2
  and the Attic funeral orations, 63–4, 85
  in comedy, 47–8, 87
  as effeminate, 48, 70, 80, 122n69
  and failure to appear at muster, 59
  in the lawcourts, 46–7, 87
  motives for, 48–51
  as a neglected topic, 46
  and the *oikos*, 81–5
  opportunities for, 52–62
    through abuse of exemptions, 54–7
    through feigned disability, 54–5
    through personal influence, 57–8
    through transfer to cavalry, 57–8
  Plato on, 63
  and politicians, 47, 58, 128
  prosecution for, 51, 59–61, 62
  scope of, 48, 53, 64
  and self-interest, 50–1
  as social concern, 46–8, 65, 85
  and tax evasion, 203–4
  in tragedy, 45, 65–87
  and wealthy men, 55, 56, 57–8, 61n45
  See also dokimasia rhētorōn; *graphē astrateias*
duty. *See* citizenship; compulsion

economy, Athenian, 145n4
egocentrism. *See* self-interest
Ehrenberg, V., 6
eisphora, 2, 13–14, 30, 42, 51n19, 134n92, 143, 146, 147–8, 150, 170, 185
  administration of, 147–8
  establishment of, 162, 170
  no exemption from, 149, 196
  generals as administrators of, 148–9
  and the liturgical class, 154
  metic payment of, 148
  minors' payment of, 151
  during the Peloponnesian War, 161–4
  reforms of, in fourth century, 165–6, 170
  selection of payers of, 148–9
  unpopularity of, 162–4, 165–6, 178
  unpredictability of, 174
  See also proeisphora; *symmoriai*, for the *eisphora*; *timēma*
ephēbeia, 90
ephebes, 85
Ephebic Oath, 88, 91
epibatai, 49n15
Epic Cycle, 85
epidosis, 168–9
epitaphios, 28. *See also* funeral orations, Attic.
Epizelus, 115
Eponymoi, 93n14
equality, 25, 28
eranos, 29, 29n43, 29n44, 30n45
erastai, 29
Eriphyle, 66–7
Eteocles, 22
ethelontai, 64
Euktemon, 132
Eupolis, 48
Euripides, 48, 73, 125n76, 160n41
euthynai, 195, 200
evasion. *See* draft evasion; liturgies, avoidance of; tax evasion
exemptions
  from hoplite service, 53–4
    abuse of, 54–7
  from liturgical service, 151–3, 158–9, 161, 170, 181, 188, 196–7
    abuse of, 151n21, 195, 197, 203
  See also skēpsis
exetasis, 138, 139

father-beater, 2
freedom, 9, 25, 27, 28, 41, 42, 43, 43n69, 63, 64, 77, 85–6, 124, 205–9
"free riders," 34
free speech, 42, 127
funeral orations, Attic, 12, 26n32, 27–9, 32n50, 42, 49, 63–4, 77, 83, 84, 85, 90, 125–8, 134, 177. *See also* ideology, Athenian civic

generals, 12, 40, 41, 50, 52, 53n23, 54n23, 54n25, 57n33, 57n34, 60n39, 62, 72, 92, 93–5, 95n16, 98n25, 99, 105, 108–9, 110, 112, 114, 119, 120, 128–32, 139, 148–51, 179, 181, 194–5, 197
Glaucon, 40n64
gossip, 117n61
graphē astrateias, 57n32, 60, 118–21

graphē deilias, 118–21
graphē lipostratiou, 95, 117n60, 118–21
graphē lipotaxiou, 118–21. *See also lipotaxion*
greed, 5n9, 17n3, 20n15, 23n24, 31, 34n53

Hecuba, 80
Helen, 67, 68, 70, 79
Helenus, 73, 74
Hermione, 79
Herodotus, 27
Hiero, 41n67, 59, 115
Homer, 85
honesty, 35
honor, 10, 12, 30, 40, 46, 48, 51, 72, 74, 74n71, 79–80, 88, 92, 100, 106, 110, 112–16, 141, 176–80. *See also philotimia*
hoplites, 1, 5, 10–13, 27–9
  armor and weapons of, 45, 54
  homecoming of, 112
  number of, 45
  placement in ranks of, 98–9
  See also conscription, of hoplites; exemptions, from hoplite service
horoi, 192
human nature. *See* self-interest, and human nature
hypocrisy, 36

ideology, Athenian civic, 51n18, 77, 85–6, 98, 122–4, 125, 126n79, 127n79, 128, 141, 144, 184, 203, 205–9. *See also* citizenship, ideology of; funeral orations, Attic
Idomeneus, 97
individual and state, tensions between, 3, 14, 18, 31, 32
Iolaus, 22, 65, 66n55, 66n56
Iphigeneia, 70–1, 79–80

Jason, 21, 22

katalogos
  for the cavalry, 58n35
  for hoplites, 52, 53n23, 54n23, 57, 57n34, 93n14, 150n17
katastasis, 58n35
Kennedy, J. F., 29n41

kerdos, 22, 22n20, 22n21, 74
kinaidos, 2
Knemon, 23n24

Laches, 105
lamprotes, 178
law(s), 43, 64, 64n53, 123–4. *See also* compulsion
lawcourts, 18, 19–21, 25, 35, 39, 40, 42, 180–1, 182–4
leitourgia, 183. *See also* liturgies
Lemnos, 71, 73, 75
Leocrates, 26n32, 136n98
Leptines, 152n22, 170
lipotaxion, 136, 137, 138, 139
  prosecution for, 59, 60n41, 105, 118–21, 132, 133, 134n93
liturgical class, the, 154–5, 174, 193
liturgies, 2, 13–14, 42, 51n19, 53, 56, 128n80, 143
  and aristocratic values, 156–7, 177
  assignment to, 149–51, 194–8
  attitudes of wealthy men toward, 170–1, 190
  avoidance of, 144, 163–4, 190–204, 205–9
  claims concerning, 180, 200–2
  and class tensions, 164, 184–7, 189–90
  costs of, 173–4, 199–200
  deme, 173
  under the early democracy, 156–61
  exemptions from, 151, 151n21, 153, 158–9, 161, 170, 187, 188, 196–7
  festival and military, 146–7
  history of tensions concerning, 155–64, 165–70, 171
  personal demands of, 175, 188–9
  and popular rule, 159–60, 161
  strategies concerning, 190–203
  visibility of, 179–80
  and voluntarism, 146, 195–6, 201–2
  See also antidosis; *chorēgia*; *philotimia*; *skēpsis*; trierarchy; wealthy men
Lycomedes, 69, 78, 79, 82
Lycurgus, 136n98, 183
Lykos, 22n21
Lysicles, 118n63, 136n98

Mantitheus, 47, 99, 107–9, 128
Marathon, 113–14, 115, 116n58
Meidias, 119, 121, 132–3, 134n92, 151n21, 186
Menelaus, 68, 79, 80, 124n72
Menoecus, 82n92
metics, 148, 151
Meton, 55
military discipline, 95n16
military service. *See* conscription; courage; cowardice; draft evasion; hoplites
Miltiades, 113–14
Myronides, 59, 93–4

Neoptolemus, 69, 72, 75–9, 82
Nicias, 30–1, 89n4, 118n63, 130, 172

Odysseus, 22, 38n62, 39n62, 39n63, 55, 68–80, 84, 86, 112
Oedipus, 21
oikos, 25n28, 51, 65, 81–5, 86
Old Oligarch, 20n16, 161, 185
Orestes, 81, 103
ōthismos, 101

Palamedes, 68
Paris, 67, 68
Pasio, 192n86
patriotism, 3, 3n7, 6, 6n13, 7–8, 9, 28, 30n47, 31n47, 42, 63, 73, 78, 81–4, 85, 138, 204
patris, 26, 30n46
Peisander, 58n37, 129, 129n83, 129n84
Peisistratids, 27
Peloponnesian War, 13, 17, 18n7, 45, 81, 129, 158, 161–4, 165, 169, 170
performance culture, 38
Pericles, 29, 30, 30n47, 31n47, 32, 126, 129, 130n85, 204
Persians, 63n49, 110n49
personal influence, 37
  and draft evasion, 57–8, 203
  and liturgy avoidance, 159, 194–5, 203
  See also bribery
persuasion, 10, 15–16, 40–4, 63, 65, 70, 71, 74, 76, 77, 78, 82, 85–6, 205–9
Philip of Macedon, 36n58, 137, 190
Philoctetes, 68, 69, 71, 72, 73–8
philotimia, 38, 51n19, 144–5, 171
  in honorific decrees, 177
  limits of, 170–1, 190, 204
  and self-interest, 171, 178
  See also honor
Phocion, 94–5, 130, 131, 134n92
Phoenix, 78, 78n86, 79
Plataea, 115n57
Plato, 19, 23n23, 24, 43n69, 63
Plutarch, 7
politicians, 13, 31, 34n55, 35, 58, 73, 128–41, 180–1. *See also* generals; *rhētores*
Polybius, 59
Polyeuctes, 131
Polyneices, 22, 67, 177n66
Polyphantes, 22
Polyxena, 79–80
ponēria, 38
Praxagora, 33
Praxithea, 82–3
Pritchett, W. K., 6, 46
proeisphora, 147, 147n8, 149, 154, 165, 166, 186, 188, 199
prosecution, volunteer. *See* volunteer prosecution
prothumia, 64, 64n51
psilos, 54n24
public discourse, 19, 42
public services. *See* liturgies

rational choice theory, 34n54, 145n4
recruiting motif, 65
Rhesus, 82
rhētores, 50, 58, 128–41, 181. *See also* politicians
rhipsaspia. See cowardice, and abandonment of one's shield
Roman military practices, 59, 105n37, 113, 115n56
rowers, 2n2, 45n2, 95

Salamis, 156, 157
Sannion, 60, 62
scapegoats, 8, 129, 141
scars, battle, 115
self-interest, 3, 5–6, 7–8, 9–10, 77
  Aristotle on, 23n23, 24

self-interest (*cont.*)
in the Assembly, 21
central to Athenian thinking, 19
citizenship and, 15–16, 24–34, 35–40, 171
in comedy, 23–4
and democracy, 16, 17
and draft evasion, 50–1
and the empire, 17, 24, 49
enlightened, 22, 26, 35, 42
Greek views of, 17
and honor, 51n19
and human nature, 16–24
in the lawcourts, 19–21
in modern egalitarianism, 17n4
and *philotimia*, 171, 178
Plato on, 19, 23n23, 24
and self-preservation in war, 100, 104, 106, 107
short-term vs. long-term, 23n22
in the social sciences, 16n1
and the sophists, 18–19
in tragedy, 21–3
and volunteer prosecution, 61
See also shrewdness
Seven against Thebes, the, 50, 66–7, 83–4
shame, 12, 91, 99, 101, 106, 123, 126n79, 127, 127n79, 140, 141
shrewdness, 5n9, 7–8, 9, 15, 16, 35–40, 41, 54, 65, 68, 69–71, 74, 76, 77, 86, 144, 190–203, 205–9
Simonides, 41n67, 59
skēpsis, 13, 153, 153n25, 159–60, 170–1, 195, 196, 201–2
Skyros, 66n57, 69, 70–1, 78n86
Social War, 170
Socrates, 95–6, 105, 110, 178
Solon, 17n3, 160n41
Sophanes, 114, 115n57
sophists, 18–19
Sophocles, 23, 67n58, 73, 78n83
Sparta, 25, 30, 32, 35n56, 42, 43, 43n69, 52n21, 56n30, 62, 62n47, 63, 82n94, 96–7, 98, 110n49
stasis, 186
Stephanus, 57n32, 60
strategic behavior. *See* shrewdness
stratēgoi, 128. *See also* generals
sykophant, 2
symmoriai, 147n8
for the *eisphora*, 147, 148–9, 165, 167, 170–1, 194
naval, 147, 150, 152n24, 154, 167, 168, 170–1, 184
synchorēgia, 164, 169
synēgoroi, 182
syntrierarchy, 147, 164, 167, 169

tax evasion, 3, 5, 13–14, 36, 37, 39, 42, 44, 203–4, 205–9
taxiarchs, 52, 57, 60n39, 71, 98, 99, 109, 113, 134
taxis, 138, 139
Telemachus, 68
Tenedos, 72
Theater of Dionysus, 19, 39, 42, 135
Theopompus Comicus, 48
Thermopylae, 96
Theseus, 50, 83–4, 103
thetes, 49n15
Thetis, 69, 82, 82n91
Thrasybulus, 108–9
Thrasyllus, 116n59
Thucydides, 18, 18n9, 30–2, 111n50
Thurii, 122n69
timē, 171. *See also* honor
timēma, 147, 148, 150, 161, 166, 193
Tresantes, 122, 123
trierarchy, trierarchies, 13, 53, 133, 143, 144, 146–7, 170
agents and, 175, 199
assignment to, 149–51
costs of, 146–7, 175
demands of, 157–8, 175
establishment of, 156
generals as administrators of, 149–51
history of tensions concerning, 157–8, 161–4, 166–8
number of, 146–7, 156
profit from, 200
reforms of, in fourth century, 167–8, 170–1, 190
skimping on, 199–200
temporary exemption from, 152, 158, 167, 195
visibility of, 179–80
See also liturgies; syntrierarchy

Trojan War, 45, 48, 51, 55, 67–81, 112, 114
trophies, battlefield, 110, 113
tuchē, 116, 125, 140
Tyndareus, Oath of, 67, 67n58, 68, 70, 70n61, 71, 80

veterans, 112
Vietnam War, 58n37
voluntarism, 38, 49, 49n15, 64, 85, 146, 150, 157, 161, 195–6, 201–2
volunteer prosecution, 11, 42, 60–1, 118, 120–1

wages, daily, 146n7
war tax. *See eisphora*
Washington, George, 30n47, 31n47
wealth, measurement of, 161. *See also timēma*
wealthy men
- their anxiety over liturgies, 175–6
- their attitudes toward liturgies, 170–1, 172–87, 188–90, 203
- bad citizenship of, 144
- and *charis*, 180–4
- city's increasing assertion of authority over, 155–71, 185
- city's slow recognition of wealth differences among, 154, 170–1, 187
- conflict with city over financial obligations, 155–71
- and empire, 157
- and honor, 176–80
- levels of wealth among, 154
- as the liturgical class, 154–5
- political collaboration among, 190
- and self-interest, 144–5, 178, 191, 202–3
- their self-presentation of liturgical records, 180, 200–2
- their sole responsibility for financial obligations, 143–4, 184–7, 188
- and status competition, 156–7
- strategic behavior of, 190–203

women, 30, 32, 81–5

Xenocleides, 57n32, 60
Xenophon, 59, 111n50, 123, 189